Voyage to Siam 1685

THE
VOYAGE
of
SIAM
London Printed 1688.

A Relation of the

Voyage to Siam

Performed by Six Jesuits Sent by the French King to the Indies and China in the Year 1685

With an Introduction
by

B. J. Terwiel

White Lotus Press

First published in 1688.

Every effort has been made to retain the character of the 1688 edition, to the extent of retaining much of the original punctuation and some abbreviations, even when this does not conform strictly with modern usage—especially so in the case of the profligate use of Capitals—which has been tempered somewhat. Changes in nomenclature and archaic or foreign spellings, including that of proper nouns, have been made only where the meaning of the text will benefit, and these have been recorded in the notes.

White Lotus Co. Ltd.
G.P.O. Box 1141
Bangkok 10501
Thailand

Telephone: (662) 332-4915 and (662) 741-6288-9
Fax: (662) 741-6287 and (662) 741-6607
E-mail: ande@loxinfo.co.th

Typesetting and map reproduction by Ua-fua Literary Services.
Printed in Thailand.

ISBN 974-8434-34-6 pbk. White Lotus Co., Ltd., Bangkok

VOYAGE DE SIAM,

DES PERES JESUITES,

Envoyez par le ROY aux Indes & à la Chine.

AVEC LEURS OBSERVATIONS Astronomiques, Et leurs Remarques de Physique, de Géographie, d'Hydrographie, & d'Histoire.

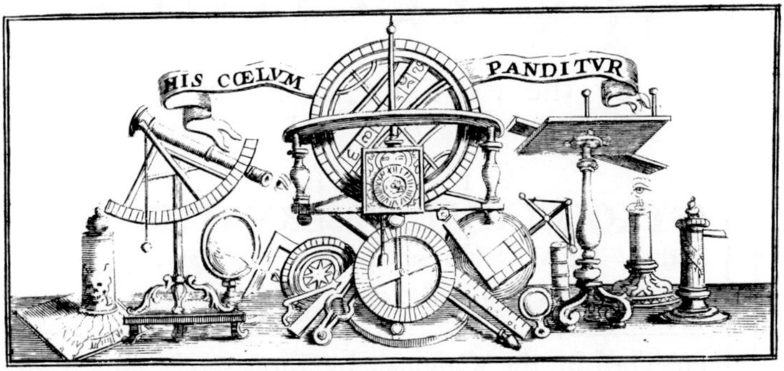

A PARIS,

Chez { ARNOULD SENEUZE, ruë de la Harpe, à la Sphere. ET DANIEL HORTHEMELS, ruë de la Harpe, au Mécenas.

M. DC. LXXXVI.

PAR ORDRE EXPREZ DE SA MAJESTÉ.

A RELATION OF THE VOYAGE TO SIAM

Performed by

SIX JESUITS,

Sent by the FRENCH KING, to the *INDIES* and *CHINA*, in the Year, 1685.

WITH THEIR ASTROLOGICAL OBSERVATIONS, and their REMARKS of *Natural Philosophy*, *Geography*, *Hydrography*, and *History*.

Publiſhed in the Original, by the expreſs Orders of His moſt Chriſtian Majeſty.

And now made Engliſhed, and illuſtrated with SCULPTURES.

LONDON, Printed by T. B. for *A. Churchil*, at the *Black-Swan* in *Ave-Mary-Lane*, 1688.

Contents

Illustrations

Introduction to the new edition

The first French Embassy to Siam which set out on March 1685 was a remarkable event. A series of unusual circumstances surrounded it. In the first place, the embassy was triggered off by the express request of the Siamese King Phra Narai, who for years had been extraordinarily interested in making contact with the King of France. At the end of 1680 Narai had already sent a fully-fledged embassy to France on the *Soleil d'Orient* a vessel of the French Oriental Company. That first attempt ended disastrously when the ship foundered near the eastern coast of Madagascar with the loss of all people and its valuable cargo. In 1684 another two Siamese courtiers were sent, accompanied by Father Bénigne Vachet, of the Missions Étrangères and it was his enthusiastic accounts of the Siamese and their enlightened king that succeeded in focusing French interest upon this exotic kingdom.

Secondly, this occurred at a time when Louis XIV, various influential courtiers as well as a number of members of the French Academy were all keen to gather more detailed information about various countries lying so far eastwards. The answer to the Siamese overtures therefore grew into a regular scientific expedition to the East, whereby it ought to be noted that the chief aim was not Siam, but China. They took an assortment of the most modern instruments, and detailed instructions were formulated as to what sort of observations were thought most interesting, what information about foreign art, architecture and science had to be collected. The expedition was equipped by the Royal Academy of Paris with scientific apparatus that contained an assortment of the largest telescopes ever to be carried across the oceans; they ranged from twelve to eighty feet in length. In addition, the Jesuits carried thermometers, barometers, quadrants, magnets, orreries, mirrors, compasses, magnifying glasses, clocks, globes, maps and scientific tables.

Thirdly, an important faction at the French court, which included the King's confessor the Jesuit Père de La Chaize and the King's mistress, Françoise d'Aubigné,[1] interpreted the Siamese overtures as a heaven-sent opportunity to boost the spreading of the Christian religion in Asia. The efforts to christianise the East had already met with a measure of success in the sixteenth and early seventeenth century, but the generation of priests that had accompanied Father de Rhodes in the 1650s had almost all died and in order not to lose the advantages that had been achieved these needed to be replaced. There can be little doubt as to the sincerely of the proselytising nature of this first French embassy. Alexandre de Chaumont, who was chosen by Louis XIV to head the mission, had recently abjured Calvinism in favour of Catholicism and apparently was full of zeal to celebrate his new religious convictions.[2] Françoise-Timoléon de Choisy, who was the second in rank, had been a notorious youth, but he was also reputedly a reformed character since 1683, when he had recovered from a serious illness.[3]

These circumstances help explain why such an unusually large group of cultured Frenchmen, among them a dozen young members of the French nobility, four missionaries, six Jesuit priests as well as an engineer, were interested in taking the risk to travel to Siam. This is also the reason why the mission was exceptional in its lavishness and size. The warship *Oiseau* turned out to be too small to carry all the presents, troops and scientific equipment so that the frigate *Maligne* had to be added to the mission.

Many of the participants were aware of their good fortune to be part of such an expedition and therefore the voyage and the subsequent visit to Siam has given rise to various books, each author describing the adventure from his own perspective. The ambassador le Chevalier de Chaumont left an account, le Comte de Forbin after returning to his country wrote a book in which this journey is depicted and also the Abbé de Choisy was quick to publish his travel impressions.[4] Thus there are four independent accounts which makes for a fascinating comparison.

Tachard's account has in common with that of Choisy that it brims with goodwill towards the Siamese, he exalts in the beauty of the things he observes and generally exudes optimism. Claude de Forbin, on the other hand, depicts the Siamese generally in negative terms.[5] The reason for these differences can be easily understood. As will be clear from the latter part of this foreword, during the course of the negotiations in Ayutthaya, Father Tachard did become deeply involved with a secret plan to change the history of Siam. In order to supervise and make the necessary steps to execute that secret plan he left his fellow Jesuits, who all continued their journey to China, and returned with the new embassy of King Narai to the French court.[6] Le Comte de Forbin, on the other hand, wrote in a bitter mood, after he had been forced to withdraw the garrison from the fortress Bangkok and there was for the time being no chance of expanding French influence.

Information about the person Tachard, and what may have prompted him to join the special company on a world voyage is scarce. Guy Tachard was born on the 7th of April 1651 in Angoulême, the capital of the Department Charente. At the age of seventeen he joined the Jesuits, the order that during the seventeenth century flourished in several European countries. The Jesuits were a proud and combative order that had gained various important privileges that assisted them in pursuing their goals. Jesuits valued their image as highly educated people who could be assigned to educate youth, to play diplomatic roles at various European courts, to attack with vigour all forms of Protestantism and to propagate the Catholic religion anywhere in the world. Like most members of a religious order, Tachard's career was largely determined by his superiors. At first he was active teaching grammar, humanities and rhetoric as well as mathematics in various colleges. From 1680 to 1684 he was attached as almoner to the French expedition to the Antilles, which was led by Vice-Admiral Jean d'Estrées. Tachard was therefore 34 years old and had already considerable knowledge of the larger world when he became one of the six Jesuits chosen to join the French expedition.[7]

All six Jesuits who were selected to make this journey had, from the very outset, cause to be particularly pleased, for each of them was presented with a Letter of Patent in the name of King Louis XIV, naming him to be a Royal Mathematician for the Indies and China, as well as a travel grant of twenty thousand *livres*. These six were Fathers Jean de Fontaney,[8] Jean François Gerbillon, Louis Daniel le Comte, Claude de Visdelou, Joachim Bouvet[9] as well as Guy Tachard himself. While Tachard returned to France with the new Siamese embassy, the other five Jesuits continued their tourney to China where most of them studied aspects of Chinese culture and many books and articles from these scientists assisted in broadening European knowledge about this part of the world.[10]

The opening part of Tachard's book deals with the preparation of the expedition, at least from the perspective of a priest-scholar. The captain of the *Oiseau* obviously had quite different concerns: he saw it as his duty to press for a speedy departure in order to make use of the seasonal winds. The furnishing of the two ships took much more time than foreseen, but finally both vessels set out on March 3, 1685 with their precious cargo. Tachard's account of the sea voyage succeeds in the first place to convey the atmosphere of pious joy. The great number of priests, under the leadership of the convert de Chaumont created an atmosphere in which an extraordinary amount of communal prayer took place during the months at sea. In moments of danger, or when it was felt that there was a dire need for divine intervention, it was decided to stage a special nine-days' devotion to the Holy Virgin.

Clearly this book conveys the impression that with so many ordained persons on board, a direct channel to God and the saints, or some sort of direct divine guidance was guaranteed. This also supports the idea that at the outset the religious aims of this embassy may have taken on a larger priority in the mind of the Chevalier de Chaumont than his official instructions lead us to believe. His written brief, dated 21 January 1685 told him that he should procure all possible mercantile advantages for French subjects and that he should examine in detail as to how the French could be employed there.

At the same time Tachard and his fellow Jesuits were trained scientists and their interest in observation and measurement are reflected in the account of meteorological conditions, in the story of the discovery that dolphins have no gills and that they breathe with their lungs as well as in other remarks about fishes, birds and seaweed. At night the king's mathematicians observed the sky, noting with growing enthusiasm the riches that the southern hemisphere had to offer the astronomer. They found the existing stellar charts to be shockingly inaccurate; unfortunately the irregular movements of the ship made it impossible to construct a proper stellar chart.

A particularly interesting chapter deals with the time when the two ships rested and refurbished their provisions at the Dutch colony at the Cape of Good Hope. Here the Jesuit mathematicians were well received; they obtained a lodging where they were allowed to set up a temporary observatory and where they managed to establish the true position of the Cape with the latest astronomical methods, by observing the movements of Jupiter's satellites.[11] Of some interest for the history of ethnology is the translation of a Latin account of a description of the peoples inhabiting the Southern African parts that had recently been discovered by the Dutch. This may well be the earliest written account of the Khoisan Nomads.

The stay at Cape Town was used to take in fresh water and victuals, but it may be doubted that much attention was given to improve the diet of the ships' occupants, for soon after setting out in the Indian Ocean many became sick of scurvy, the symptoms of which are accurately described by Tachard. It was not until much later that a connection was made between the intake of fresh food—particularly lemons—and the prevention of scurvy.

The reception of both ships by the Dutch at Batavia was also friendly. Throughout the eight days of their stay the expeditionary ships were given fresh meat and fruit. The Jesuits used the same tactics that had been so successful at Cape Town to assure a warm welcome by offering to make detailed astronomical observations. Unfortunately meteorological conditions did not permit a clear view of the night sky.

Finally, on 22 September 1685, more than six-and-a-half months after having set sail, the embassy reached the mouth of the Chao Phraya River. The very first character introduced by Tachard is not a Thai, however, but a Greek, here in this book identified as Monsieur Constance, and by Tachard described as a Minister of State in the Siamese administration. The prominent position accorded to this figure is related to what may have been Tachard's chief motivation for writing this book. Monsieur Constance is none other them Constantine Gerakis, better known as Phaulkon, a well-known figure in Thai History.

Phaulkon was born in 1647 on the Greek island of Cephalonia. In 1660 he had left his native country as member of the crew on an English trader. He managed to accumulate sufficient resources to be able to trade for himself before taking up employment in the Thai capital of Ayutthaya where his linguistic capabilities gained him a position at the Krom Phrakhlang, the Trade Department. In 1685, when Tachard met him he had been given the relatively high administrative rank of "Phra". He had gained direct access to King Narai and therefore occupied an important role at the Siamese court. Tachard exaggerates somewhat when he describes him as a fully-fledged Minister of State.

Probably it was because of his four years' experience in the Americas that Tachard spoke Portuguese and that he became indispensable as the go-between between Phaulkon and members of the French mission.

Tachard describes with approval with what honours the embassy was received by the Thais. We note the growing suspense during the slow journey upriver, each rest stop a little more luxurious until they were lodged in what appeared to Tachard to be a temporary palace outside Ayutthaya.

Here they waited until the first audience with the Thai king. It was a proud and hopeful procession carrying the personal letter by Louis XIV that on October 18, 1685 slowly moved to the chief royal reception hall,. Phaulkon seems to have exulted in being allowed to guide and conduct the largest and most impressive group of Europeans that had hitherto visited this country towards the man who held absolute power.

Tachard gives the text of the speeches that the French delivered, in which the sincere wishes to assist with a speedy conversion of the Thai king to Christianity take a prominent place. The overt proselytizing nature of the address may well have been somewhat embarrassing to Phaulkon, who must have known that Narai's interest in Christianity was no greater than his wish to know more about Islam. Since Phaulkon served as interpreter on this occasion, he had the opportunity to temper the language and so avoid causing insult. Later he takes much trouble to warn the embassy against an over-hasty approach.

The stay in Ayutthaya was made interesting to the French visitors when they had occasion to visit the Minister of Trade (the Phrakhlang) and when they made extensive sightseeing tours in some of Ayutthaya's Buddhist temples. For Tachard, however, the highlight of this first stay in Siam was the excursion to the nearby town of Lopburi (which was called Louvo by the Europeans) where the king maintained a large palace and spent much of his time. King Narai's Lopburi palace has been restored and readers are well advised to spend some time there and to attempt to picture the place as it was in Tachard's time, the elephant stalls occupied, and the women's quarters firmly closed. The ruins of Phaulkon's residence are not far away, its size is still apparent and it does not take much imagination to fill the ponds with water and picture the Jesuits strolling in its gardens.

It was here in Lopburi that the Jesuits seized the opportunity to examine an elephant, employing the eye of the scientist; one of the long list of tasks which the Royal Academy of Paris had asked them to do. They noted that the elephant indeed possessed five nails. It was there at Lopburi that the Jesuits were put in contact directly with King Narai who was interested in their skills as scientists. Upon hearing that they were to be given the chance to directly talk to him they wrote an address that is a statement of faith both in the Christian religion and in science. The highlight for the group of the French king's mathematicians was the observation of the eclipse of the moon on December 11, 1685. Up till then they had not been able to practice their skills for the ground was too wet and the houses too unstable to provide a solid base for their sensitive instruments. However, a proper site was provided and a temporary observatory installed. Tachard's account of King Narai's questions whilst using the telescope are of particular interest for they demonstrate the Siamese monarch's depth of knowledge and understanding. It would not be until the middle of the nineteenth century that Siam would again be reigned by a person with such wide interests and a keen regard for astronomy.

It was at Lopburi that Phaulkon discussed with the king a plan to establish a proper observatory, which would have to be manned by a group of Jesuits. It was at this moment that Tachard was asked whether he was interested in returning to France accompanying the new envoys of Narai to the French court. This meant that he would have to abandon his fellow-Jesuits who would all continue their voyage to China. This episode was undoubtedly a crucial moment in Tachard's life, for during the years that followed he would be devoted to matters concerning the Thais while his fellow Jesuits were henceforth occupied with China.

Tachard describes in a few words how this plan came about. King Narai was obviously impressed with the scientific instruments and their methodological display, so that Phaulkon seized the opportunity to suggest founding an observatory, just as the Chinese emperor in Peking possessed such a building. The version that was discussed at Lopburi, however, would be a modem European institute. King Narai agreed to allow twelve Jesuit mathematicians to settle down there on the understanding that they would teach the best that Europe had to offer in the arts and sciences.

However, in reality it appears that Tachard's change of plans was part of a rather sinister plot which is not mentioned in this book. After numerous conversations with him, Phaulkon had selected Tachard by name to become the key figure in a much more grandiose plan in the near future. When on the 18th of December the *Oiseau* set out for the return journey to France, this time carrying a letter from the Siamese king, Tachard tells us that Phaulkon called him aside and presented him with a rosary whose beads were made of a costly wood. He omits to tell us that on the same occasion he was handed a document in which Phaulkon had written down what he and Tachard had discussed in secret and which contained detailed instructions. This letter is highly relevant, for it throws light upon what Phaulkon's real intentions towards Siam were. The information it contained also helps explain why Tachard did not continue his journey to China, but returned to France as Phaulkon's agent to prepare for nothing less than the conversion of the whole of Siam.

This letter provides some of the background that may also explain why Tachard devoted so much of his energy to writing this book. It also assists us to understand the role Tachard played during the preparation of the second French embassy of 1687–8 as well as his conduct during subsequent negotiations between the French ambassadors and King Narai. Therefore it is here presented in full:

> 'Your reverence [Tachard] will use all possible despatch to secure the interest of the Pope and of Père la Chaise[12] with Louis XIV, in order to give immediate effect to the following recommendations which are calculated to establish the Christian religion in Siam along the lines which we have often discussed together in secret.
>
> Sixty or seventy men of good character and well versed in affairs should come out in the French fleet to Siam. They must have sufficient means to be independent of a salary, and must accept voluntary service with the State, so as to

circumvent any attempts that may be made to interfere with their promotion. If the General of the Jesuit Order desires to include any of his priests, they must come out ostensibly as laymen, and must be unrecognizable even to the people who know them.

I undertake to give them all the support they may need, and through my influence I will obtain for them the most important positions in Siam, such as governorships of provinces, cities and fortresses, or the control of forces on land and sea. I will introduce them into the palace and into State affairs, not excepting even the royal household, and I will employ them as my advisers in negotiations of State, following the plan which I have frequently expounded to Your Reverence.

To ensure that success be swift and certain, Your Reverence must impress upon the King the importance of occupying Singora[13] without delay. Two good colonies with soldiers are needed. Once the establishment is effected, there will be nothing to fear. The merchants will acquire the habit of trading there; all the Missions of Cambodia, Annam and Tonkin will be nearer to supplies and assistance, and the trade of Siam will be diverted to that place without much effort.

It would be desirable that the men who come out should be owners of the ships which they bring with them. I would give them facilities for conducting a successful trade, such as they could never obtain with the Company's ships.

All that is needed to secure the success of this scheme is speed, secrecy and the right men. Provisions abound here. We have all the tin, iron and copper we require for the manufacture of every imaginable article, even cannon; and what is more, it is ready to hand, as I have explained already to Your Reverence.

> If the objection is made that the King of Siam may die, and that the venture would thus be doomed to failure, I promise and undertake that the king's successor shall be even more ready than His Majesty King Narai to grant us everything; also that under him Christianity will enjoy even greater favour.[14]
>
> All these matters must be treated with profound reserve and with the utmost despatch, as I have already insisted in conversation with Your Reverence. I adjure you, therefore, by the bowels of the Lord Jesus Christ and by his wounds, that you pursue these negotiations with the King through the medium of his Confessor, and I wish you a good voyage and a speedy return.'[15]

This letter shows clearly that Phaulkon had developed, probably during the course of this first French embassy and after having been given permission by King Narai to bring in a group of Jesuits to establish an observatory. Obviously these are much bolder plans. They amounted to formal secret proposal to the French that he, Phaulkon, would use his position of influence at the Siamese court to provide them with a chance to take control of the whole region. With this secret document in his hands, Tachard must have felt himself to have been the real envoy. In his hands lay the possibility to further the cause of religion as well as that of France.

It is the effect of this letter which accounts for the glowing report on the Siamese kingdom that Tachard published so soon after returning in France. The first edition of this book appeared under the title *Voyage de Siam des Pères Jésuits, Envoyez par le Roy aux Indes & à la Chine: avex Leurs Observations Astronomiques, et leurs Remarques de Physique, de Géographie, d'Hydrographie, & d'Histoire.*

The work is of consummate interest for those who are interested in how at the end of the seventeenth century a French Jesuit observed the world. For scholars who are more interested in the history of Thai culture, the sixth and final part of the book which contains general information of the Siamese may be of the greatest interest. It rests upon deep knowledge of Siam and its inhabitants. Many accurate details that would have escaped the casual visitor must have derived from long discussions between Tachard and Phaulkon. Here we find for the first time an accurate translation of the chief vernacular names of the Thai capital Ayutthaya. Here is also an impressive description of the manner the Thais dress, we learn about the use of the betel nut, the preparation of tea and the medicinal qualities of ginseng.

The account of the Buddhist theory of karma in this part is, as far as I am aware, the first accurate and detailed description of Buddhist metaphysics in any European language. The Thai and Pali words and concepts are all easily decipherable. Thus "Pphukan Pprasamen" is a Thai expression, "Phukhau Phrasumen", the central post of the universe, Mount Sumeru, "Sommonokhodom" represents the Thai pronunciation of Samana Gautama, words designating the historical Buddha, "Prayomppaban" is Phra Yommaban, "Niruppan" is recognizable as Nirvana, "Thavip" is the Thai pronunciation of the Sanskrit word "Dwipa", which means island, or continent. "Ppra Rasi" are the legendary wizards, which are still called Phra Rishi. "Ton ppo" is Thai for Ton pho, the Bodhi tree under which the Buddha achieved enlightenment. "Thevatat" is a fair representation of the Thai pronunciation of the Pali name Devadatta, and the ominous role of this person in the Buddha's lifestory is retold by Tachard with many accurate details.[16] Also, the pages that deal with the heavens and hells may be regarded as a fair summary of the book on the Three Worlds, Traiphumikatha, which apparently was written in the fourteenth century and which remained a key document to understand traditional Thai cosmology.

After publishing this book on the first French diplomatic mission Tachard became attached to the second French embassy to Siam which took place in 1687 and 1688 under the leadership of Simon de La Loubère and Claude Céberet. This was an even grander event, with five vessels instead of two, carrying even more presents, fifteen Jesuits and hundreds of soldiers. In light of the secret letter printed above it seems clear that this time the French came with the purpose to greatly extent their influence. Tachard also has published an account of this second travel.[17]

When Tachard returned from the second embassy he still had no idea that his plan had foundered. King Narai had become too ill to reign and he had appointed Phra Phetracha, the general who was chief of the Elephant Brigade, to be acting head of government. This general seems to have more than an inkling of Phaulkon's duplicity and he sensed the danger of having French troops in the country. Thai history tells that he found proof of a plot against the ailing King, but it may well be that Phetracha had a hand in causing this proof to be found. Phaulkon and Narai's adoptive son, obliquely mentioned in the above-mentioned letter, were compromised. Realising that without the king's protection he was vulnerable and that a confrontation was at hand Phaulkon made a final attempt to call the French troops to come to his assistance but when they hesitated he was arrested, tortured and finally on June 5, 1688 summarily executed. Most of the French troops had since the arrival of the second French embassy occupied Bangkok and after Phaulkon's death they were beleaguered until they were forced to withdraw. The French bishop at Ayutthaya was incarcerated and all French influence came to an end.

When news of the disastrous end of the attempt to extend French influence finally reached France, Tachard was of course forced to abandon his master plan and all agents that he had already recruited had to be employed otherwise.

It is possible that the dream to convert Siam, which had been Tachard's secret wish and in which he had invested so much energy, did not readily disappear from his mind. According to a letter written April 7, 1713,[18] the intrepid priest called in at Siam in 1690, from where he went to Pondicherry where he was taken prisoner by the English. After the treaty of Rijswijck in 1697 he returned to France, and in 1698 he travelled for the last time to Asia. Once more he visited Ayutthaya, armed with a letter of Louis XIV, but it is doubtful that he was well received by King Phetracha. Tachard then settled down in the French East Indies where he died October 21, 1712.

This book, Tachard's first was quite influential. It was the first of a large number of French works concerning late-seventeenth century Siam. Apparently it was avidly read, the first three French editions date from 1686, 1687 and 1688, the first edition in the Dutch language dates from 1687, this English version appeared in 1688 and an Italian edition came out in 1693. When Engelbert Kaempfer visited the Dutch trading station at Ayutthaya in June and July 1690 he found, read and annotated a copy of this book and it can be established that in his later writing on Siam he benefited from some of Tachard's observations. It was a work that helped stimulate the French appetite to invest in a short-lived military adventure.

It is a book that still deserves attention, its mixture of scientific curiosity, methodical enquiry and religious zeal is typical for the period. The information it contains, in particular that which Tachard collated in the final part, provides us with an exemplary document on Siamese seventeenth-century culture.

B. J. Terwiel
Hamburg University

Notes to the Introduction

[1] Perhaps she is better known as the Marquise de Maintenon.

[2] The strong religious character *of* the first mission is also described by the Abbé de Choisy in his account, *Journal de Voyage de Siam fait en 1685-6 par M. I'Abbé de Choisy,* Paris chez Sebastien, 1687.

[3] For an account of the noble background and aspects of his licentious youth, see *The Transvestite Memoirs of the Abbé de Choisy and the Story of the Marquise-Marquis de Banneville* (Translated from the French by R. H. F. Scott). London: Peter Owen, 1973.

[4] In the eighteenth century some doubt was expressed as to the authenticity of the journal of the Abbé de Choisy, because extracts were found among the papers of Father Gerbillon, one of the Jesuits who shared the journey. However, these notes proved to be in a handwriting that differed from that of Father Gerbillon.

[5] Forbin is quite aware of this difference when he writes (p. 30): "...je dirai franchement que j'ai été surpris plus d'une fois, que l'Abbé de Choisy et le père Tachard qui ont fait le même voyage, et qui ont vu les mêmes choses que moi, semblent s'être accordés pour donner au public, sur le royaume de Siam, des idées si brillantes et si peu conformes à la vérité."

[6] What the Thai envoys experienced in France can be read in Michael Smithies, 'The Travels in France of the Siamese Ambassadors 1686-7', *Journal of the Siam Society,* Volume 77, Pt. 2, 1989, pp. 59-70. It is quite astounding that this scholar, as also all other European scholars cited in the

article, appears to be unaware of the fact that the diary of Kosapan, in which he describes in some detail what he observed and experienced, has been published in facsimile edition, together with a good transcription in modern Thai. See "Banthuekraiwan khong Okphra Wisutsunthon (Kosapan) Rachathut Thai pai Farangset samai Ayutthaya" *Sinlapakon,* Vol 27, B.E. 2527, pp. 27–145

[7] Much of the information about Tachard comes from Carlos Sommervogel (ed.), *Bibliothèque de la Compagnie de Jésus,* Brussels, Oscar Schepers, (9 Vols, 1890-1900) hereafter BCJ, Vol. 7, pp. 1802–5. Other relevant data were brought to light by Dirk van der Cruysse, *Louis XIV et le Siam,* Paris: Fayard, 1991.

[8] In the English editions the name is falsely printed as Fontenay. Father Fontaney was at the time a famous astronomer who, during the previous eight years, had taught mathematics at Cremont, the Parisian Jesuit college. He was put in charge of the party of six Jesuits.

[9] In English editions of Tachard's first voyage to Siam, the name is usually falsely printed as Couvet.

[10] Gerbillon later published a method of using the astrolabe in order to observe eclipses (BCJ, Vol 3, 1346–7). Claude de Visdelou, who was only 19 years old and just ordained at the time of embarkation, became particularly well versed in reading Chinese characters (BCJ, Vol 8, pp. 838–43). Le Comte probably became best known in Europe because of his books, which were translated in several languages (for details see BCJ Vol 2, pp. 1356–62).

[11] The results of these astronomical observations were published by Father de Fontaney as "Observations faites au Cap de Bonne-Espérance en 1685, sur les étoiles méridionales et sur la Voie Lactée", *Histoire de l'Académie des Sciences,* 1733, p. 30.

[12] La Chaize, the above-named confessor of Louis XIV.

[13] The southern port city of Songkhla. Subsequently the plan was altered in favour of the occupation of Bangkok.

[14] Phaulkon was assured of Mom Pi's willingness to cooperate with him. Mom Pi was King Narai's adopted son and who could be expected to have had a real chance to become Narai's successor.

[15] This is the English translation of a note, written in the Portuguese language, dated December 18, 1695, which carries Phaulkon's signature. It is held in the French Colonial Archives. (C. 22, fol. 183–184.) The translation is by E. W. Hutchinson, *Adventurers in Siam in the Seventeenth Century,* London: Royal Asiatic Society, 1940, pp. 112–114.

[16] Tachard identifies Devadatta as the Buddha's brother, while according to Buddhist tradition he was a cousin, the son of the Buddha's maternal uncle. However, since the Buddha, when he was still Prince Siddhattha, married Devadatta's sister Bhaddakaccana, he was also his brother-in-law.

[17] *Seconde Voyage du Père Tachard et des Jésuites envoyez par le Roy au Royaume de Siam. Contenant diverses remarques d'Histoire, de Physique, de Géographie, & d'Astronomie,* Paris: chez Daniel Horthemels, 1689.

[18] BCJ, Vol 7, p. 1802.

Book 1

The Voyage from Brest to the Cape of Good Hope

Since the time the King settled a Royal Academy at Paris, for improving arts and sciences within his Kingdom, the members that compose it have not hit upon any means more proper for accomplishing that design, than the sending out of learned men to make observations in foreign countries whereby they might correct the geographical maps, facilitate navigation, and raise astronomy to its perfection. In that prospect, not a few of the learned men of that illustrious society, were, by His Majesty's orders, sent into several Kingdoms: some went into Denmark, others to England; some were sent to the Isle of Cayana, and other Isles of America, Cape Verd, nay, and to the chief ports and coasts of the Kingdom, whilst others in the observatory at home, kept pace, and entertained all necessary correspondencies with them.

It was desired that an occasion might offer of sending more observators into several parts of Europe, to the Isle of Foroy, where they have fixed the first meridian, the East-Indies, and chiefly into China, where it was known that arts had flourished for these four thousand years, where there are books upon all subjects, and libraries that may compare with the fairest in Europe, from which the King's bibliotheque might be enriched.

This Father parted from Macao, December 1681, in a Dutch ship, and arrived in Holland in October 1682

This desire grew stronger in the chief members of the academy, after they had conversed with Father Philip Couplet, a Flemish Jesuit, who upon his return from China, posted by Paris on his way to Rome, whither he was sent about the affairs of the mission.

The Marquis de Louvoy, minister and secretary of state, who besides the affairs of war, and oversight of the King's buildings, was likewise charged with the concerns of arts and sciences, ordered, in His Majesty's name, the members of the Royal Academy to draw up a memoir of the most remarkable things they desired to be informed of from China, to be given and recommended to Father Couplet, who was to return thither the year following.

The Duke of Mayne favoured also the design with a great zeal for religion, and a curiosity suitable to his wit, calculated for knowledge, and far above his years.

But the King surpassing all in zeal for the improvement of arts and sciences, especially of such, which in those countries might most contribute to the growth of religion, being affected with the necessity of missions, was resolved to assist them with his protection and liberalities. He was informed by Father Couplet that almost all the French Jesuits, who above thirty years since went to China with Father Alexander of Rhodes, were dead, labouring in the missions of that Kingdom; that there were but a very few missionaries remaining; that the Emperor, in the mean time, continued to them his protection, and that in imitation of him, the viceroys and governors of provinces were also very kind to them; and that in short, there was a great want of gospel-labourers, not only for cultivating the Christians, who were already very numerous there, but also for reaping the fruit of the certain hopes, which at present more than ever, good men have of spreading the faith in that vast empire. He had already gone so far, as to assign a considerable sum of money for the French Jesuits who were to accompany Father Couplet; and all the care was, how they might be sent under His

Majesty's authority, when divine providence presented a most favourable occasion for it.

Hardly was Father Couplet departed for Rome, when two Siam Mandarins, with a priest of the foreign missions settled in Siam named Monsieur le Vachet, arrived in France. They were sent by the Ministers of the King of Siam, to learn news of the embassy which the King their master had sent to His Majesty, with magnificent presents, on board a ship belonging to the East-India Company, called the *Sun of the East*, which was reported to have been cast away.

His Majesty perceiving what advances the King of Siam made in seeking his friendship, and that there was hope besides he might turn Christian, if there were an ambassador sent to him, resolved to do it; and by the same way send Jesuits to China, which had a great commerce with the Kingdom of Siam, from whence it is not above five or six hundred leagues distant.

The King ordered six Jesuits, mathematicians, to be sent to China

The King having thereupon declared his intentions to the Marquis de Louvoy and Father de la Chaize, they forthwith demanded of our superiors, four fathers at least, that might be capable of labouring in consort with the Academy Royal, in the improvement of arts and sciences, and at the same time employ themselves with the missionaries of China in advancing the Christian religion; adding, that they must needs be ready to depart within six weeks, in the ship that was to carry the French ambassador to Siam.

It was no hard matter for our superiors to find men that were willing to contribute to the furthering of the design. Amongst many who offered themselves, six were chosen, who, though of different provinces, were happily at that time in the Jesuits College at Paris, as if divine providence had only brought them together for obtaining a happiness which they earnestly longed for. The superior named to be over them was Father Fontenay, who for eight years past taught the mathematics in that college. The other five were, Father Gerbillon, Father l'Compte, Father Visdelou, Father Couvet and myself, Father Gay Tachard.

The preparations for their departure

So soon as the thing was resolved upon, we had private notice given us, to prepare for our departure within two months at farthest. Next day we went together to Mount-Martre to thank God by the mediation of the Holy Virgin and Holy Martyrs, for the favour that was done us, and to offer ourselves up to Jesus Christ more particularly in that place where St. Ignatius and his companions made their first vows, and which is looked upon as the cradle of the society, that from its birth had devoted itself in a most particular manner to foreign missions. That's the reason that they who constitute it, have ever since consecrated themselves to that duty by a solemn vow; so that everyone thinking himself in particular destined to it, ought accordingly to prepare himself from his youth upward, by all the exercises of piety and mortification, and by the study of the sciences and long voyages that may most fit him for it. And this is practised with so great a blessing, that the same vigour of spirit that was at first may be said still to be in the order.

They were admitted into the Royal Academy of Sciences

The design of our voyage being made public at Paris, the members of the Academy, who concerned themselves most in it, did us the honour to admit us into that society, by a particular privilege; and we took our places there some days before our departure. The most proper means for executing the orders of the King were thought on, and it was resolved that besides the instructions which the Marquis of Louvoy had prepared, to be given to Father Couplet, when he should return to China, and which was forthwith put into our hands, the chief members of the Academy, should furnish us with particular memoirs relating to the observations that might be proper to be made in China, and the things that were to be sent home to France, as well for enriching the King's library, as for the improvement of arts.

Divers instructions are given them for the improvement of Arts and Sciences

Every one of these members took upon themselves to furnish us with such as concerned the arts and sciences they were most versed in; and we thereupon had several conferences with them. We agreed upon the astronomical observations that we should make in China and on our voyage. They gave us the tables of the satellites of Jupiter, which have been made with so great labour, and which at present serve for determining the longitudes of places. They also presented us with several large telescopes of 12, 15, 18, 25, 50, and 80 foot, whereof we were to leave some in the observatory of Peking. They imparted to us besides, several memoirs in Natural Philosophy, Anatomy, and concerning plants. There were sea-charts of the course we were to follow in the King's library, which had served in other voyages, we had copies of them given us, and they proved very useful to us in our sailing. They gave us very good and ample instructions concerning navigation, architecture, and other arts, concerning the books that were to be sent to France, and the observations that it would be proper for us to make. In short, of all the members of that learned academy, there was none who appeared not in that affair with particular zeal and application, seeing the success of it would not a little contribute to the glory and satisfaction of the King. All these memoirs being examined in several meetings of the Academy Royal, were given in to us before our departure. And these gentlemen having promised to communicate their discoveries to us, we engaged ourselves to send them our observations, to the end that acting in consort, and making but one body of academicians, some in France, and others in China, we might jointly labour in the increasing and improvement of sciences, under the protection of so great a Monarch.

The various instruments they take with them for their observations

In the mean time we were much taken up in preparing all the instruments that were necessary for us; and seeing we were to leave Paris within a month, we had made for us in that time, two quadrants of ninety degrees, the one of eighteen inches the radius, and the other of twenty six; three great pendulums with seconds, an instrument for finding out at the same time the right ascension and the declination of stars; and equinoctial dial that marked the hours to the very minutes, having underneath a large compass for finding out all hours of the day the declination of the load-stone. All these instruments were to be made use of in astronomical observations.

We had also two bows or half circles, divided very exactly into six and six minutes, for geometrical operations, the one had only sights, and the other glasses. When we went to take our leave of the Duke of Mayne, he had the goodness to give us a third and bigger, divided by three and three minutes, which he had made for his own use. We cannot sufficiently acknowledge the obligations we have to that prince for the goodness he expressed towards us on that occasion.

Besides the engines I have been mentioning, we carried with us two repetition-pendulum-clocks, burning-glasses of twelve, and twenty inches diameter, load-stones, microscopes, several thermometers and barometers, all the tubes and machines that serve in making experiments of vacuity, a dial upon an inclining plane, the two machines of Romer, one of which represents the motion of the planets, and the other the eclipses of the sun and moon. They gave us also for our use several books out of the King's library.

In the mean time our pensions were settled by orders from the King, who caused also his letters patents to be expeded for us, whereby His Majesty made us his mathematicians in the Indies and China.

The arrival of the Chevalier de Chaumont at Brest

We arrived at Brest, February 10 and some days after orders came from court to hasten our embarking, because the season was already far spent. They were obeyed with so much diligence, that everything almost was in a readiness, when the Chevalier de Chaumont named by the King for the embassy of Siam arrived at Brest. This gentleman well known in the Kingdom for his particular merit, and the nobility of an ancient and illustrious family, was in his youth bred up a Calvinist, but God did him the grace to convert him and his brothers one after another at different times. The last of all having for many years served in the armies with the approbation of a brave gentleman, and good officer, being at length cloyed with the world, and desirous to work out his own salvation, put himself into our society, where he lived and died like a saint, having edified all that knew him by rare examples of all sorts of virtues, and especially of an heroic patience under the pains and trouble which he felt by the wounds that he had formerly received in the wars. The Chevalier de Chaumont of whom we are now speaking, was his elder brother. At first he served at land, where his singular merit made him known, and particularly beloved of the King whilst he was but young. He was afterwards sent to Toulon, there to command the main-guards or reformades, and to instruct them in all exercises necessary for gentlemen who are to command His Majesty's ships. Since that he was made captain of a man of war, and Major General of the King's naval-forces in the Levant. His zeal for his prince's service had nothing lessened his continual application to the service of God; and all gave him his due when they looked upon him as a man of singular prudence and piety. Therefore it was that His Majesty, who proposed to himself chiefly the good of religion, and the conversion of the King of Siam by the embassy which he resolved to send to him, pitched upon the Chevalier de Chaumont for so glorious an employment; being persuaded that the good example which he would give in that country, would be so many proofs of the sanctity of Christianity, that might fully convince that King of the truth of our religion.

The King sends the Jesuits patents of mathematicians

Next day after he came we had the honour to salute him in his lodgings, and received from his hands the patents which it pleased the King to give every one of us in particular, sending us in quality of his mathematicians into the Indies and China. They were signed and sealed with the great seal of yellow wax, and conceived in these terms.

> LOUIS by the grace of God King of France and Navarre: To all who shall see these present letters; greeting. Being very willing to contribute on our part to anything that may more and more establish the security of navigation, and improve arts and

sciences; we have thought that for the surer attaining to that, it was necessary to send to the Indies and China some knowing and learned persons, capable of making there the observations of Europe: and judging that for that effect we could not make a better choice than of F.N. a Jesuit, by the particular knowledge we have of his extraordinary capacity. For these and other causes thereto moving us, of our special grace, full power and Royal Authority, we have ordained and constituted, and by these presents signed with our hand, do ordain and constitute the said F.N. our mathematician. Our will is, that in that quality he go to the Indies and China, there to make all observations necessary, for the improvement and curiosity of arts and sciences, the exactness of geography, and the surer establishment of navigation.

We therefore charge and command our most dearly beloved son the Count of Toulouse Admiral of France, our vice-admirals and lieutenant-generals in our naval forces, commanders of squadrons of the same, particular governors of our towns and strong places, mayors, consuls, and all our other officers to whom it belongs to give to the said F.N. all the aid, favour and assistance that is needful to him for the execution of these presents, without permitting any let or hindrance to be given him that may retard his voyage, for such is our will and pleasure. In witness whereof, we have caused our seal to be put to these presents; we pray and require all kings, princes, potentates, states, republics, our friends, allies and confederates, their officers and subjects to give the said F.N. all sort of succour and assistance for the accomplishment of a design which equally concerns the advantage of all nations, without suffering anything to be exacted from him contrary to the liberty of his function, and the customs and rights of the Kingdom.

Given at Versailles January 28, 1685 and the two and fortieth year of our reign. Signed Louis, and upon the fold, Colbert.

A Frigate is joined to the first ship

Though all things were ready for embarking, and the wind very fair for putting out to sea, yet it behoved us to stay, till the frigate called the *Maligne*, mounted with thirty guns which was lately ordered by the King to accompany the first ship, should be fitted and made ready to follow us: when the news of these orders came to Brest, it caused so much joy amongst all that were to go [on] the voyage, and was received with so great applause; that it was in everybody's mouth, that now we could not but expect a prosperous voyage. The truth is, without that assistance it would have been impossible to have carried the King's presents, the equipage of the Ambassador, and of the officers of the ship, and passengers, and above all, necessary provisions for so long a voyage, not to speak of a great many bales of all sorts of curiosities which the King of Siam had sent for, both from France and England.

The King ordered his ambassadors at Lisbon to demand passports for the Jesuits from the Kingdom of Portugal.

About that time we had advice that at Lisbon, they had granted the passports which had been demanded for us, and which we earnestly desired; because the differences that happened betwixt Portugal and the French ecclesiastics not being as yet made up, we were in fear lest the Portuguese Officers might from thence take occasion to stop us on our way. Monsieur de Saint Romain, extraordinary ambassador from the King in Portugal, who very well knew the Kings mind as to that, took notice of it in a discourse he made to the King of Portugal for obtaining the passports. These were his very words.

SIR,

I have by the last courier from France received orders, to acquaint Your Majesty with the resolution the King my master has of sending by sea an ambassador to the King of Siam, in correspondence with the civilities of that prince; and that taking advantage of that occasion, he'll send on board the same man of war six

French Jesuits who are to go from Siam to Macao in China. These religious have in commission to observe in their travels by sea and land, the longitudes of the chief places, the declinations and variations of the needle, and all that can serve to certify and improve our charts and navigation, and to make an exact search of all sorts of curious books for the library of the King my master. I am commanded to tell Your Majesty that they have express orders to entertain a good correspondence with your subjects in what place soever they may meet them, and to have all due deference and submissions for the Portuguese prelates. The King my master makes no doubt but that Your Majesty desires also on your part, that your subjects in the East should give to these religious the succours and assistances that they may stand in need of for the accomplishment of their voyage and commission: and to the end they may be informed of it, the King my master has ordered me to demand, as I do with confidence, of Your Majesty, a passport for these religious, in the most ample and favourable form that may be. The ship that is to carry the Ambassador of France and the Jesuits to Siam, will infallibly set out before the end of March and I most humbly beg Your Majesty that it would please you to order that passport speedily to be expeded, and presently after delivered.

The letter of Father la Chaize to Father Verbiest at Peguin

In the same packet they sent us this letter, which Father la Chaize wrote in the King's name to Father Ferdinand Verbiest of our company, missionary of China and President of the mathematics in the vast empire.

Reverend Father,

With great joy do I acquit myself of the commands of the greatest King in Christendom, in addressing myself to your reverence, to recommend to you six of our fathers, his subjects, men of extraordinary merit and capacity, that under your protection they may carry to China and Tartary, the knowledge of the true faith, and get from thence all the observations of astronomy, and all the knowledge of the arts and sciences of a nation, for which the reverend Father Philip Couplet, whom His Majesty had the pleasure to see here, had wrought in him a very particular esteem. All the six besides a great zeal and rare virtue, have considerable advantage as to languages and sciences, and the skill they have in the mathematics, had made His Majesty make choice of them for his mathematicians, for which he had given them all letters patents under the great seal of the Chancery. Your reverence will have the satisfaction, by means of these fathers to contract a kind of commerce, in favour of the sciences, betwixt two of the most powerful sovereigns of the world, and the greatest protectors of sciences. There is so great a resemblance betwixt the prudence and happiness of their government, the strength and number of their armies, the economy and good order of their states, the blessing God gives their undertakings, the magnificence of their courts, the greatness and nobleness of their thoughts, that it would seem those two admirable princes finding nothing upon earth so great and august as themselves, and being both born for the glory of their age, and the welfare of their people, ought to be as much united by the same heroic virtues and qualities which they have received from Heaven, as they are separated by the vast space of seas and land that disjoin their territories on Earth, may the supreme lord of all Kings and Emperors, who had made them both the defenders of the true worship of God, and protectors of his altars, give them also the same thoughts as to religion, the same zeal for the propagation of the true faith, and the same earnestness in the publication and practice of the gospel, that the great Emperor of China may not be inferior to ours in that only essential point of true grandeur, which is wanting to the dignity of his person, and the happiness of his reign, all holy and zealous persons of this flourishing Kingdom, wherein Louis the Great does sedulously establish the unity of the Catholic faith, virtue and piety by his examples, his cares, his edicts and continual liberalities, incessantly beg of Heaven the same grace for your great Emperor: we continually offer up our prayers and sacrifices to the true God for that. We cannot believe that so many virtues as he already possesses, will be for ever without a reward, for want of the virtues of Christianity, with which we hope he will consummate that great merit, which procures him so fair a reputation all over the Earth. I beseech you R.F. that for the satisfaction of our great King, which God hath given to Europe for a defender and restorer of the true faith, and whom according to all prophecies he designs for the destruction of Mohammedanism,[1] you would still give us the best information you can, of the virtues, sentiments and actions of your great Emperor, for whom he had already conceived so particular an esteem. I likewise adjure you to protect, assist and favour, as much as lies in your power, those zealous and learned missionaries whom he hath sent you, and at whose head he has placed Father Fautenay, whose merit you know, and who was looked upon by all the learned mathematicians of the Royal Academy of Sciences, that is here entertained by the liberalities of His Majesty, as an extraordinary man, and one that was an honour to their nation. They bring you all the observations and curiosities of the sciences of Europe in their greatest perfection, and are sent to you as pledges of other greater matters that His Majesty would do, and without doubt will do hereafter for the satisfaction of your great Monarch, and of yourself in particular, so soon as he hath heard how his mathematicians have been received and treated in China and what aids and assistances have been given them for putting in execution the orders that are enjoined them. I cannot express to your reverence what advantageous consequences I do presage from the sending of these fathers to you, if it please God to give a blessing to it. Since they all set out from court, and the capital city of this realm, where they have been bred for some time, and highly considered for their merit; they will acquaint you with many things that will content your zeal and curiosity, better than I can relate them in writing, above all things I beg of your reverence to believe them, when they assure you that no man living is more respectfully and more cordially than I am in the union of your sacrifices, and of your apostolic labour,

reverend Father,
your most humble
and obedient servant,
DE LA CHAISE.
of the Society of Jesus.

Monsieur de Vaudricourt made captain of the ship

Some days after, they adjusted the number of those that were to go in the ship with the Ambassador. Besides the Abbot of Choisy who is well known in France by his birth and merit, and who was to continue with the King of Siam in quality of ambassador until his baptism, in case he should be converted. The two Siamese mandarins, Monsieur le Vacbet, who came with them into France, four other churchmen, and the six Jesuits, were also taken on board. Monsieur le Vaudricourt commanded the ship; he is one of the oldest and ablest sea-captains the King has; and has distinguished himself on several occasions, both in the Channel against the Dutch, and in the Mediterranean in the war of Messina, during twenty years that he had served at sea, having never missed a campaign wherein he was not actually in His Majesty's service. We are particularly obliged to him for his civilities, and the good offices he did us during our whole voyage in such a manner as engages us to the highest acknowledgement. M. Coriton was our second captain; we had two lieutenants, M. de Forbin, and M. de Cibois, and an ensign called M. de Charnorean.

Of the twelve gentlemen named by the King to wait on the Ambassador, three were put on board of us; and the rest of the frigate commanded by Monsieur Joyeux, lieutenant of the port of Brest, who had already made several voyages to the Indies.

The Ambassador goes on board the Oyseau

In fine, the day of embarking being come, on the first of March my Lord Ambassador accompanied by the Count of Chasteau-Renaud commander of a squadron, and most of the nobility and gentry that were then at Brest, went into the King's chaloop, and so on board, with sound of trumpets. Monsieur de Vaudricourt, with all the officers at the head of the soldiers and seamen, was in readiness to receive him on board with the colours, streamers and pendants abroad. Upon his entry the ship saluted him with thirteen guns, and the frigate with nine. The companies of both vessels by their many reiterated huzza's showed the joy they had to perform the voyage under a commander of so great worth; all the day following was allowed for preparing to be gone.

Departure from the road of Brest

We weighed anchor in the night time, and Saturday morning, the third of March by break of day made sail. So in leaving France we parted with the sweetness and repose of a religious life, which till then we had enjoyed, that we might go to the end of the world, to find an occasion of glorifying God and consecrating ourselves to the conversion of infidels, in prosecution of the orders laid upon us by our great Monarch.

As we put out of the road of Brest we had a fair wind; but it failing us by that time we were got seven or eight leagues from the port, about noon we dropped anchor, until five or six o'clock in the evening that the wind blowing again from the same corner, we again set sail.

The Gullet is a very strait passage from the road of Brest to the sea

The entry and coming out of the Gullet as ships put out from Brest, is a very difficult passage, by reason of hidden works which run out a good way into the sea, on both sides of the shore; but our pilots being well acquainted with the coast made no scruple to put out in the night time.

From that time till within five or six degrees of the line, we had as good weather, and as favourable winds as we could have desired; divine providence taking pleasure, it seems, to savour a voyage undertaken for the sake of religion, in a time when the most expert sea-commanders were of opinion that we had let slip the season proper for setting out by three whole weeks. We had at first so strong a wind on poop, that with a single sail abroad we made above threescore leagues in four and twenty hours. So that without any danger we doubled Cape Ushant and Cape Finistere so dreadful to our seamen, because of the frequent storms that arise about those places. The truth is, we found a very rough and rolling sea there.

Thursday the eighth, at the height of Cape Finistere, we saw a Dutch vessel standing in to the Channel of England which had been forced to lie by and drive because of the contrary winds. Both our pilots and officers assured us that ships were many times above three weeks before they could double that cape.

They who have been at sea well know how great trouble and sickness men endure, the first time they meet with a rough sea; but it is impossible to make those who never felt it sensible of the same: one finds himself quite stunned with a violent headache, the stomach retches, the heart faints, and it would seem that the roiling of the ship overturns the whole frame and constitution of the body, such pains it causes in the bowels. We were almost all of us grievously tormented with this sea-sickness for the first five or six days.

How the Churchmen and Jesuits spent their time during the voyage

From that time forward until we arrived at Siam we said mass for the most part[2] every day, and I make no doubt but that the happy success of our voyage ought to be attributed to that august sacrifice which was so often offered up on board, and to which all came with singular devotion. There passed no Sunday nor Holy-day whereon several did not participate of the Holy mysteries. This zeal was the effect of the good examples of my Lord Ambassador, who communicated once every eight days with extraordinary humility and piety. Every Holy-day and Sunday before public vespers which were sung with much devotion, the secular and regular churchmen by turns made a sermon to the ships company. A Jesuit took the care upon him of catechising the officers men, soldiers, and seamen, three times a week. That exercise was begun and ended by a spiritual hymn, sung by two seamen who had pretty good voices, and all the rest made answer upon their knees about the main-mast. These good examples, these regular instructions and exercises of piety, besides the visiting of the sick, and the small assistances that were given them several times a day, so wrought upon the hearts of those poor people, that there was none of them almost but that made a general confession, and came to the sacrament on the principal Holy-days.

Calms under the torrid zone

Before we came to the Cape of Good Hope, we had a little calm and much contrary wind, which made the Ambassador resolve to have nine masses said to the honour of the Holy Virgin, that by her intercession we might obtain favourable weather, because the heats which are commonly left in those places, began to occasion many diseases in the ship.

The devotion of the whole ship's company towards the Holy Virgin

One of the Jesuits laid hold on that occasion to introduce on board a laudable custom of saying the litanies of the most Holy Virgin, which is practised on board the ships that are commanded by the Marshall D'Estree: five or six soldiers, and as many sea-men divided into two companies upon the poop and fore-castle began that devotion a little before the first watch was set in the evening, and within a few days, all were ready to join in it, so that upon our return it was made, as it were, a public exercise of obligation, which was performed so zealously, that neither cold nor rain could hinder it.

To all these Holy practices we added the chaplet. Our fathers took the pains to divide themselves into several parts of the ship to cause it to be said, and God so blessed their zeal, that there was hardly any seaman or soldier but who every day said his beads. Besides the time that we allowed to public instruction, we daily said our breviary together, and we had an hour of conference about cases of conscience; the rest of the day was employed in study with as much application and assiduity as if we had been in our colleges. These were our ordinary exercises during the whole voyage.

Sunday the eleventh we past in sight of the Isle of Madera, where we plainly observed a great deal of snow upon the hill that was nearest to us.

In sight of the Isle of Madera

After noon three small English vessels returning into Europe past to the leeward of us; it was thought they came from the Canaries, because they had not as yet haled in their boats. Much thereabouts we met with the trade-winds so much desired by the seamen, and so agreeable to all people; being winds that blow always one way betwixt north and east, the ship does not require much working; besides being temperate they qualify the heats of the zone, which otherwise would be insupportable. They are commonly met with about the latitude of Madera. The sea then becoming smooth, and the wind steady and fixed, ships carry a great deal of sail, and make commonly betwixt forty and fifty leagues from noon to noon without any roiling of the ship or sea; so that if sailing were never more troublesome nor dangerous, voyages to the Indies would be but long and pleasant recreations.

In sight of the Isle of Palmas

The thirteenth we discovered the Isle of Palmas and sailed within four or five leagues of it, according to the reckoning of our pilots: there we called to mind the happy lot of Father Ignatius Azebedo and his nine and thirty companions all Jesuits, who going together to preach the gospel in Brazil, had all the happiness to die in sight of this isle, which was literally to them a fortunate island, since there they found the palm of martyrdom, which they were going to look for in the new world. They were all put to death in hatred of the faith by Calvinist pirates, who having made themselves masters of the ship wherein they were, called the St. James, put them all to death either by water or sword, to hinder, as they said, these papists the declared enemies of their reformation, from going to infect the barbarians with their pernicious doctrine. One and all of us envied the happy lot of these generous defenders of the Catholic faith, and would have been ravished to have finished our course for so holy a cause: but it is not just to desire the crown before one hath run the race. We saw also the Isle of Fera, the most western island of the Canaries, where our geographers have placed their first meridian, afterwards we doubled Cape Verde, and the isles of that name, which are ten in number.

The maps of the south part of the Heavens are not exact

According as we drew nearer and nearer to the line, we took pleasure to observe that as the stars of the Arctic Pole lowered those of the Antarctic Pole were elevated over our heads, of all the new stars which we discovered to the south, we were at first most taken with those of the crosiers, so called, because the chief four are so disposed that they make a kind of cross. The biggest of all is twenty seven degrees from the Pole; by these seaman steer their course, and sometimes take their latitude.. Seeing our course stood still on that way, and that we daily discovered new stars, we had time enough to consider them, and to compare that new region of the firmament with the astronomical map of Father Pardies; but we found little or no conformity betwixt them. That map needs much to be reformed, and one might begin with the crosiers, the arms whereof are more unequal in the firmament than in the map. The Wolf and Centaur are so carelessly and unfaithfully set down in it, that with much ado can one know them in the Heavens, though, in the mean time, they render the place they possess very bright and sparkling, by reason of the great number of stars that compose them, and which seem to make but one constellation. But in the map it is nothing less, where the two constellations, can, at most pass but for ordinary. The stars of the Southern Triangle, seem indeed to stand in the firmament in that very situation which the map gives them as to one another; but they seem to be ill placed in relation to other constellations. The stars of the Bull are nothing near so fair as they appear to be in the map, though the disposition of them be much the same, the Crane, in my opinion, is the constellation the best represented of any on that side, and to see it once upon the map, is enough to make one immediately find it out in the Heavens: the Bee, the Apodus or Bird of Paradise, and the Chameleon, though they be small, yet are pretty well set down. Something also would be reformed in the figure and situation of the clouds and other Meridional constellations, wherein many more defects might be found out by means of instruments. If we had the pleasure, as you may see, to observe the grosser faults, we had the trouble at the same time, that we could not tell how to remedy them; the tossing of the ship not suffering us to make use of our instruments, for reforming that map, so as to make it a new one, which otherwise would not have been hard to be done. However we made a new one only by the eye, which, though it be not so defective as the former, yet cannot be so exact as such works require to be, wherein one can not well succeed without the assistance of instruments.

Plenty of fish about the Equinoctial Line

This was our usual employment for the first hours of the night and an hour or two before day, when the sky was clear. However that was not all our diversion; for in the daytime we had the pleasure of fishing. It is true we did not begin to find plenty of fish till we came within five or six degrees of the line. Before that we had taken a kind of tortoise which the seamen call a turtle, weighing about three of four score pound weight, which was brought to table three or four times, several ways dress't. Many liked the taste of it pretty well, and others could hardly endure the smell thereof. But in the whole space of twelve degrees; that is to say of 120 leagues on each side of the line, we daily saw, for the most part, a vast quantity of all sorts of fish, and especially of porpoises which swam in shoals about the ship. To see the fishing of these, which was the most common, served to recreate us after our studies.

The way of catching porpoises

In several parts of the ship, and especially in the head, there were many seamen with each a harping-iron, which is a kind of big javelin fastened to the end of a line about the thickness of ones little finger. As the porpoises past by them, they struck them so home, that sometimes they pierced them through and through. When once they had darted the harping-

Iron, they left it sticking in the wound, keeping hold of it by the line to which it was fastened, and which they veered out to play the wounded fish, until the porpoise weakened by the loss of blood, suffered itself to be hauled aboard without any resistance, we took many in this manner. They were about four or five foot long and proportionally big. It is an animal that much resembles a pig, not only in the flesh and fat, but also in the internal and external figure; the flesh of it is not delicate, and tastes oily.

The blood of porpoises is hot We had a fair occasion then to undeceive a great many who having never seen porpoises could not believe that their blood was hot, or that they breathed, tho' they had sometimes heard those who had made trial of it say so; some of those had the curiosity to thrust their hand into the belly of the fish when it was opened, and they averred that the entrails of it were very near as hot as those of a pig. Nor did they make any more doubt but that they breathed, when they saw that it had lungs as fit for respiration, as the lungs of animals that live out of the water are. And indeed nature having given it no gills like other fish; but only two holes on the two sides of the head to let in the air; that undoubtedly is the reason, why these fish every now and then raise the head, and sometimes the whole body above the water, and that they always swim against the wind. Hence also it is that when seamen see the porpoises move any way during a calm, they fail not to say that they will have the wind from that corner which they swim towards. Whatever presentment they may have, we sometimes luckily found the seamen's predictions to be true.

Porpoises devour one another I have been often told, nay and have observed in a voyage that I made to America, that when one of these fish is mortally wounded, and has strength enough to struggle itself off of the harping-iron, the rest follow it by the tract its blood makes which it sheds in abundance, and never leave it till it be dead, that so they may devour it. I was confirmed in that opinion; for one day a porpoise which had been struck kept so great a struggling, that it wrought the harping-iron out of its belly, and escaped out of our hands. At that time there were many more about the ship; but so soon as this which had been wounded, fled for it, all the rest disappeared, and there was not one more to be seen all that day.

A *description of the shark*

Now we are upon fishing, I must here speak of what sport we had that way, and of the fish we saw, which are not so well known in Europe. I will begin with the shark, because it is a fish often seen, and most easily taken. We have some times taken six of them in one day. This fish is a kind of sea dog which hath a very large and flat head, the mouth very low because of the lower jaw which lies a great way under the upper; so that when it would bite, it is forced to lie upon one side, and sometimes upon the back. Those we took were about four foot long, and very thick, a little below the head the skin of it is a kind of chagrine, that hath a very rough grain, with six openings on each side, which are shut by means of a kind of very thin skin, that stands it instead of gills. It is certainly the most voracious animal living; tho' it hath been struck with the hook three or four times, and the mouth of it be all bloody, yet still it returns again with the same greediness, until it be taken, or hath carried away the bait. Now if it chance to seize a man, he is gone, it never quits its hold, and therefore it is, say some, that the sea men call it shark. The cause of that extraordinary greediness is the greatness of its liver; it consists of two lappets drawing round at the ends, being a foot and a half long and four fingers broad, but not at all thick; besides it hath but one gut, and that a very short one too and almost straight. We found one with a piece of board in its belly four fingers broad and a foot and a half long. It hath no lungs, and the heart of it is placed in a concavity made by the concourse of two bones near the head. It hath three rows of teeth, of which some do bend, some are straight, and others of different figures, nay it hath also a row of triangular teeth which are very thin, and terminate like a saw. There are three concavities in the head of it, one on each side, which contain a white substance that hath some consistence; it afterwards grows hard, and is called the sharks stone: our chirugeons[3] attribute great virtues to it, and I take their word. The third concavity, that is in the middle of the head holds the brain, which is much about the bigness of a pullets egg. The substance thereof appeared to us to be very waterish, and it was with much ado that we could distinguish the callous body, from the medullary. It hath a very little cerebral, and betwixt the brain and the cerebral, a very soft glandule which bears upon two other smaller ones.

Sucking-fish called by the seamen pilot-fish

The shark is always attended by several small fish that make its retinue, and which adhere so inseparably to him, that they will choose rather to be taken with him than to abandon him: they are called his pilot-fish; because it is pretended, that they serve him for guides to lead him to those places, where they discover any prey. It is a vulgar error to imagine that these fish perform that good office to him without any interest; they only stick so close to him, because of the food they find there. For besides that, they make the best of the reversions of his prey, they stick close to his skin by means of a cartilaginous little skin of an oval figure, which they have upon the head and which is straked and armed with a great many fibres, wherewith belike they attract some juice; and that's the reason why some call them sucking fish. When they have a mind to swim off, they must keep without reach of his teeth, otherwise they would fare no better than other fish do. I have seen some sharks attempt to catch them, and it was well for the sucking fish that they got as soon as possibly they could to their usual sanctuary. When they are pulled up with the shark it is no easy matter to separate them; if they be put upon a table, they will stick to it as they do to the sea-dog; and in that situation which is natural to them, the under-side of their gills and their belly is upwards. There are two kinds of them, some white, which are much of the shape of rochet-fish, and others blackish that are very small: of these last chiefly I speak.

The bonito pursues the flying-fish

We found also a great many bonitos thereabouts which are the implacable enemies of the flying-fish, whom they continually pursue. It is the best sort of fish that we took in all our voyage: they are about the bigness of our largest carps, but much thicker, have no scales, but the skin a little silvered, and the back marked with long, obscure, and gold-like streaks. We also took albacores, so called by the Portuguese because of their whitish colour. They are a kind of bonito, but three times bigger than the others: the fish, colour, and taste are much the same. Seeing both of them are great lovers of the flying-fish, the seamen make a thing like a flying-fish, which they fasten to the end of a line to catch them with. They make that figure dance upon the surface of the water before the bonitos and albacores, which leap out of the water so greedily to snap it, that many times they will take thirty or forty of them in an hours time with two or three lines only.

We met not with so many bonitos as sailors commonly do, because, perhaps, the number of flying-fish was not then so great in those seas. However, we saw many shoals of them rise up in the air eight or ten foot high, and fly fifty or sixty paces before they fell again into the water to moisten their wings, and recruit their strength to avoid the bonitos, which many times catch them at their fall, or leap out of the water and take them upon wing. They meet with certain birds of prey also that fall upon them, when they rise out of the water to escape from the bonitos.

One of these fish being hotly pursued one day leaped into our ship and struck against one of our mates heads. Tho' I had seen of them before, yet I took pleasure to consider it: it was of the shape, colour and bigness of a herring, the back somewhat thicker, and the fore-part of the head round like the pocket-fish with wings much like to those of bats.

Those are the sorts of fish that we saw most about the Line. We had the sun a'peek, that is to say, just over head the nine and twentieth day of March towards the third degree of the north latitude.

The weather being very clear that day; we had the pleasure to observe, that at noon the masts and everything else in the ship made no shadow, after that we were becalmed for seven or eight days, and we made the remaining three score and ten leagues to the line, only by short gusts of wind, which clouds and tempests brought with them. After all, we heard none of those great-thunder-claps thereabouts, wherewith they threatened us so much in France: but we saw much lightning in the night time, and so frequently, that the sky and sea seemed to be all on a fire.

Seeing we were not very much incommoded by the heats and calms in those climates, we had but very few sick men on board, and in all our passage from Brest to the Cape of Good Hope, we lost but one man; nay, and he too came on board, tho' nobody knew of it, with a bloody-flux upon him, whereof he died.

God's particular protection of all that were in the ship

It was certainly our duty to give God great thanks for the good weather He was pleased to send us about the line: for had we been stopped by the calms so long as many times ships are weather-bound there, all our water, bread, and victuals would soon have been spoiled and have occasioned many distempers, that must needs have carried off many of our men; as it happened this year to a Dutch ship. This vessel put out from Europe above two months before us, and nevertheless they found us at an anchor before Batavia;[4] where we were informed that the ships company had been so incommoded with calms about the line, for six whole weeks time, that most part of them falling sick, thirty seven of about forty eight that were aboard died; among whom were the captain and two chief mates: so that the surviving eleven not being able to sail the ship to the port whither they were bound, were obliged to put in to the Isle of Sumatra, and to look for men there to carry them to the road of Batavia, where we saw them come in.

April 7. Passed the Equinoctial line

Our victuals and water were not spoiled, nor did we hardly suffer anything by bad weather nor calms; and the heats of the torrid zone appeared not to us to be much greater than the heats that are felt in France about midsummer. Thus without any incommodity we passed the line the seventh of April, being Saturday, with an easy north-west-wind, about the three hundred and fifty eighth degree of longitude. It being already late, the solemn ceremonies which seamen never fail to perform upon that occasion, was put off till next morning after mass. It is an invention devised by the masters, mates, and other officers of ships, to get a little money to buy fresh provisions with for themselves and company, to which they give, (but very improperly), the name of Baptism.

The Ambassador would have no ceremonies acted that did any ways allude to sacred things. Everyone gave what he thought fit; and the rest came off for some buckets full of water which were thrown upon their bodies: but it being very hot there, they were not much the worse for it.

From the time we passed the line, till we came to the tropic of Capricorn, we had bad winds, and sometimes none at all; for we were becalmed about the twentieth degree of south-latitude, where we suffered the scorching heats of the torrid zone until the thirtieth of April that we passed the tropic.

What Travadas and the fire of S. Helme are

After that we had for the most part changeable winds and so easy that a small boat might have followed us without any danger. It is true that under the zone we met two or three times with those boisterous gusts which the Portuguese call Travadas or Troadas; because they are always accompanied with thunder and lightning: but seeing we had them astern of us, they did us but little harm, and made us run a good way on head. During one of these Travadas, there appeared several times[5] upon the masts, yards, and guns of our ship, some of those little fires of a pyramidal figures, which the Portuguese call the fire of St. Telme and not St. Helme. Some seamen look upon them as the soul of the saint of that name, whom then they invoke with all their might, joined hands, and many other marks of respect. Nay, there are some of them, who take them for a certain sign that the storm will soon be over, without doing them any damage. These are the very same fires which heretofore the Pagans adored under the name of Castor and Pollux; and it is strange that that superstition should be introduced also amongst Christians.

March 12. About noon we discovered one of those phenomena called a weather-gall or ox-eye because of its figure. They are looked upon commonly at sea as certain forerunners of a storm. It is a great round cloud opposite to the sun and distant from him eighty or ninety degrees; and upon it the sun paints the colours of the rainbow, but very lively. They appear, perhaps to have so great a lustre and brightness, because that weather-gall is environed on all sides with thick and dark clouds. However it be, I dare say that I never found anything falser than the prognostics of that apparition. I formerly saw one of them when I was near the continent of America, but which was followed, as this was, with fair and serene weather, that lasted several days.

Several Phenomenas observed during the voyage

Since we are speaking of phenomenas or apparitions, I must not here forget a pretty rare one which we observed betwixt the line and tropic of Capricorn; and which seems to be difficult to be explained. It was one of those great whirl winds which the seamen call spouts or water-dragons. They are like to long tubes or cylinders made of thick vapours which with one end touch the clouds, and with the other the sea that seems to boil all round it. Much after this manner are these dragons formed.

The manner how spouts are formed

At first you see a great thick cloud, from which a part breaks off; and this separated part being driven by an impetuous wind, insensibly changes its shape, and takes the figure of a long pillar, which descends as low as the surface of the sea; continuing so much the longer in the air, as the violence of the wind retains it there, or as the lower parts of it support those that are above. So when that long spout of water comes to be out by the yards or masts of the ship entering into it, when one cannot avoid the same; or the motion of the wind comes to be interrupted by rarefying the neighbouring air with canon or musket-shot: the water being then no longer supported, falls in prodigious quantity, and immediately all the dragon is dispersed.

W*hich are dangerous to be met with*

They do all they can at sea to avoid them, it being dangerous to meet them in their way, not only because of the water which falls into the ship, but also by reason of the sudden violence and extraordinary weight of the whirlwind that blows it, which is able to unmast the greatest ships, and even put them in danger of being lost. Though at a distance these spouts seem to be pretty small, and like to pillars of six or seven foot diameter, they are nevertheless of far greater extent. I saw two or three of them near the Berlingues in Portugal, within a pistol-shot of me; and they seemed to me to be above an hundred foot in circumference.

S*pouts of another kind*

We observed besides other phenomenas not much different from these last: they are called siphons because of their long figure pretty like in shape to some pumps: they appear about sun-rising and sun-setting, towards the same place where the sun then is. They are long and thick clouds environed with other clear and transparent ones, and fall not; but in process of time are all confounded together, and by little and little scattered, whereas the dragons are impetuously driven, last a long while, and are always accompanied with rash and whirlwinds, which make the sea to boil and cover it with froth.

E*xtraordinary rainbows to be seen at sea*

The rainbows of the moon in these places have far more lively colours then those that are seen in France. But the sun forms rare ones upon the drops of sea-water which are driven by the wind like a very small rain, or like fine dust when two waves beating against one another break. When one looks down upon these Iris's from a high place they seem to be reversed, and sometimes it happens that a cloud passing over it, and being ready to dissolve into rain, another rainbow is formed, the extremities whereof seem to be continued with the extremities of the reversed Iris, and so makes a circle of rainbow almost entire.

Phenomena that are to be seen in the water of the sea

The sea hath its phenomena as well as the air, fires many times appear upon it, especially betwixt the tropics: we have seen it sometimes in the night-time covered all over with sparks, when it is a little high and the water breaks with a topping sea: we observed also a great light astern of the ship, especially if she made quick way; for then the wake or tract of the ship appeared like a river of light, and if anything were thrown into the sea, it glittered and shone all over. I think the cause of that light need no where else to be searched for, but in the very nature of the sea-water itself, which being full of salt, nitre, and more particularly of that water whereof the chemists make the chief part of their phosphorus, which being agitated is immediately inflamed and appears luminous, ought also by the same reason to sparkle when it is put into motion. So small a matter is enough to make fire come out of sea-water, that handling a line or small rope that hath been steeped in it, one will force out an infinite number of sparks like to the light of glow-worms, that is to say, lively and bluish.

Lights that come out of the sea in the night time

It is not only when the sea is in agitation that these glancings are to be seen, we saw of them near the line, in a dead calm after sunset they seemed to us to be like a vast number of small flashes of faint lightning coming out of the sea and immediately after disappearing. The cause of that we attributed to the heat of the sun, who having in a manner impregnated and filled the sea in the day time with an infinite number of igneous and luminous spirits, these spirits uniting together in the evening, that they might get out of the violent state whereunto they were forced by the sun, endeavoured in his absence to regain their liberty, and formed those little flashes as they made their escape by the favour of the night.

Besides these transient glances of a minutes continuance, we saw others also during calms, which might be called permanent, because they are not dispersed as the former were. There are of them of different sizes and shapes, round and oval above a foot and a half diameter, which passed along the ships side, and were kept in view above two hundred paces, by what one could guess in seeing them pass nine or ten paces from the ships side. They were thought to be only slime or some unctuous substance, which by some natural cause or other unknown to us might be formed in the sea. Some would needs have had them to be fish asleep, and these glitter naturally. It is true that twice in the morning we had seen above twenty such glittering things following one another in a straight line, and shaped like our pikes; nay many who had been much at sea took them to be real fish, but one cannot be positive as to that.

An English ship made off at sea

Let us now pursue our course again, the tenth of May in the morning we made a small English ship, which hailed and spoke to the *Maligne* that was nearer it than we. She was returning from the Isles of America, and going to take in slaves at Madagascar. They did what they could to keep up with us, but the wind being good, and we carrying much sail, the same day we lost sight of her.

May 17. We were got into the 33rd degree of south latitude, and the 19th of longitude according to our mates reckoning. There we began to see fowl of various shapes and weeds with great greenish rushes ten or twelve foot long which they call trunks, because [of] their stalk which grows and tapers insensibly to the top where it ends in leaves of the same colour, represents pretty well the shape of an elephant's trunk. The sea-weeds are a kind of herb inclining to green, not unlike to hay, whereof the sprigs are very long and interwoven one within another. Some think that these weeds come from the bottom of the sea being by the waves forced from thence, and raised to the surface of the water. Others will have them to grow in the water, because they see them far out at sea, and they cannot believe that the sea can be so agitated as to carry its waves to the bottom and so beat off the weeds from thence. Besides that they are found in so great plenty upon the surface of the sea, that it looks like a great meadow. Lastly, others maintain, and that is the opinion which seems to me most plausible and consonant to truth, that these weeds come from the neighbouring coasts, from whence the waves force them so that they are carried out into the open sea, but not very far from land, either by the tides, currents, or the prevailing winds. Upon that persuasion it was that Christopher Columbus, so famous for his discoveries in America, seeing one night the sea about his ship all covered over with these weeds, encouraged his men who thought themselves lost, taking those weeds for flats, and promised to make them suddenly see land; which accordingly he did two days after.

Marks to know the nearness of the Cape of Good Hope

These extraordinary birds, trunks and weeds, are the surest signs of ones approaching the Cape. This shows that men have intimations of it at a pretty good distance, seeing the first time that we saw of them, we were in the nineteenth degree of longitude, and the thirty third of south latitude, that is to say, that we were near three hundred leagues from the Cape of Good Hope.

They said that if instead of keeping along the coast of Africa, as we did, we had stood out to sea, to the west-ward, we had met with those signs farther off at sea. This made me judge that the currents that carry them along with them run stronger towards the west than north. We found the same things two days after we set out from the Cape of Good Hope, steering away east south-east, but in far greater quantity. That continued all the third day, though we had a good wind, and made a great deal of way.

Divers birds to be seen at sea in approaching to the Cape of Good Hope

The days following we saw the same birds in a greater number, which forsook us not till we were got a great way beyond the Cape. Some of them were black on the back, and white on the belly, the back of their wings beings speckled with those two colours, much like to chequer, and therefore the French call them *damiers*; they are somewhat bigger than a pigeon. There are others bigger than these, blackish above, and all white below, except the tip of their wings which appears to be of a velvet-black, and therefore the Portuguese call them *mangas de veludo*, velvet sleeves. After these we saw flocks of others somewhat less than the former. The Portuguese call them *boralhos,* because they are of an ash-coloured-grey. I shall not speak of certain big fowls which because of their whiteness may be called sea-swans, nor of the ravens and rooks which are to be found in these places, nor yet of a kind of bird which they call boobies, because they are so little upon their guards, that they suffer themselves to be taken with the hand.

The north-wind blowing much stronger, on the twenty eighth we were obliged to lie under a main course for fear of running ashore, which we did not think to be far off. Indeed next day about noon a seaman that was aloft to look out, with all his force cried *land*, *land*, and presently came down to ask of my Lord Ambassador the reward which be had promised to him who should first make land. He confidently affirmed that he had made it before in the morning, not daring to say so, because he was not very sure of it, but that at present it was past all doubt: nevertheless hardly anybody could discern the mountain which he saw, and it was a long while before they would believe him. But, at length, three or four hours after we easily saw the mountains of the Cape of Good Hope, which might be fifteen or twenty leagues ahead of us.

Next day, the one and twentieth, the day of our Lords ascension, after we had said our usual prayers and sung mass to thank God for the good success of our voyage; we viewed the land with our glasses, and saw it distinctly, not being above three leagues off. How barbarous and barren soever it seemed to be to us, it was nevertheless a delightful sight for men who had seen no land from the Canary Islands, which we sailed by the thirteenth of March.

Book 2

The Voyage From the Cape of Good Hope, to the Isle of Java

The Cape of Good Hope, as those that come from Europe make it, is a long ridge of mountains reaching from north to south, and ending in a point in the sea. The first two which we made at, ten leagues distance from that point, are the mountains of the Table, and of the Lion. We made the Table land first, and it is called by that name because the top of it is very flat, and much resembles a table. The Lion-land or mountain is so called, because it hath a great deal of the shape of a lion, couchant upon the belly: though it run farther out into the sea than the other, yet we did not see it till after; at a distance it would seem that they were but one single mountain, and, indeed, they are not very remote. At the foot of these mountains a great bay of an oval figure runs up towards the east, two or three leagues within land; it is almost two leagues over at the mouth, and about nine in compass. On the south side towards the mountains it is all a safe coast, everywhere else it is dangerous near shore. The Commissary General of the East-India company, of whom we have much to say in the sequel, told us one day, that he was many times afraid, seeing us stand in so near to shore, upon the tacks we made, insomuch that he was thinking to fire a gun with a bullet, to give us warning by that signal, that we should keep off, and wait for a fairer wind.

Towards the middle of this bay, the Dutch have built a pentagon fort below the Table-land, which covers it to the south, and behind the Lion-mountain, that secures it to the west, a league from land or thereabouts. In entering the bay, you leave a pretty low island on the left-land, called Isle Robin, in the middle where the Hollanders have put up their flag. Thither they send those of the country, and the Indians also whom they would punish with banishment, and force them to make lime there of the shells that are cast up by the sea.

Danger of being forced upon a rock as the ship was coming to anchor

The weather being fair for putting into the bay, we were in hopes of being at anchor by ten of the clock in the morning, but the wind failing us all of a sudden at the entry, we were becalmed, and met with a current that carried us a great pace upon a rock towards Isle Robin, where we saw the water break with much violence. Immediately two boats were launched to tow us off, and get us clear of that rock but notwithstanding the foresight of the officers, and diligence of the crew in obeying their orders, we were in great danger of running foul of it, the current or tide carrying us violently upon the same, and we were not half a league from that break, when suddenly we had a land-breeze which obliged us to tow in our boats again, and soon put us out of danger; we lost, however, two top-sails there, which were split by the violence of the wind. Being obliged all day long to beat to and again in the mouth of the bay, with a great deal of trouble, we could not get to the place of anchoring before the beginning of night. Nay we were obliged next morning to weigh again, that we might lie under the mountains secure from the west winds, which are extremely violent, and reign there in the winter time, as then it was.

Our ship came to an anchor amidst four Holland's vessels

We came to an anchor, then, next day about an hundred and fifty yards from the fort. There were in the road of the Cape four great ships, arrived there about a month before from Holland, though they had been at sea at least two months before us. The first carried an admiral's flag, as a mark of the supreme power and command that the Dutch East-India company take to themselves in the Indies. She was commanded by the Heer van Rheeden, who was sent by the East-India company with the title of Commissary General, to

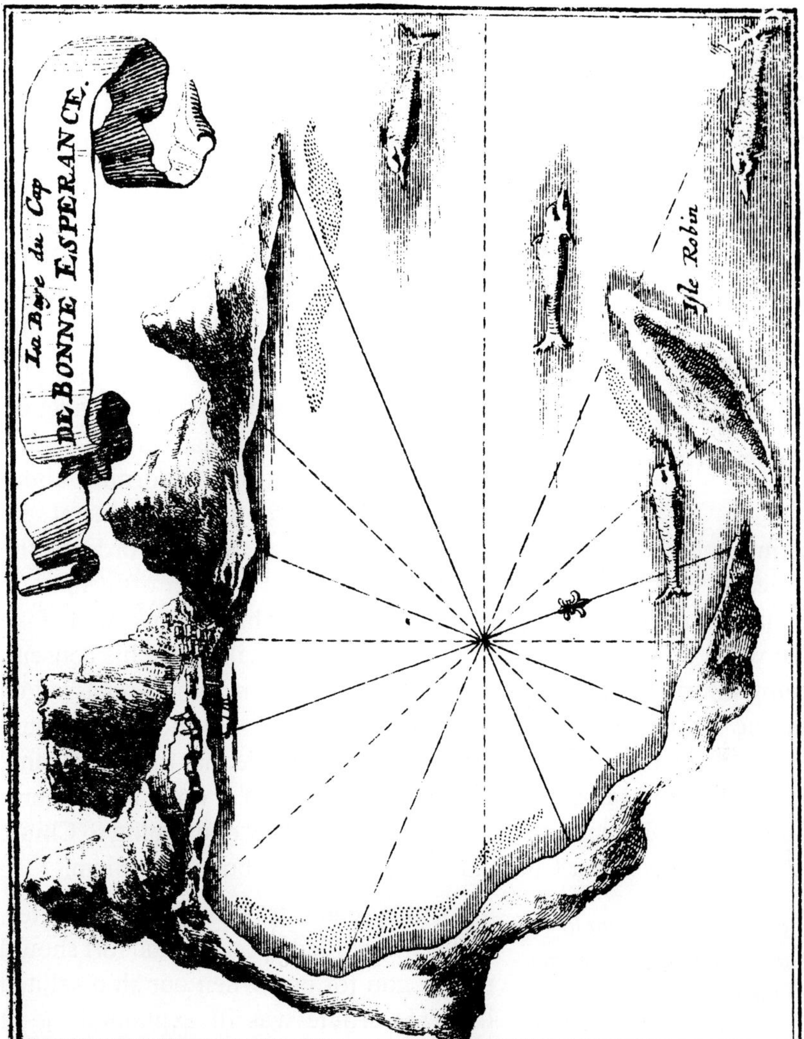

Plate 1. The bay of the Cape of Good Hope

visit all the places which they hold in that country. He hath full power to order all things, to change the officers of factories, nay, and the governors of places also, if he thought fit. The second was commanded by the Heer St. Martin, a Frenchman by country, and Major General of Batavia, in that quality commanding all the forces the states have in the Indies. One Bocheros an old sea captain, and counsellor to the Heer Van Rheeden, during the time of his commission, commanded the third, the fourth attended the Heer St. Martin, who was to make all haste to Batavia.

All these gentlemen and M. Vanderstellen Governor, or to use the Dutch word, commander of the Cape, are men of worth, and it was a happy encounter for us, that we had such men to treat with, during the stay that we made there.

The Dutch send to know from whence our ships

No sooner were we come to an anchor, but two boats came on board of us, to know who we were, and next morning about seven o'clock the Commissary General sent and complimented my Lord Ambassador, who on his part ordered the Chevalier de Forbin, lieutenant of the ship, and three other officers to go ashore and salute him, and withal, to desire leave of him that we might take in fresh water and necessary provisions. He very civilly gave his consent, and being informed that there were several gentlemen in the Ambassadors retinue, he invited them to come and hunt ashore. He inquired if there were any Jesuits on board our ship, and it is probable that they who came the day before had taken notice of us, and talked of it upon their return. Monsieur de Forbin made answer, that there were six of us going to China, and that there were other Churchmen on board also bound for Siam.

The Ambassador sent to complement the Governor of the Cape

Then they came to speak of the salutes, and it was agreed upon that the fort should render gun for gun when our ship saluted it. This article was ill explained, or ill understood by these gentlemen, for about ten of the clock my Lord Ambassador having ordered seven guns to be fired, the Admiral answered only with five guns, and the fort fired none at all. Immediately the Ambassador sent ashore again, and it was determined that the Admiral's salute should pass for nothing, and so the fort fired seven guns, the Admiral seven guns and the other ships, to salute the King's ship, which returned them their salutation, for which the fort and ships gave their thanks. After that we made ready our boats, and thought of nothing now but of going ashore to refresh ourselves.

The Jesuits visit the Governor of the Cape

So soon as we arrived in the bay, we found it to be so proper a place for making observations, that we instantly resolved to use all means that we might observe: for that end there was a necessity of taking a commodious house, carrying thither our instruments, and having leisure to ply it both day and night during the short time we had to stay there. There was difficulty in this; Jesuits, mathematicians, and several instruments carried ashore might offend the nicety of Dutch commander, in a pretty new colony, and make him suspect something else than what we pretend. Nay, we were advised to disguise ourselves, and not to appear to be Jesuits; but we did not think it fit, and we found by what followed, that our habit did us no injury at all.

After we had a little considered on it, it was resolved, that Father Fontenay and I, should go visit the Commissary General and the Governor of the place before the rest went ashore, and that if in discourse we found occasion to open our design, we should lay hold on it. We went straight to the fort then without any other recommendation. The sentinel stopped us at the first gate, according to the custom of garrison-places, until an officer of the guard being come, and having informed himself that we were come to pay a visit to the Commissary General and governor, he commanded us to be let in, and gave us a soldier to conduct us to their apartment.

The climate of the Cape of Good Hope is very temperate

This house consists of a large pile of building, two story high, and very solidly built. It is covered with a very fair terrace, paved with broad free stone, with balconies and iron rails all round; thither they commonly go to take the fresh air. This country has so temperate an air, that it is never very cold there, but when a south wind blows; and though it was the depth of winter then in relation to that climate, yet it was so hot in the day time, that they were glad to go take the fresh air in the evening.

We went first into a great hall where they preach every Sunday until the Church be finished that was begun to be built without the fort. On both sides of that hall there are pretty handsome apartments; they had us in to that which was on the left-hand, where we were received by Monsieur Vanderstel, and whither presently after the Heer van Rheeden came to see us. He is a man of quality about fifty years of age, handsome, civil, wise, and learned, and who thinks and speaks well on all subjects. We were extremely surprised to meet with so much politeness at the Cape of Good Hope, and much more at the civilities and many testimonies of friendship which we received at that first interview. Father Fontenay, whose interpreter I was at that time in Portuguese, finding so lucky dispositions for our design, told the Commissary General that there were six Jesuits of us who were bound for the Indies and China, that not being at all accustomed to the fatigues of sea, we stood in need of taking a little air on land, that we might be recruited after so long a voyage; that we durst not do so, before we knew their minds, whether they would be contented with it or not. The Commissary General did not suffer me to interpret all that Father Fontenay had said to him but presently interrupting me: you'll do us the greatest pleasure imaginable, Fathers, said he, in Portuguese, to come and refresh yourselves at land, we will contribute all that lies in our power to your refreshment and recovery.

The Jesuits are extremely well received by the Dutch

This answer was so favourable that we went a little farther; we told him, that being ashore, we should be glad to employ ourselves for the public good, and then to communicate to him our observation; thereby to acknowledge in some manner the civilities that he had shown us: that we had brought with us from France several mathematical instruments, amongst which there were some very proper for finding out the true longitude of countries through which one passed, without any need of the eclipses of the sun and moon, we explained to him the new way of observing by the satellites of Jupiter, of which the learned Monsieur Cassini hath made so good tables. I added that thereby we would render a very considerable service to their pilots, by giving them the certain longitude of the Cape of Good Hope, which they only guessed at by their reckoning, a very doubtful way that many times deceive them, and that very considerably too. He told us that we would thereby oblige him, and that seeing we had a mind to labour in that discovery, he offered us a place every way proper for observing. At the same time he ordered a summer-house that is in the company's garden to be made ready for us to lodge in, so long as the Ambassador should continue in the road.

The civilities of Monsieur Van Rheeden

We made answer that the civility which he showed us should not rest there, and that we hoped my Lord Ambassador would have the goodness to thank him, and take it as a kindness done partly to himself. Then we showed him our patents for being the King's mathematicians. You increase my joy, Fathers, replied the commissary, in letting me see that I comply with the will and orders of so great a King, for whom I shall entertain a profound respect so long as I live. However I am not vexed that you did not speak to me of that before I obliged you to accept of a lodging, which I offer you freely, and with all my heart. They brought us tea, as it is the custom amongst the people of the East-Indies, and after a pretty long conference about indifferent matters, we took leave of these gentlemen, and withdrew. The commander followed us to conduct us to the apartment that was offered us in the company's great garden.

The description of a lovely garden which the Dutch East-India company have on the Cape of Good Hope

We were mightily surprised to find one of the loveliest and most curious gardens that ever I saw, in a country that looks to be one of the most dismal and barren places in the world. It lies above the habitations betwixt the town and the Table-land, and on the side of the fort, from which it is but about two hundred paces distant. It is fourteen hundred and eleven common paces in length, and two hundred thirty five in breadth.

The beauty of it consists not as in France, in compartments beds of flowers, nor water-works. They might have them if the East-India company would be at the charges of it; for a brook of running water falling from the hill, runs through the garden. But there you have walks reaching out of sight, planted with lime[6] trees, pomegranate-trees, and orange- trees, which are covered from the wind by high and thick hedges, of a kind of laurel, which they call *speck*, always green, and pretty like to the Filaria. By the disposition of the walks, this garden is divided into several indifferent big squares, some of which are full of fruit-trees, and amongst them, besides apple-trees, pear-trees, quince-trees, apricot-trees, and other excellent fruits of Europe, you have also ananas, banana-trees, and several others that bear the rarest fruits to be found in the several parts of the world, which have been transported thither, where they are most carefully cultivated and looked after. The other squares are sowed with roots, pulse and herbs, and some with the most esteemed flowers of Europe, and others that we know not, which are of a singular good smell and beauty. The East-India company, to whom it belongs, as we have already said have caused it to be made, that they may always have in that place a kind of magazine of all sorts of refreshments for their ships that go to, or come from, the Indies, which never fail to touch at the Cape of Good Hope.

All Dutch ships are ordered to touch at the Cape of Good Hope

The ships that come from the Indies arrive there in the beginning of March, either alone or several together in company, and there they stay for the fleet of Europe, which comes in the month of April. By that means they have the news, whether or not they be in wars, and set out all together, that by the great number and strength of their ships, they may be in a condition not to fear what hurt pirates or their enemies can do them.

There is a great pile of building built at the entry into the garden, where the company's slaves live, to the number, as it is said, of five hundred, of whom, part are employed in cultivating the garden, and the rest in other necessary work. About the middle of the wall, on that side which looks to the fort, there is a little banqueting-house where nobody lives; the lower story of it consists of a porch open to the garden and the fort, with two little halls on each side; over that there is a pavilion open every way, betwixt two terraces paved with brick, and railed about; the one looking towards the north, and the other to the south. This pavilion seemed to be purposely made for our design: for on the one side we discovered the north, the view whereof was absolutely necessary to us, because it is the south in relation to that country. Whilst they were a preparing that pavilion, which with the Dutch I shall call our observatory; we went on board to give the Ambassador and our fathers an account of all that had passed.

The Ambassador and Commissary General interchange many civilities

Next day the commissary and commander sent us on board all sorts of refreshments. The officer who was ordered to make that present to the Ambassador in their behalf, told us that these gentlemen had also sent us a boat to carry us and our instruments ashore. Having in the night time prepared those which we thought we might stand in need of, we put them into the boat, and so went to the observatory the second of June, in the year one thousand six hundred and eighty five.

We began to make our observations

A pendulum clock with seconds, made by Monsieur Tharet at Paris, being set at to hour, as near the true hour as we could guess, not having as yet corrected the clock, we began the following observations.

The first satellite appeared in the evening at eleven and three minutes of the clock not as yet corrected, distant from Jupiter, somewhat less than the diameter of the same Jupiter.

By the telescope we saw two parallel bands or streaks upon the body of Jupiter, the one larger towards the southern border, and the other narrower towards the northern.

The first satellite began to touch the border of Jupiter at 11 o'clock 37 M. 30 S. At eleven o'clock 58 M. 5 S. the satellite was no more to be seen. These observations were made with an excellent telescope twelve foot long, of the late Monsieur le Bas: the hours are still of the pendulum not rectified.

We constantly observed Jupiter until two of the clock five minutes after midnight, at what time he was hid behind the Lion mountain, which limited our sight towards the west, so that we could not that day see the emergence[7] of the first satellite.

The third of June, 1685.

For rectifying the hour of the clock.

Heights before noon.			Hours of the clock.		
Deg.	Min	Ser.	Hour.	Min.	Ser.
20	16	0	9	35	38
22	56	20	9	34	47
24	11	0	10	4	50
24	39	55	10	8	48

A dubious observation

Heights after noon.			Hours of the clock.		
Deg.	Min.	Ser.	Hour.	Min.	Ser.
24	39	55	0 The observation failed.		
24	11	0	2	50	19
22	56	20	2	57	40
0	26	0	3	16	38

These elevations were taken with a quadrant of ninety degrees, of eighteen inches the radius, made by Mr. Butterfield at Paris.

It is to be observed that these heights of the sun were not of the same border; in the morning we took the height of the superior border, and in the evening of the inferior only, which is to be taken notice of.

F*or the Variation of the needle* By Mr. Butterfield's equinoxial dial, which carries a great compass under the Meridian: the variation of the needle was found to be eleven degrees and a half north-west.

Having no particular observations to make in the evening, we considered several fixed stars with the telescope twelve foot long.

Plate 2. The Dutch Fort at the Cape of Good Hope

Several observations concerning the southern stars

The foot of the Crozier marked in *Bayer* is a double star, that is to say, consisting of two bright stars distant one from another about their own diameter only, much like to the most northern of the twins; not to speak of a third much less, which is also to be seen, but farther from these two.

Under the Croziers there are several places of the milky way, which seem to be filled, if you look through the telescope, with an infinite number of stars.

The two clouds which are near the south pole appear not to be a cloud of stars, like the *Prasepe Cancri*, nor yet a duskish light, as the cloudy part of *Andromeda*; nothing hardly is to be seen there with great glasses, though without a glass one may see them very white, especially the great cloud.

No constellation in the Heavens looks so lovely as those of the *Centaur* and *Ship*. There are no fair stars near the pole, but a great many little ones, *Bayer* and other books that speak of them, omit a great many, and most of these they set down appear not in the Heavens in the same situation.

The Fourth of June, 1685.

For rectifying the hour of the clock.

Heights before noon.			Hours of the clock.		
D.	M.	S.	H.	M.	S.
22	23	0	9	50	47
23	31	50	10	0	32
24	37	30	10	9	18½
25	53	20	10	20	29

Heights after noon.			Hours of the clock.		
D.	M.	S.	H.	M.	S
25	53	20	2	32	33
24	37	30	2	43	38
23	31	50	2	52	47
22	23	0	3	1	38½

The horizontal thread of the telescope was not exactly parallel to the horizon, we always endeavoured to supply that in the certifications of the clock, by making the border of the sun pass by the same place of the thread, or as near as could be to it.

You are always to mind that they are the heights of different borders of the sun, in the morning of the superior border, and in the evening of the inferior.

An interview betwixt the Ambassador and Commissary General.

Monday after dinner we went to the fort, to see the gentlemen, and communicate to them the observations which we had already made, and acquaint them with that we were to make that evening, according to which alone one might regulate the true longitude of the Cape. Upon our return all these gentlemen would needs go along with us, to be spectators of that observation. We were together upon the terrace taken up in showing them our instruments, which seemed very pretty and curious to them, when we perceived my Lord Ambassador, who having come incognito the day before to walk in the garden, found it so pleasant, that he returned again next day to divert himself there, with most part of the officers of both ships, and the gentlemen of his retinue. The Ambassador and commissary had mutually interchanged many civilities from the very day of our arrival, and no day passed without sending one another presents. The Heer Van Rheeden perceiving him, went immediately down from the terrace, where he was observing with us, and after two or three turns, meeting the Ambassador as by chance, they entertained one another to their mutual satisfaction.

The emergence of the first satellite[8] of Jupiter observed

When the Ambassador was gone, the commissary with the Heers, St. Martin, Vanderstel and Bocheros stayed with us in the observatory till ten o'clock at night. The emergence of the first satellite happened at ten hours, five min. forty sec. of the clock not rectified. We took the meridian line of the northern terrace, and the meridian elevation of the sun; but we could not make use of that; because the operation was not sure.

After the emergence of the first satellite from under the shadow of Jupiter, having compared together the heights of the sun, taken morning and evening the third and fourth of June, and considered the difference of time amongst the same heights of the superior and inferior limb or border of the sun, because in the morning we had observed the superior border, and in the evening the inferior, we found that the pendulum went faster than the sun both days, by eight and twenty minutes.

At the instant of the emergence of the first satellite it was by the pendulum ten hours, five min. forty sec. from whence having subtracted twenty eight minutes.

Remains the true time of the emergence, nine hours, thirty seven min. forty seconds.

The Ephemerides of Monsieur Cassini calculated to minutes gave the time of that emergence in the meridian of Paris to be at eight hours, twenty six minutes.

But his Tables of Eclipses calculated to seconds, gave the same emergence at eight o'clock. seven min. forty seconds.

Having deducted them from the hours observed at the Cape of Good Hope, nine hours, thirty seven min. forty seconds.

The difference of meridians betwixt the Cape of Good Hope and Paris

There remains the difference of meridians betwixt the Cape of Good Hope and Paris of an hour twelve minutes, which make eighteen degrees difference of longitude; and supposing the longitude of Paris taken from the first meridian, that passes by the Isle of Fera the most westerly of the Canaries to be twenty two degrees and an half according to the same author, the longitude of the Cape of Good Hope taken from the same meridian, will be forty degrees and an half, not much different from what the modern charts assign to it.

Next day being Tuesday the fifth of June about ten of the clock, these gentlemen came back to the observatory, and stayed there till towards two in the afternoon, to see us take the height and distance of Table mountain, and to view our instruments. We showed them particularly the use of the equinoctial dial, by means whereof we found again that day the variation of the needle to be eleven degrees and a half north-west.

Advantages that may be drawn from the observations made at the Cape

So that two advantages may be drawn from these observations. First the variation of the needle which we found with the astronomical ring to be eleven degrees and half north-west, and then, the true longitude of the Cape, which we regulated according to that emergence of the first satellite of Jupiter, which being to appear at eight of the clock twenty six minutes upon the horizon of Paris, and having been observed at the Cape at nine o'clock, thirty seven minutes, forty seconds difference betwixt the two meridians of the two places, which being converted into degrees, make eighteen, and make the Cape more easterly by near three degrees than in reality it is. The Abbot of Choisi would needs be a witness of our observations, and for some time led the life of an observator with us.

The Governor sends several presents to the Jesuits

Towards the evening we had notice sent us ashore, that we must come aboard next morning betimes; we went immediately all six of us to the fort to take leave of the Dutch gentlemen, and give them our thanks. For, indeed, we could not be more civilly, nor more kindly used than we were. Besides when we went on board we found presents of tea and canary wine, which the governor sent us, taking it kindly that we had left with him a microscope and a small burning glass.

Curious fish brought from Japan

These gentlemen seemed all much affected at our departure. We pray God, said they, embracing us tenderly, that the designs for which you are going to China may succeed, and that you may bring a great number of infidels to the knowledge of the true God. At length we parted, very much touched also with their good desires and civilities. As we passed by the Governor's apartment he showed us in a tub full of water, two little fish, no longer than ones finger. The Portuguese call one of them the Goldfish, and the other the Silverfish; because, in reality, the tail of the male seems to be of gold and the females of silver. He told us that these fish came from China, and that the persons of quality of these countries as well as the Japanese hath an extraordinary esteem for them, and kept them in their houses out of curiosity. We saw some of them afterward in the palace of the General of Batavia, and at Siam in the house of the Lord Constance, Chief Minister of that Kingdom, and of some Chinese Mandarins.

We reimbarked in order to sail

The Ambassador had prayed the Heer Van Rheeden Commissary General to write to the General of Batavia, that he would give us a pilot to conduct us to Siam, and he having undertaken the commission, sent the Ambassador, next day, a very obliging letter for that general, wherein towards the end he added of himself; without any solicitation from us, an article in our favours. We spent the night in packing up our instruments again, and next morning before day we put them into a chaloop, which the commander ordered to be in readiness for us, and so we went on board again.

What care was taken of the Catholics at the Cape. The sentiments of the Catholics on the Cape upon our arrival

This is all that passed at the Cape of Good Hope in relation to our observations. Though we plied them day and night, yet they were not our only employment. No sooner had we got possession of our little observatory, but the Catholics of that colony, who are pretty numerous, had notice of it, and were thereat exceedingly rejoiced. In the mornings and evenings they came privately to us. There were some of all countries, and of all conditions, free, slaves, French, Germans, Portuguese, Spaniards, Flemings, and Indians. They who could otherwise express themselves; because we understood not their language, fell upon their knees and kissed our hands. They pulled chaplets and medals out of their bosoms to show that they were Catholics, they wept and smote their breasts. That language of the heart much more touching than words, wrought great compassion in us, and obliged us to embrace those poor people, whom Christian charity made us look upon as our brethren. We comforted them the best we could, exhorting them to persevere in the faith of Jesus Christ, humbly and faithfully to serve their masters, and to bear their troubles with patience. We commended it to them particularly that they would examine their consciences at night, and honour the holy Virgin, who was ablest to procure them more grace to live Christianly, and to keep them from heresies. They who spoke French, Latin, Spanish, or Portuguese were confessed. We visited the sick in their houses and in the hospital. This was all that could be done for their consolation in so short a time, they not having the liberty to come on board of us and hear Mass, nor we to say it to them ashore.

The Jesuits are suspected of administering the sacraments

Nevertheless it must have been suspected at the Cape that we carried them the sacrament. For two of our fathers returning one day from on board with microscope in one of their hands covered with Spanish leather gilt, two or three of the inhabitants walking upon the shore, imagined it to be the holy sacrament which they were carrying to Catholics in a box. They drew near to the father to know the truth of the matter; the father told them what it was, and to convince them, made them look into the microscope. Then one of them told him, sir, I thought it had been so, because I know that you are the greatest enemies of our religion. We could not but smile at that saying, but without making answer we kept on in our way straight to the fort.

To conclude all that concerns the Cape of Good Hope, it only remains that I relate what we learned of the state of the country. For some of our fathers were charged to inform themselves of that, whilst the rest were taken up about their observations. In that prospect we made it our business to get out of M. Vanderstellen in the several conversations we had with him all that could contribute to our information; and we made acquaintance with a young physician of Breslon in Silesia, called Mr. Claudius, whom the Dutch for his great capacity entertain at the Cape. Seeing he had already travelled into China and Japan, where it was his custom to observe everything, and that he designs and paints animals and plants perfectly well, the Hollanders have stopped him there to assist them in making their new discoveries of countries, and labour about the natural history of Africa. He hath completed two great volumes in folio of several plants, which are drawn to the life, and he hath made a collection of all the kinds which he hath pasted to the leaves of another volume. Without doubt the Heer Van Rheeden who had always these books by him at home, and who showed them to us, has a design to give the public shortly an *Hortus Africus* after his *Hortus Malabaricus*. Had these books been to be sold, we would have spared no cost to have bought them and sent them to the King's library. Since this learned physician hath already made some progresses sixscore leagues up into the country towards the north and east, there to make new discoveries, it is from him that we got all the knowledge we have of that country, of which he gave us a little map made with his own hand, with some figures of the inhabitants of the country, and of the rarest animals, which here are inserted. The most remarkable things we learnt are what follow.

The Dutch settling on the Cape

The Dutch finding that an establishment in that place would be convenient for their ships, which they yearly send to the Indies, treated with the chief heads of that nation, who consented for a certain quantity of tobacco and brandy, to surrender that country to them, and to withdraw farther up into the continent. This agreement was made about the year 1653, and since that time they have taken a great deal of pains to make a firm settlement on the Cape. They have at present there a great town and a fort with five bastions which commands all the road. The air is very good, the soil excellent, and corn grows there as well as in Europe; they have planted vines which yield almost delicate wine.

The different animals that are to be found on the Cape

Wild game they have every where in abundance. Our officers returned from hunting and fowling with wild goats, antelopes, pheasants and abundance of partridges as big as the woodhens of France, and there are four sorts of them. The oxen and the sheep are got farther up amongst the wild natives of the country; but that is a traffic which the company reserves to themselves, who buy them up for a little tobacco, and sell them again to the inhabitants of the Cape, and to strangers that put in there for fresh provisions. We saw sheep there that weighed fourscore pound weight, and were very good meat.

A prodigious elephant

They have there also civet-cats, many wildcats, lions and tigers which have very pretty skins and especially huge great apes that comes sometimes in troops down from the tableland into the gardens of private persons, and carry away their melons and other fruit. Nine or ten leagues from the Cape eastward there is a chain of hills full of lions, elephants, and rhinoceroses of a prodigious bigness. Men of credit who have travelled there assured me that they had found the foot trace of an elephant two foot and a half in diameter, and that they had seen several rhinoceroses as high and big as an ordinary elephant. All that I can say as to that, is that I have seen the two horns which that beast carries on its nose, fastened together as

Plate 3. Wild game at the Cape: Zebra

they are naturally, of a bigness and weight that inclined me to believe that what they told me of it was true.

A property of the Rhinoceros The lieutenant of the castle who went on that progress, told me that the rhinoceros being in rage runs his greatest horn into the ground and continues to run a kind of furrow with it, till he come up with him that has smitten him. The skin of that beast is so hard, that it is musket-proof, unless one take his time to hit it, when it shows its flank, the only place of its body where fire-arms or halbards, that the travellers carry, can wound it. There are horses and asses there of extraordinary beauty. The first have a very little head, and pretty long ears. They are covered all over with black and white streaks that reach from their back to their belly about four or five fingers broad and are very pretty to look on. I saw the skin of one that had been killed, which my Lord Ambassador bought to carry with him into France as a very curious thing. As for the asses, they are of the body like the horse, full of pretty broad streaks, blue, yellow, green, black and white, all very lively.

Stags are so plentiful there that they are seen feeding in flocks like sheep, and I heard the commander's secretary say, and the commander himself too, that they had seen ten thousands of them together in a plain which they found in a wood. There are not so many lions nor tigers as stags, but yet there is a great many of them, and I can easily believe it because of the vast number of those beasts' skins wherein they trade at the Cape. They keep not so close to the woods, but that they come sometimes to places inhabited, where they set upon anything they meet, and even upon men themselves. There happened an instance of this while we were there, and the Commissary General told us it. Two men walking at a distance from their habitations perceived a tiger, one fired at it and missed it, upon which it made a spring at him and brought him to the ground. The other seeing in what extreme danger his comrade was, fired at the tiger and wounded his friend in the thigh. The tiger in the meantime having received no hurt, left his prey, and made after this man; the first getting up again came in, in the nick of time and killed the tiger. They say that this beast had such an instinct that amongst an hundred men it will single out him that fired at it, and leave all the rest. A month before, the like accident almost happened of a lion who tore to pieces a man and his servant, pretty near the habitations, and was afterwards killed himself.

Several sorts of fish at the Cape

At the Cape we took a great many excellent fish. Amongst others mullet, and of those fish which in France they call *dorades*, or gilt-heads and are far different from the dolphin which is much bigger and better deserves that name, because of its yellowish colour and golden specks, that make it pass for one of the loveliest fish that swims in the sea. We took also great numbers of seals, and some cramp-fish. The cramp-fish is an ugly fish, and very soft, which hath the virtue, when they fish for it, to cause a numbness in the hand and arm. We saw many sea-wolves there, which seem to be well enough named. There are penguins there also. These are water-fowl, without wings, and are constantly almost in the water, being truly amphibious.

Golden mines on the Cape

In the year 1681, the Heer Vanderstel settled a new colony, consisting of fourscore and two families, nine or ten leagues farther up in the country, and called it by the name of Hollenbok. Some affirm that there are gold mines on the Cape. They showed us stones found there which seemed to confirm that opinion; for they are ponderous, and with a microscope one may discover on all sides small particles that look like gold.

But the most curious thing we found on the Cape was an exact map of the places about newly discovered by a Hollander, with a Latin relation of the nations that inhabit them. Both were given us by a man of credit who hath set down nothing but what [he] himself was an eye-witness of, the translation of it follows.

A translation of a Latin relation of the places about the Cape

"The South point of Africa is no less remote from Europe, than the manner of its inhabitants are different from ours. For

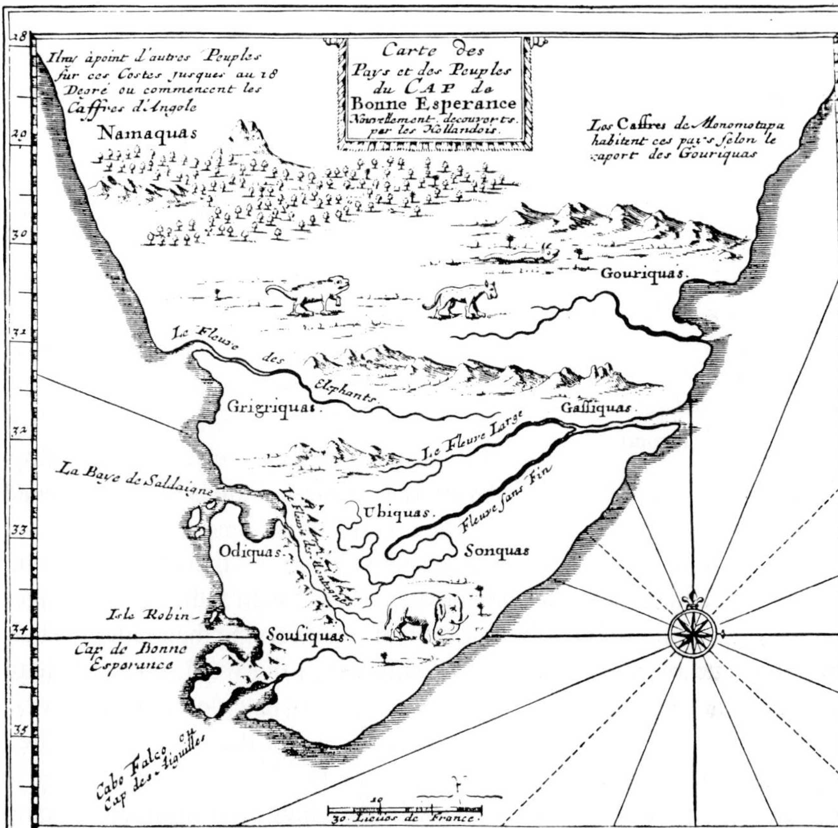

Plate 4. Map of the country and the peoples of the Cape of Good Hope

these people are ignorant of the creation of the world, the redemption of mankind, and the mystery of the most Holy Trinity. However they adore a God, but the knowledge they have of him is very confused. In honour of him they kill cows and sheep, and offer him the flesh and milk in sacrifice, as a token of their gratitude towards that deity, who grants them as they believe, sometimes rain and sometimes fair weather according as they stand in need of it, they expect no other life after this. Notwithstanding that they have still some good qualities which should hinder us from despising them: for they have more charity and fidelity one toward another than is to be found commonly amongst Christians. Adultery and theft are with them capital crimes always punished by death. Tho every man has the liberty to take as many wives as he is able to maintain, yet none of them, not of the richer sort, is to be found with more than three."

The manners of the inhabitants of the Cape. Their Arms. Their food

"These people are divided into several nations, who have all the same way of living. Their ordinary food is milk and the flesh of the cattle which they keep in great quantity. Every one of these nations have their head or captain whom they obey, that office is hereditary, and goes from father to son. The right succession belongs to the eldest, and that they may retain the authority and respect, they are the only heirs of their fathers, the younger having no other inheritance, but the obligation of serving their elders. Their clothes are no more but plain sheep skins with the wool, prepared with cow's dung and a certain grease that renders them insupportable both to the eye and smell. The first Nation in the language of the country, is called Songuas. The Europeans call those people Hotentots, perhaps because they have always that word in their mouth when they meet strangers. Seeing they are nimble, strong, bold, and more expert than others in handling their arms, which are the javelin and arrows, they go and serve other nations as soldiers, and so there is not one nation who besides their own natives have not also Songuas in their militia. In their own country they live in deep caves, and sometimes in houses as others do. They live much by hunting, at which they are very dextrous: they kill elephants, rhinoceroses, elks, stags, antelopes, wild goats and several other beasts, of which there is a prodigious quantity on the Cape, they gather also at certain times the honey which the bees make in hollow trees and rocks."

Their blindness as to matters of religion. Their opinion as to their own way of living, and that of strangers

I will make a little digression from this relation, that I may give an account of what we ourselves have seen of those people, or what we learned of them from very sure hands. The Hotentots being persuaded that there is no other life after this, labour as little and take as much ease as they can in this world. To hear them talk even when they are serving the Dutch, for a little bread, tobacco, or brandy, they look upon them as slaves who labour the land of their country, and as people of no courage who shut themselves up within houses and forts to secure them from their enemies, whilst their people encamp securely in the open fields without stooping so low as to labour land. By that way of living they pretend to demonstrate that they are masters of the Earth, and the happiest people of the world, because they alone live in liberty and repose, wherein they place their felicity. Whilst we were in the company's garden, a leading man amongst them seeing how civilly we were used by the chief of the Dutch there; came to the observatory, and there meeting Father Fontenay, he presented him with two oranges, saying to him in Portuguese, "Reverendo Padre, geral dos Ottentots a Vossa Senhoria." Thereby intimating that his captain and nation congratulated our arrival.

The apparel of the men and women

Whatever good opinion they may have of themselves, they lead a wretched life. They are nasty even to excess, and it would seem that they study to make themselves hideous. When they would deck themselves, they rub over their heads, face, and hands, with the soot of their kettles, and when that is wanting, they have recourse to a certain kind of black grease, that makes them stink and look so horridly that there is no enduring of them. Hence is it that their hair which is naturally almost as woolly as the hair of Negroes, runs into little round knots, to which they

Plate 5. The Hottentot inhabitants of the Cape of Good Hope

fasten pieces of copper or glass. Those amongst them of greatest note, to these ornaments add great ivory rings which they wear about their arms above and below the elbows. Their food is far more surprising than all the rest for they make a delicious dish of the vermin that breeds in the skins wherewith they are clad. We have seen this oftener than once, otherwise we could never have believed it. The women, besides this apparel, encompass their legs with the guts of beasts, or small skins which they cut for this use: they do it to preserve them from the prickings of thorns, when they go through the woods, and to have always a present remedy against hunger if they should be put to a pinch. Their attire consists of several strings of beads made of shells or bones of different colours, whereof they make themselves necklaces and girdles, and some thicker rings which they wear about their arms.

Their moral virtues

However barbarity has not so totally effaced all the tracts of humanity in those people, but that there remains still some footsteps of virtue: they are trusty, and the Dutch allow them free access into houses without any fear of being robbed by them. Nevertheless it is said, that they are not so reserved as to strangers, or to the Dutch who are newcomers, who know them not so well as to get them punished for it. They are beneficent and helpful, and keep nothing wholly for themselves. When they have anything given them, if it can be divided, they give a share of it to the first of their acquaintance they meet, nay they'll hunt about for them for that purpose, and commonly keep the least share of what they have to themselves.

The manner how they punish crimes

When any one amongst them is convicted of a capital crime, as of theft or adultery, the captain and chief men assemble, and having fairly tried the prisoner, they themselves are the executioners of their own sentence. They knock him on the head with cudgels, every one coming in order and according to his quality to give him a blow, after the captain in honour hath given him the first; or otherwise they run him through with their javelins.

The knowledge they have of the Heavens and natural things

They say, they are astrologers and herbalists, and men of credit assured us that they pretty well understood the disposition of the Heavens, and that they would distinguish simples, even in the night-time by the touch and smell.

They are so accustomed to liberty, that they cannot live under the least constraint

They are excessively jealous of their liberty, and the Dutch commander told us that he had a mind to tame one of them by making him his domestic servant in his tender age. However when he was grown up, there was a necessity of giving him leave to be gone, which he instantly desired, saying, that he could not submit to the rack of regular life; that the Dutch and such other nations were slaves to the Earth; and that the Hotentots were the masters of it that they were not forced to stand with the hat continually under their arm, and to observe a hundred uneasy customs; that they ate when they were hungry, and followed no other rules but what nature taught them. After all they are merry, sprightly, brisk in their words, and seem to have wit.

The hunters live in the woods and the shepherds in cottages. A description of these cottages

They have some very odd and whimsical customs. When a woman has lost her first husband, she ought afterwards to cut off as many joints of her fingers beginning at the little finger, as she marries new husbands. The men in their youth make themselves half eunuchs, pretending that contributes much to the preservation and increase of bodily agility. They are all either hunters or shepherds, these dwell in caves, and live on their prey: these feed on their flocks and their milk. They lodge in huts made of the branches of trees, covered with skins and mats like to tents; the door of them is so low, that there is no entering but upon all fours, and the roof so little raised, that one cannot stand upright in them. Four or five families lodge in one of these hovels, which is not above five or six geometrical paces in circumference. They make the fire in the middle, and the apartments are only distinguished by holes dug in the ground two foot deep. But let us now go on with the relation which we have interrupted.

Namaqua Peuples nouvellem.t decouverts vers le Tropiq du Capricorne.

Plate 6. Namaqua peoples newly discovered living about the Tropic of Capricorn

The Namaquas lives in villages, and are politer than the rest

The second Nation is that of the Namaquas, the figure [illustration] of whom is here represented. The first time we discovered them was in the year 1682. We entered their village, and by some caffres[9] that served us for guides, we sent their captain tobacco, a pipe, brandy, a knife and some bits of coral. The Captain accepted our presents, and in gratitude sent us two fat sheep each of whose tails weighed above twenty pound weight, with a great vessel full of milk, and a certain herb which they call *Konna*; it is probable that famous plant which the Chinese name Ginseng, for Monsieur Claudius who had seen it at China, affirms that he found two plants of it upon the Cape, and showed us the entire figure of it which he had drawn to the life, and which Monsieur Thevenet lately gave me a sight of. They use *Konna* as frequently as the Indians do betel[10] and areca.

Their music and instruments

Next day one of their captains came to us: he was a man who for the tallness of his stature and a certain fierceness in his looks, was respected by his country-people. He brought along with him fifty young men, and as many women and girls. The men carried each of them a flute in their hand made of a certain reed very well wrought, which rendered a pretty pleasant sound. The Captain having given them the sign, they fell a playing altogether upon these instruments, with which the women and girls mingled their voices, and a noise which they made by clapping of their hands.

Their way of dancing

These two companies were drawn into two rings one within another. The first, which was the outmost, and made up of the men, encompassed the second or the ring of the women, that was within them, both men and women danced thus in a round, the men turning to the right hand and the women to the left, whilst an old man standing in the middle with a stick in his hand beat the time and regulated their cadence. Their music at a distance seemed to be pleasant nay, and harmonious too,

Plate 7. Rhinoceros

but there was no kind of regularity in their dance, or rather it was a mere confusion.

Their strength, courage, and manners

The Namaquas are held in great reputation amongst those people, and are accounted brave, warlike, and potent, though their greatest forces exceed not two thousand men bearing arms. They are all tall of stature and strong, have good natural sense; and when any question is put to them, they weigh their words well before they answer, and all their answers are short and grave. They seldom laugh, and speak very little, the women seem to be nasty, and are not near so grave as the men.

The Ubiquas are given to thieving

The third Nation are the Ubiquas. They are by profession robbers, and rob the Africans as well as strangers. Though they are not able to send five hundred men into the field, yet it is not easier to root them out, because they retreat into inaccessible mountains.

The different nations discovered by the Dutch

The Gouriquas make the fourth Nation which is but of small extent. The Ilassiquas makes the fifth, and are more numerous: they are rich and powerful, little versed in the art of war; contrary to the sixth Nation, I mean, the Gouriquas who are great warriors. The seventh Nation are the Sousiquas, and the Odiquas are their allies.

The sea-cow

In the great rivers there is a monstrous creature which they call a sea-cow, and equals the rhinoceros in bigness, the flesh, or to say better, the lard of it is good to eat, and hath a very pleasant taste. I have here given you a cut[11] [illustration] of it.

As to trees, plants and flowers, there are infinite numbers of them, and those very curious, not only for their beauty, but for their particular virtues also.

The Governor of the Cape made a progress up into the country

In the progress they made which lasted five months, they advanced as far northward as the tropic; that is to say, they

Plate 8. A Cape buck

Plate 9. Hippopotamus

discovered two hundred leagues of the country, keeping always within ten or twelve leagues of the western ocean. The commander Vanderstel was there in person, accompanied with fifty eight men well armed. His calesh came after him and forty wagons with twenty eight horses, three hundred sheep, and a hundred and fifty oxen. These last carried the baggage and drew the wagons, and the sheep served for food to the travellers. He set out with his company from the Cape of Good Hope about the latter end of May, which is the winter time in that country, and he chose that season, that he might not want water and forage in the deserts which it behoved him to cross over. They discovered some different nations [at] the eight and twentieth degree of latitude, who live in a pleasant country abounding in all sorts of fruits and animals. Before they got thither, they found many deserts and mountains, one of which was so high, that the commander assured us they were forty days in mounting up to the top of it.

The danger he was in of losing his life

They were all both man and beast like to have been killed with thirst, and were many times in danger of being devoured by the wild beasts which they met in troops. He had much ado to save himself from a rhinoceros of a huge bigness that was within three steps of him ready to tear him in pieces, had he not escaped it by flinging himself to one side, and getting out of sight of the beast, which sought about for him a long while to have rent him.

Their music, instruments and dancing

But when they came to the 27th degree of latitude about ten or twelve leagues from the coast of the ocean; they met with a very numerous nation, and far more tractable than any they had met with till then. M. Vanderstel had with him two trumpets, some hobois, and five or six violins, and so soon as the people heard the sound of these instruments, they came flocking about them, and sent for their music, consisting of near thirty persons, who hath almost all different instruments. He that was in the middle had a very long cornet made of the gut of a bullock dried and prepared. The rest had flageolets[12] and flutes made of canes of different lengths and thickness. They bore their instruments much after the same manner as ours are, but with this difference that there is but one hole, which reaches from one end to the other, and is much wider than that of the flutes and flageolets commonly used in France. To tune them together, they make use of a ring that hath a little opening in the middle, which they move up or down in the pipe by means of a little wand, according to the note they would have it tuned to. They hold their instrument with one hand, and with the other press their lips against the instrument that so they may blow full into the pipe. That music is simple, but it is harmonious. He that is master of the consort having made all the other musicians tune their instruments according to the key and note of the cornet, which he has by him, bids the tune that is to be played, and with a great stick beats the time so as he may be seen of all.

The music is always accompanied with dances, which consist in leaping, and certain motions of the feet, without budging out of the place they are in. The women and maids, making a great ring about the dancers, only clap their hands, and sometimes knock with their feet in cadence. None but the players on the instruments change their place in dancing, except the master of the music, who stands motionless that he may keep them in tune and time.

The men are well shapen and robust; they have long hair, which they suffer to hang down and dangle about their shoulders. Their arms are the arrow and javelin, which hath some resemblance with the lance, their apparel consists in a long cloak of a tiger's skin, that reaches down to their heels, some of them are as white as the Europeans, but they smut themselves with grease and the powder of a certain black stone, wherewith they rub over their face and whole body. Seeing their fields and woods abound with very rare simples of all sorts, they are all herbalists. Many of them are very skilful in minerals too, which they know how to melt and prepare, but they have no great esteem for them, perhaps, because there are a great many gold, silver and copper mines in their country. Their women naturally are very fair, but to please their husbands they make themselves black as they do.

Their apparel

Married women have the upper part of their head shaved, and upon their ears long sharp pointed shells. They cover themselves with the skins of tigers, coloured rats, which they tie about their bodies with thongs. That nation highly value a certain kind of pith of stone, which is not to be found but in the heart of some rock, and is pretty hard and of a very dark colour. Experience hath taught them that mineral is of a wonderful virtue to bring women to bed when they are in labour, and to make their cows, sheep, and goats easily bring forth. When the Dutch blew up a great rock with a minc they sprung, they were vexed and complained of it as if they had been robbed of a great treasure. Upon my return I had a piece of that mineral given me with some of the other sorts that have been found in that country.

There are many other sorts of animals and insects to be found there, whereof these are the figures [illustrations]. The first is a serpent with horns, called the cerastes, which has not been hitherto seen, and whose poison is extremely dangerous. Secondly, a chameleon that changes it self into all colours. And has a cry like to a rat. Thirdly, a lizard, when one strikes him he makes a moan like a child that cries, and growing angry bristles up his scales wherewith he is rough all over. His tongue is bluish and very long, and when any body comes near him, he is heard to blow with great violence. There is another lizard also to be found there, that is marked with three white crosses, but the bite of it is not so dangerous as that of the first.

The misfortunes of those idolatrous people, and the small hopes there is of converting them

From all that hath been said, it plainly appears, that part of Africa is no less peopled, less rich, nor less fertile in all sorts of fruits and animals, than the other parts already discovered, though it hath been so long neglected. The people who inhabit it are neither cruel nor wild, and want neither docility nor wit, as appears more and daily, by the commerce that the Dutch entertain with them. But it is their great misfortune, and not

Plate 10. The Horned Serpent

Plate 11. Chameleon

Plate 12. Small lizard of the Cape of Good Hope

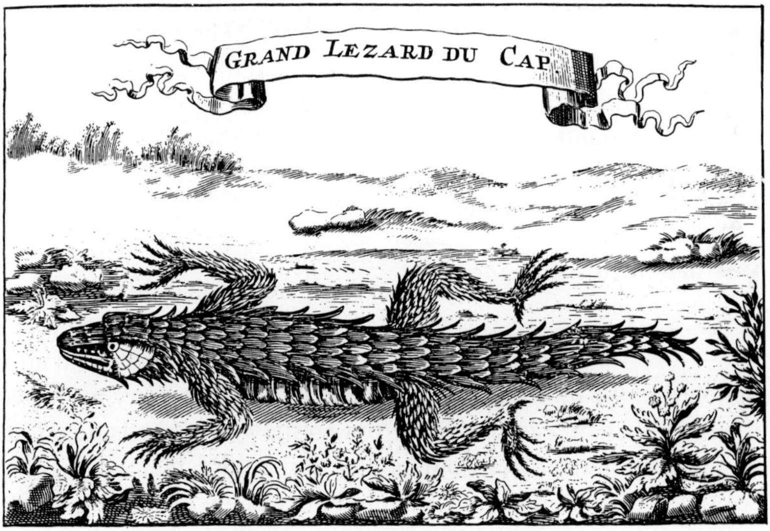

Plate 13. Great Cape Lizard

enough to be lamented, that being so numerous a people, they have no knowledge of the true God, and that nobody endeavours to instruct them. Men, indeed, travel over all their country, and even visit them at their habitations in the thickest forests, they cross over their scorching deserts, and with much hardship, charges and danger, climb over their steepest mountains. But this is only done to discover their mines, to examine the plentifulness of their provinces, to learn their secrets, and the virtues of their simples, and to grow rich by their commerce. The truth is, such an enterprise, and the execution of so great and difficult a design would be very laudable, if zeal for the salvation of their souls came in for a share, and if in trading with them, one did teach them the way to Heaven, and the eternal truths.

Zealous missionaries, who would look upon those people as ransomed by the blood of Jesus Christ, and for all they are such savages, as capable of glorifying God to all eternity, as the nations who are most polite, would be very necessary in that remote part of Africa. In the first place, they would be assistant to the Catholics of the Cape, who are many years without masses and the sacraments, for want of priests. They would at the same time instruct the Hotentots, already known, and the more easy to be won over to Jesus Christ, that they have no considerable vice that may divert them from Christianity. In process of time they might advance up to the more distant people, of whom, by God's grace, many might be brought in to the sheepfold of our Saviour.

Our departure from the Cape of Good Hope

These are the particulars concerning the Cape which we learned during our abode there. We had resolved to weigh anchor the sixth of June, and for that end all were got on board in the morning, but we wanted a wind to carry us out. Next day, the seventh, a breeze-blowing from north, we weighed and put under sail about seven of the clock, and having beat a little, that we might stand clear of the tail of the Lion; we doubled the Cape without any difficulty. They affirm this to be one of the most dangerous places in all the ocean.

The truth is, there is very rough sea there, and there is always danger with a contrary wind; but, thanks be to God, we found none, because we had a fair wind. We had, indeed, always very high seas, and our ship rolled and made so much travel, that we could neither stand nor sit without something to hold by, and far less rest in the night-time. However we easily took heart, because we made a great deal of way with these high west and south-west winds. This continued about eighteen days, in which time we ran near seven hundred leagues. Nay, we had made more, but for the currents which we met near to the Isle of Madagascar, that were contrary to us: we ran at first to the thirty seventh degree of south latitude, that's to say, on the sixteenth about eleven o'clock in the morning, at the height of thirty six degrees south latitude, whilst we were making pretty good way with a fair gale, on a sudden the wind changed right on head, and back-filled our sails with so much violence, that we were like to have failed all our masts, and had much ado to bring the ship about and get our sails in the wind again.

Navigators ought to be always on their guard about the thirty sixth degree south latitude

The Heer St. Martin warned us that we should tell our pilots not to stand to the south, but as little as they could, and that so soon as we should find the west-winds, make the best of our way, and bear away straight east. He assured us that the Dutch had observed, that the more they stood to the southward, the more violent winds they found, and that sometimes they changed so suddenly from stern to stem, that many times they had their sails blown away, and their masts brought by the board. But there was no necessity of giving this last advice to Monsieur de Vaudricourt, for there never was a more vigilant and industrious commander, and we fared the better for it, especially that day; for if the ships company had not been looking out, and the officers upon the deck, we had run great risk of losing, at least our masts and our sails.

Necessary remarks for those who are bound to the Indies from the Cape

Hereby it is apparent enough, that the less ships stand away to the southward, the better it is, and that if they met with westerly winds at the height of the Cape, they should steer their course, without giving themselves the trouble of running into more latitude, because of the winter season, and the accidents I have been speaking of, which without caution and circumspection, are not to be avoided. It is not the same in coming back, as we found it in our passage off of the Isle Maurice, and I heard also a Dutch pilot, whom we took in at Batavia to carry us to Siam, tell my Lord Ambassador so. He said, that in the summer time, which we took to return again to the Cape, the best way was to stand away southward to the thirty fifth or thirty sixth degree of latitude, for avoiding some furious gusts of wind, which happen commonly near the Isles Mauritius[13] and Madagascar; that these gusts are like Hurricanes, which endanger the best ships. That was a very discreet warning, and two violent storms that we met with in those very same parts, as I shall relate in its proper place, convinced us of the truth of it.

I have already observed that we were put in vain hopes, that being past the line, we should find at the height of six or seven degrees south latitude, fair winds to carry us to the Cape of Good Hope. We were no less deceived after we had doubled the Cape, in our expectation of the westerly winds, that were so confidently promised us, if we stood off to the thirty sixth or thirty seventh degree south. We followed these instructions; but we found that what the Heer Van Rheeden said was true, when he assured us that their pilots had observed within these four or five years, that the seasons and winds were extremely altered, and that there was no trusting to past experience, but to sail with all circumspection.

Seeing our pilots steered their course according to the instructions that were given them in France, they bore away south to the thirty seventh degree of latitude and farther, that they might preserve the west winds, but there we lost them; for having met with them upon our setting out from the Cape, they failed us at the thirty fourth degree. Nay, they began to be both so contrary and so high, that we never met with so rough a sea as we had then; nothing but mountains and abysses, and the waves broke against the ship with so much violence, that they made almost as great a noise as a canon shot, so that had not she been a strong ship, and had the weather lasted many days longer, she would have been in great danger of springing leaks, and of being foundered. The waves ran so high, and broke so violently, that they went clear over our stern, and poured in several tons of water at a time betwixt decks, which was very uneasy and tiresome to the ships company.

Prayers made for obtaining of fair weather

After six or seven days, these winds did indeed abate a little, but then they became contrary. This obliged us to have our recourse to the Holy Virgin, to whom the whole ships company vowed a novenary, or a nine days devotion, to pray her that she would obtain a fair wind for us, because having made little or no way for near a fortnight, we were afraid of being forced to put into the coast of Malabar or the Isle of Ceylon, or at least to come too late to Batavia, for making the voyage of Siam that year.

Sickness amongst the ships company

We had the more cause to dread that delay, for that we began to have a great many sick on board, not only because of the bad weather, but also of bad victuals, which now began to be spoilt. We had at least sixty sick at a time from the Cape to Batavia, most of them of scurvies, a distemper which rotted their legs, their mouth, and made their teeth drop out. We had then a fair occasion to assist those poor wretches in the work of their salvation. We did all we could to administer to them spiritual comfort in their troubles, by teaching them to make a good use of them. It was easy to make them resolve to resign themselves to the will of God, in the violent pains they endured, especially when they were dressed; the chirurgeons being obliged to scarify their gums, even to the palate of their mouth, and then make them wash their mouth with vinegar or brandy to stop the putrefaction, and hinder a gangrene.

The patience and piety of the sea-men

We were sometimes surprised to see in what tranquillity they were amidst their pains; how indifferent as to health or sickness, life or death, desiring nothing in this world, but that God's will might be fulfilled. They showed so much earnestness to hear mass and to communicate, that getting their messmates to carry them up upon the deck, you might see them faint away, and yet return satisfied, though far sicker than before they had performed their devotion. Doubtless this was a great comfort to us, which was much increased by the conversion of two poor seamen Calvinists, who were shipped without the Ambassador's knowledge. Had it been known that they were heretics, they would never have been suffered to make their voyage, but Divine providence made use of the curiosity they had of going to Siam, to bring them into the way of salvation. They had much ado to resolve upon it, but at length, being gained and instructed by one of our Fathers, they publicly renounced the errors of Calvin. Father Fontenay having made a short exhortation to them to confirm them in the resolution of living and dying good Catholics, received their abjuration the third Sunday after Whit-Sunday. They were afterwards farther instructed to prepare them for their first Communion, which sometime after they performed with much piety, and since that time both of them have lived very exemplarily in the ship.

God grants fair weather at the intercession of the blessed Virgin

We began then our novenary the seventh of July, and next day our prayers were heard. There arose so favourable a wind, that we made fifty leagues in less than four and twenty hours; after that we saw weeds and fowl in greater number than usually, for we had not failed of having, their company all the way from the Cape to Batavia. It was thought they came from the Isle of St. Paul of Amsterdam, which is towards the thirty sixth degree of south latitude, and the eighty ninth of longitude.

A caution not to be neglected in that course

Having run near a thousand leagues eastward, we steered away our course northward, that we might make the Isle of Java, which lies within six degrees of the line southward. Nay, for some time we had a fresh fair gale, but July the fifteenth it began to slacken so much, that we hardly made any way at all. The seventeenth of the same month, in the night-time, we re-passed the Tropic of Capricorn, and from that day forward we sailed as near as we could upon a wind, until we came in sight of the Isle of Java. For we were afraid of falling too much to the northward, and by consequence to the leeward of the strait of the Sound, which would have mightily perplexed us, because the trade-winds and currents that are in those parts, not suffering us to enter it, we would have been obliged to put into the Isle of Ceylon or Sumatra. Therefore we desired winds that might suffer us to bear away more to the east, to the end we might come up with the land of Java. However, perceiving that the contrary winds still continued, on Wednesday the five and twentieth of July, we held counsel to determine, whether or not we should bear away still north-east, that we might pass betwixt the Isles of Cocos and the Trial, or if we should go and make New-Holland.

The Trial are three pretty low islands

Two of our pilots were of this last opinion, trusting to particular instructions that set off the course so, and they alleged that the winds changed not, and that if we went and made these lands, they would be fair for us for entering into the strait of the Sound. The other three were against it, because of the dangers that are to be met with along that coast, and the many shipwrecks that happen there; besides, they made it appear that it was very difficult to pass betwixt the Trial and the land, and that so it was better to make up to the Isle of Java. They said that in a short time the winds would change, or that at worst we might put in to Sumatra, that this course, though irksome enough, was nevertheless safe, and that it was better to resolve upon it, than to run the risk of being cast away. This last advice was followed, and it proved to be the best, as may be seen in the sequel. The truth is, the winds, became no fairer afterwards than they had been before; but seeing the Isles of Java was not so far from us as our pilots, relying upon their charts, imagined, in a short time we found ourselves a good deal higher than the strait of the Sound, and we entered it as you shall hear. We would not trust to the experience and good advice of Monsieur de St. Martin, who assured us that the Isle of Java was ill placed in the common maps and that it was about a hundred leagues nearer the Cape, and much more to the leeward than was believed.

The wind being contrary, we betook ourselves to prayers again

We held on that course then, steering north-east, in hopes of a fairer wind; but seeing after long sailing the wind changed not, we vowed another novenary, which we began with fresh zeal and devotion. About one half of the ships company were dangerously sick, and the rest were so feeble and spent, that they could not work the ship. The seamen who belonged to St. Malo, resolved to give some token of their devotion towards St. Saviour their patron. They sent two or three of their number to one of our fathers, to pray him that he would assist them in their good desires, and prescribe to them what was to be done for rendering their vow acceptable to their Holy patron. This custom they have amongst them, which they inviolably observe, that when they are in any danger at sea, they promise to St. Saviour to go and visit his Church in Linnen, that's to say, in their shirt, to communicate there, and to have a solemn mass sung. They had already agreed among themselves to make this vow, many of their townsmen, who were sick of the scurvy, put that thought into their minds, and egg'd on to the performance of it.

The seamen of St. Malo show a particular devotion

When they had proposed their design, they were told that they must begin by confession and communicating, that so they might be in a condition to have their prayers heard. They prepared themselves accordingly during the rest of the week, and on Sunday all of them confessed and communicated. When they had done so, the father to whom they had applied themselves, went up upon the forecastle, and having made them to kneel, published aloud the promise which they made to God, if by the intercession of St. Saviour, they obtained a fair wind, and a happy return into their own country.

Providence, without doubt, is in all places wonderful, but I dare be bold to say, and I have often found it by experience, that it shows itself in a particular manner at sea. We had never begged fair weather with greater confidence, and we never thought we stood more in need of it, during all our prayers, and we were astonished to find ourselves already at the end of our novenary, without any the least sign of the change of weather.

Gods special protection of our ship

But we were soon happily undeceived, and we found that after all our vows and prayers, we must resign ourselves to the providence of God. For had our prayers been heard, and had God granted us the wind which we so earnestly begged; on the twelfth of August, in the night-time, we had infallibly run foul of a little low island, and been in great danger of being cast away. We did not make that Isle before next morning at break of day, when we had already passed almost one half of it, being no more but about two leagues of on it: so that if that night we had a fair wind to carry us straight north-east, as our pilots thought best for us, we could not have avoided being lost; because that Isle lies almost in the tenth degree of latitude. For some time we took it to be the Isle of Cocos, which we thought we had already passed, and the rather, because it is marked in the sea-charts to lie in the twelfth degree of south latitude.

The perplexity we were in before we come to the Isle of Java

We could not imagine that it should be the Isle of Mony, the most southern, and most eastern of the two isles, which lie near the coast of Java, either because Mony is set down in the common charts to be in eight degrees of latitude, or else because we did not all that day, nor next, see the other little isle which is very near to it. And so our sick men, who were in very great number, having turned out to see land, were much dejected when they found it was not that which they expected; but they had far sadder hearts, when they came to understand that we did not know where we were. In this doubt we took the surest course, and steered away east, for fear of falling to the leeward of the strait of the Sound, into which it would have been difficult to enter, by reason of the south and south-east wind that reigns there constantly in that season.

But we came to know afterward that it was Mony, when we saw exacter charts at Batavia, which placed that isle just in ten degrees eleven minutes south latitude. The Treasurer General show'd us, that the first day we went ashore, when we acquainted him with the danger we had been in, he called an old pilot who show'd us in a great chart that isle placed exactly as we found it. The signs of being near the land of Mony are three sorts of birds, which the sea-men call boobies, frigates and tropic birds, or straw in tails, according to the French. The first suffer themselves to be caught with the hand, when in the fore-part of the night they come and perch upon the yards of the ship, and the last have feathers in the tail about twenty inches long, which one would take for straws, seeing them at a distance, and that's the reason the French call them by that name.

In all that long passage we saw nothing remarkable, unless it were some porpoises pretty different from those we formerly spoke of, as to bigness, shape and colour; for they are bigger and whiter by one half, and have the snout shorter, and almost round, as you may see by the figure of them in the following map of the road of Bantam. Seeing they are fairer than the others, and that many took them at first for the dorados we thought they were the fish known to the ancients by the name of dolphins. We caught no fish from the time we put out from the Cape, the seas being too rough for fishing. We saw grampusses which are like little whales, and some others bigger, that spouted the water up in the air above fifteen or sixteen foot high, by what we could judge at the distance we saw them at.

Book 3

The Voyage from the Isle of Java to the Kingdom of Siam

Arrival at the Isle of Java

August 5. We discovered a great coast of land, and standing in with it, found it to be the Isle of Java, when we thought ourselves to be far from it. This made us observe that that island lies much more to the west, and by consequent is nearer by threescore leagues to the Cape of Good Hope than it is marked in the geographical maps.

A considerable mistake in the Hydrographical and Geographical charts

Therefore it was that we came in with the land above threescore leagues farther up than the most western point of that Isle which we looked for. An error to be imputed to the charts, and not to the inability of the pilots, who all along sailed very exactly, and always kept reckoning that we should make the land the same day that we saw it, both at the Isle of Java and the Cape of Good Hope, as we have already observed. The sight of these lands seemed somewhat rare to us; they are covered with trees of a most lovely verdure, which yield a pleasant smell to the ships that sail along the coast, at two or three leagues distance. We coasted along that isle with so good a wind, that in a day and a half's time we made the sixty leagues which we had run too far to the east, and Monday evening the sixth of August, were got to the entry into the strait of the Sound which is made by the Isles of Java and Sumatra.

But what surprised us more, and was a sign of God's particular providence upon our voyage, the same evening that we saw the entry into the strait of the Sound, we made the *Maligne*, which was separated from us by the bad weather I mentioned, June 24, in the night time, and which we hath never seen since. Though my Lord Ambassador and several others took it to be the frigate, yet we could not be sure of that, because it was already late, and the weather dark. We were not certain it was she till eight days after in the road of Bantam where we joined her again. The pilots who were aboard of her having made the strait in good time, put into it, and having a fair wind came to the place of anchoring. But it being usual to shoot the strait of the Sound betwixt the Princes Isle and Sumatra, keeping as near as may be to the Princes Isle, which we could not make plainly because of the night, we were forced to tack and stand off to sea all the night long. So that since we could not make the best of the fair weather which then we had, which would have easily carried us beyond the Princes Isle, we fell too low, and spent the rest of the week in the strait, which is not above thirty leagues in length, struggling and beating against the currents and contrary winds. One of our pilots assured us that the *Sun of the East* which he was aboard in an East-India voyage, was three full weeks stopped there, and could not get to Bantam but as she was towed with Boats.

We entered then the strait of the Sound three days after we made the land of Java, but the Princes Island lying at the mouth of the strait betwixt Java and Sumatra, and dividing it into two, we entered by the more northern passage, which is the larger and safer betwixt the Princes Isle and Sumatra. We made many tacks to double the Isle of Cacatoua (so called because of the white parrots that are upon that Isle, which incessantly repeat that name) we did, I say, all that lay in our power to double the Isle of Cacatoua, which lies pretty near to Sumatra, that so we might stand in with the land of Java: but all our attempts were unsuccessful because the wind was too weak, and currents too strong in the middle of the channel. That which causes the currents, is because the water that for several months has been forced into the straits by the south and south-west winds, which reign commonly from the month of March to September, set out again impetuously during the other six months of the year, being sent back by the east and north-east winds.

Breezes rise on Sumatra at certain hours of the day

We had the wind so cross, and the currents so contrary, that it was thought best to keep as close in as we could by the shore of the Princes Isle, by the help of some breezes that came from Sumatra, and which for some hours interrupted the great heats and dead calms that are common in that season in the straits of the Sound.

By the help of those little breezes we were in hopes by little and little to come up with the land of Java, but it behoved us first to double the Princes Isle which is pretty big, and lies in the mouth of the strait. After all, the view which we had of the land and of several small islands all decked in verdure comforted us a little, for the time which we lost in that strait.

The danger the ship was in, in the strait

Nay we were like to have been stranded one night upon the Princes Isle, as we endeavoured to bear close in with it. We had not observed that the tide which was not perceived in the middle of the strait, was pretty strong near land, and seeing we resolved to rake along very near the shore, because the coast is safe, and that within a pistol-shot of land there is no ground to be found, that night we fetched aboard into the island, that we might recover what the currents and tide had made us lose the day before. Hardly were we got out of the strength of the currents, when the officer that was upon the watch, and the seamen who were upon the deck, took notice that the ship ran apace towards land. They had only time to tack about and stand off, which was done so much in the nick, that when the ship was about, and the sails trimmed, one might easily have thrown a stone on shore, from the poop of our ship.

Extraordinary thunder and lightning at Java and Sumatra

If ships could come to an anchor in the strait, they would not be exposed to that danger; but no ground being to be found in it, at least off of the Princes Isle, we were forced to keep continually under sail, and when it was a calm to keep at large amongst the currents, which made us lose sometimes in less than three hours what with small breezes we had got in four before. Thus we spent several days in passing that island, where we had leisure enough to make trial of the extraordinary heats of that climate, and to consider Sumatra which appeared to us always covered with a black thick mist, and in the evening with continual flashes of lightning. Thunder is very common there; and amongst others we had one clap so hard and smart, that many took it for a cannon-shot, and some dabb'd down their heads, as if it had been to avoid the bullet. At length a good breeze did our work for us, made us double the Isle and carried us upon the coast of Java. When we were got in with that land, we advanced by little and little, dropping an anchor so soon as the wind left us.

The Javanese[14] came on board in their little boats

In the mean time vast numbers of the Javanese' canoes which they call prau[15] came on board of us every minute. These boats are made of one entire piece of timber hollowed and some of them are so little, that with much ado can they hold their man sitting. We were altogether astonished to see these poor people venture out so many leagues at sea, in such brittle boats, wherewith they danced upon the waves and advanced with incredible swiftness, to bring us fresh provisions. And because these prau sail in a quite different manner from other canoes, I thought fit to give you the figure [illustration] of one under sail in the road of Bantam. The Javanese are well shaped and strong, they seem to be sprightly and resolute, but the extraordinary heat of the climate obliges them to go almost naked. They who live in the middle of the isle are Idolaters, and the rest who inhabit the coasts are Mohammedans, all superstitious to excess. When they came on board, we offered them bread, wine and brandy, but there was not one of them that would take anything, saying, that it was their fasting time, and that their law prohibited the drinking of wine. Notwithstanding all this they are bold robbers and thieves. I saw one of them openly in the day time carry off a seaman's shirt which he had fastened to a line and held it by one end. It was to no purpose for him to cry out and make a noise; for the Javanese who held it only in one hand and row'd with the other, was too strong for him, and carried it clearly away. The whole nation are not subject to this vice, and there are some of them very faithful. One of them coming on board of us to sell some small refreshments, he seemed to be so honest, that some gentlemen of the Ambassador's retinue, who could not go ashore to buy some things they stood in need of, trusted him with their money. He promised to bring them what they desired against the time they had prefixed. This Javaner was so true to his word, that the Ambassador having ordered to set sail before the appointed hour, he nevertheless got into his prau with his provisions, and made so much haste that he came up with the ship, and gave an account of his commission and brokerage even to the last farthing.

The road of Bantam

We did not come to sight of the road of Bantam before the fifteenth of August, the Assumption Day of Our Lady, as we had arrived at the cape on the Ascension Day of Our Lord. This is one of the fairest and most commodious roads in the world. It is about eight or nine leagues in circumference. The land on all sides is but low, and yet there is always very smooth water in it. The town of Bantam, which is pretty big, lies at the middle of the bay, and the houses of it are all of wood. Towards the middle of the road, there is a small fort, where the King lives, and where the Dutch, since they became masters of it, keep a good garrison, till they have time to build a strong fort, which is already pretty well advanced. Bantam was heretofore a town of trade especially for pepper, where all the Europeans entertained great commerce. But for these two or three years that it is fallen into the hands of the Dutch, in the manner we shall hereafter relate, none are suffered to come to it, and all the trade is removed to Batavia. Here you have the view of it as it appeared to us after we came to an anchor.

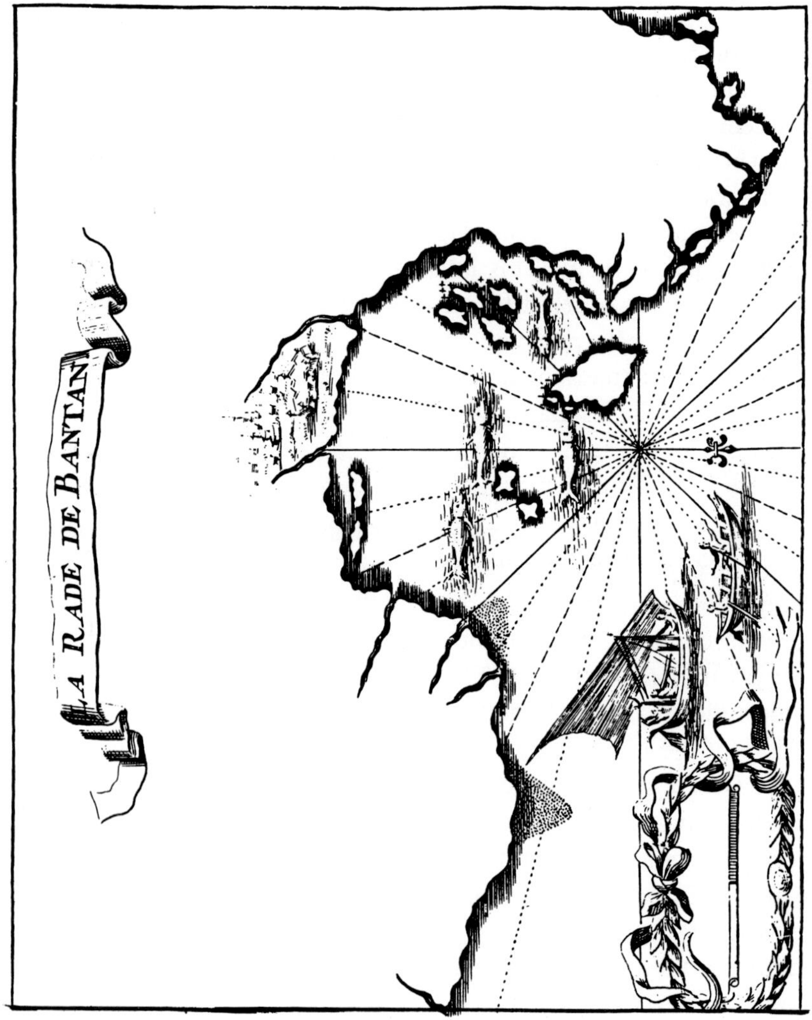

Plate 14. The harbor of Bantan

A remedy for the Land-Evil

At first we designed to go to Batavia to take in fresh provisions, but the season being already far spent, we were afraid we might lose the monsoon; that is to say, the proper time for sailing to Siam. Besides the passage from Bantam to Batavia, tho not above fourteen or fifteen leagues in length, being very difficult, because of islands, banks and rocks on all hands, it was thought convenient to stop in the road of Bantam, that we might lose no time, and get more speedy relief for our sick men, who for the most part were in a sad condition and therefore my Lord Ambassador resolved next morning to send to Bantam to him who commanded in the fort for the Dutch, and to demand permission of him to take in fresh provisions, and put our sick men on shore. That is the sovereign remedy for that distemper, which the French call the Land-evil, and which to speak properly, is nothing else but a corruption of the blood caused by bad food and salt victuals. This evil begins commonly in the gums, which at first grow very red, then black, and at last entirely rot; so that to prevent the corruption from spreading farther, the rotten flesh must every day be cut off from about the teeth, which easily drop out, if remedies be not used. This corruption gets also into the legs and thighs, which swell and become livid. There is no curing of those that are ill of it, but by putting them on shore, and giving them wholesome food. Some chirurgeons bury them up to the neck in sand for several days, others bath them in fresh water, and many times these remedies have succeeded.

The Chevalier de Fourbin is sent to the Governor of Bantam

Before we came to an anchor in the road of Bantam the Chevalier de Fourbin was by orders from the Ambassador gone to the town to pay a visit to the Governor, but he had no sooner passed a little island, behind which we lay at anchor, than he saw the frigate also at anchor, on the other side of that island within three leagues of Bantam, and steered straight towards her.

He found the Maligne *and returned on board with the Lieutenant of the Frigate*

Those who were on board the *Maligne* were overjoyed at his coming, they being more concerned for us than we were for them: because the *Oiseau* being a far better sailor than their frigate, they thought we had been already a great way beyond Bantam. But they having met with fairer winds than we did, in the course they had steered; they had been already four or five days in the road, and heard no news of us.

The bad reception those of the Maligne *met before our arrival at Bantam*

The Chevalier de Fourbin was informed of Monsieur de Joyeux captain of the *Maligne* and of Monsieur de Tertre his Lieutenant, in what manner the Governor of Bantam received their compliment. They told him that they could not have audience of the King, tho they had long waited for it, and were put in hopes by the Dutch of obtaining it; that they could not so much as speak to the Governor of their nation, whom they have settled there, nor have leave to buy fresh provisions. The lieutenant of the fort made known to Mr. de Tertre in the name of the King of Bantam, and of the Governor who was sick, that the King's affairs did not permit his Majesty, to suffer strangers to come ashore; that his throne was not yet well fixed; that his people repining at the present Government, longed for some change, that they were ready every minute to rise upon the first appearance of any succour which they were made to expect from England; and that so the French ought not to take it ill, that that Prince was upon his guard; and that the Dutch who were only concerned as his allies and friends, and who served only as auxiliary forces, should receive and obey his orders. The French officer being nettled at that answer, and thinking that he saw to the bottom of such an uncivil procedure, replied that it would be thought very strange that the Dutch who in Europe make profession of keeping and entertaining peace and good intelligence so carefully with the French, would not grant them in the Indies, that which is not refused but to declared enemies; that certainly the King his master would take it extremely ill, that they should use his ships so; and that in short, it was well enough known that they could do anything at Bantam; that the King, of whose authority they made a pretext to cloak their refusal, was wholly at their disposal, nay, and guarded by their soldiers too. To these words the Dutch lieutenant made answer, that it would be in vain for him to endeavour to remove out of Mr. de Tertre's mind the disadvantageous suspicions, wherewith he saw him prejudiced against those of his nation, that the French would be undeceived if they would go to Batavia where the Dutch were the masters, and where they would be made sensible of the respect those people hath for the King, and of their esteem for the French Nation. It was to no purpose for Monsieur de Tertre to complain; for that was all the answer he had, so was obliged to return on board again.

Mutual presents of the Governor of Bantam and the Captain of the

Next day the Governor of Bantam sent to Monsieur de Joyeux a great deal of fresh provisions of the fowl, herbs and fruits of the country; and Monsieur de Joyeux returned the civility by a present which he made him of many curiosities of France. Some days after a *pangran* came on board of the Frigate, (that is the name they give to the lords of court) attended by four halberdiers of the natives. He bid his interpreter tell the Captain that he came from the King his master, to tell the French that that Prince was surprised to see them still at anchor in his road; that they should weigh with all expedition, and be gone from his ports and lands. Monsieur de Joyeux answered very fiercely, and bid them tell the pangran, that he knew not what it was to obey any but the King of France his master, and that his answer to the King of Bantam was, that he would not be gone till he thought fit, and that they durst not send a ship to fight him as they had threatened. With that the King of Bantam's envoy withdrew without any other compliment.

The Governor's suspicion of the French

It was easily believed that the Dutch officers who were in the fort, made all those engines play, and that they used the Kings authority to drive the French away from the town. For the Governor not knowing the reasons which had obliged the King to send two men of war into the

Indies, could not think that it was only to carry an ambassador to the King of Siam, as he was told: on the contrary, the more pains was taken to convince him of it, the more ground he imagined he had to suspect that they were part of the squadron which the Kings of England and France sent to be revenged of the insolencies that both nations had lately suffered, when the Dutch raised the siege of Bantam. The rumour that was spread abroad amongst the islanders, that for a long time they had been arming in England upon that design, increased his suspicions, and he was easily persuaded that that ship at anchor, and another bigger which was seen off in the strait of the Sound, would soon be followed by the whole fleet.

The Javanese are mad to see Sultan Agoum their old King in prison

To all this it is to be added that the Javanese were furiously incensed to see the young Prince upon the throne, the Dutch masters of Bantam, and their old King kept close prisoner. It did, indeed, surprise us to hear these people speak with so much liberty, threatening to put the Dutch to the sword, and dethrone the King Regnant, if they had forces to assist them.

This news made the Chevalier de Fourbin resolve to put back again to the *Oiseau* and inform the Ambassador before he went farther. He took Monsieur du Tertre the lieutenant of the frigate with him in his boat, who himself gave the Ambassador a relation of all these things in our presence. He added that he had been assured that the monsoon was not yet far spent, and that three weeks or a month after would be time enough to set out for Siam.

The Ambassador wondered much at that conduct, however, he sent to Bantam to ask leave to take in wood and water, thinking that the Governor of the fort would have more regard to his character, and grant him a prau (a kind of very light boat which are commonly made use of in those isles) to carry Monsieur Van Rheeden's letter to the General of Batavia. The Ambassador would have no mention made of the sick, because he had already caused them to be put on shore for some days in a little neighbouring island, where they were to have tents pitched, and so be looked after till they should recover.

The Chevalier de Fourbin is sent to Bantam

The Chevalier de Fourbin being charged with these orders put off again anew for Bantam. At the same time we weighed and gave warning to the frigate by a gun to come and anchor by us in the road, at a pretty distance from Bantam, in expectation of the Governor's answer. The *Maligne* saluted our ship with seven guns, as she past by her, and we answered with five. About an hour after noon the Chevalier de Fourbin came on board again, and brought the same answer that had been given to the Lieutenant of the frigate, without being able to speak to the King, or to the Governor, who they still said was sick. He added that they told him, that they had sent on board the first ship that came to an anchor, all the fresh provisions they could find in the town. When the Ambassador had heard that surly answer, he ordered presently to put under sail, and stand away for Batavia.

We weigh from the road of Bantam and stand away for Batavia

We were two days and a half in our passage thither, being forced every night to come to an anchor, by reason of a multitude of islands, rocks and banks that lie in the way, and besides, none of our pilots had ever been there before. However we steered our course fortunately enough, by means of a very exact and large chart which by very good luck one of our pilots had found out amongst others that he had.

Several revolutions that have happened in the Kingdom of Bantam

For comprehending the reasons of this conduct, which seemed to be so strange in the Dutch, it will be pertinent to give a brief history of the Prince Regnant, who hath made so much noise in the Indies, and given occasion of discourse enough also in Europe.

The King of Bantam having resigned the crown to his son, attempts to resume it again

Sultan Agoum, the father of Sultan Agui, who reigns at present, being weary of wearing the crown, resigned over the government of affairs into the hands of his son, and confined himself for the future to his seraglio and pleasures. This young prince had a mind to govern after his own fancy, without any regard to the instructions that his father gave him at his coronation. He began by removing all those from court, who had the greatest share in the administration of affairs under the late reign; whether it was that he was displeased with their conduct, or that he looked upon them as secret spies, that would give his father an account of all that he should act in the government. Amongst others, he banished two pangrans, whom his father had chiefly recommended to him. This was a sensible blow to Sultan Agoum, who began to be convinced, but too late, that it was easier to quit a sceptre, than not to repent of it after one had laid it down. He could not forbear to complain of it to his son, and to tell him, that it surprised him to see that his recommendation, and the wise councils which he had given him, had made but so small an impression upon his mind; but the young King nettled at this expostulation, which he looked upon as a heinous reproach, sent orders immediately to have those two lords dispatched. This, conspiring with the solicitations of the ancient subjects, who looked upon themselves to be oppressed under this new government, and with the secret jealousies, as some have given it out, which people who found their interest in the bad understanding betwixt father and son, sowed betwixt them, prevailed upon the old King to take arms, and endeavour by force, to recover a Kingdom, which of his own free consent he had just before willingly resigned. He marched then at the head of a great army against his son, who was soon forsaken of all, besieged in the capital town, and upon the point of surrendering, or of being delivered up prisoner to the conqueror. Being reduced to this extremity, he resolved to put all to a risk, rather that to submit to the clemency of his so much provoked father.

The young Sultan besieged by his father, begs assistance from the Dutch

In short, seeing no other way of relief in this his distress, he implored the assistance of the Dutch by a trusty Javanese, who made his escape to Batavia, by favour of the night. General Spelman was then alive, who being a man of a quick wit, a lover of great enterprises, and not stinted to the common measures of conduct, called his council to consult what was best to be done. It was the opinion of all the council that there was no meddling in a quarrel betwixt father and son, that they could espouse no party betwixt the two Princes, seeing they were both alike their allies and friends; that if they should resolve to assist Sultan Agui, the English and French would infallibly declare against them, and that so they would bring a troublesome war upon themselves. It was to no purpose for the General to represent to them what an occasion they would lose of rendering themselves masters of so considerable a place and Kingdom, and lying so conveniently for them; that by raising the siege, which would be done without doubt, they would entirely oblige the young Sultan to their interests, and perhaps render themselves masters of his person, Kingdom, and of all the trade of the Isle of Java, which was the thing the company could most desire. None of these reasons wrought upon the council to change their opinion; they still persisted in this, that it was best to continue neutral.[16]

General Spelman sends a strong assistance to Sultan Agui besieged

Then the General, who had views of a far different nature, making use of the sovereign authority which he had on such occasions, said publicly, that he would assist the Prince his ally, that the success he would take upon himself, and get his proceedings approved by the East-India company in Holland. He presently sent for the Heer St. Martin, Major General of Batavia, declares him chief of the enterprise, and having ordered him to muster together as many forces as he could of the garrison, and townspeople, both Europeans and Indians, he put them on board twelve ships, which were then in the road of Batavia. So soon as the Heer St. Martin arrived before Bantam, he made a descent, and found but little resistance. Then, without giving the Enemy time to take breath, he marched straight to their trenches, and at the second attack forced them to raise the siege in disorder. After this victory the Sultan Agui commanded the gates to be opened, and received the Heer St. Martin with all his forces into the town.

Sultan Agui guarded by the Dutch

The Dutch finding themselves masters of the capital town, resolved to subdue the whole Kingdom, and to make sure of the persons of both kings. They set a good guard of Dutch over Sultan Agui, whom they had in their hands, under pretext of doing him honour, and securing him from the insults of his enemies. And so pursuing their victory, with sword in hand, they took the Citadel of Tangran. The old sultan having fled to the town of Cartbiace; they drove him from thence, and cut to pieces the garrison, consisting of 1,600 Macassars, the best soldiers of all the Barbarians, who after a vigorous resistance, were killed every man of them in their posts. Then they took that poor Prince, who was endeavouring to make his escape, and delivered him up prisoner to his son, who to punish his father for his revolt, would presently have put him to death; but the Dutch persuaded him not to embrew his hands in the blood of him who had given him life. So that he thought it enough to shut him up in a very close prison, without allowing him the company of his wives. Nevertheless he had remitted his severity as to this last point, since he is become peaceable possessor of the Kingdom.

The English and French leave the town by the King of Bantam's order

Some days after the young king commanded the English and French to withdraw, under pretext of jealousies he had of them, and that he had been told they favoured the party of the King his father. The French carried away their effects and left Bantam, but the English protested against the Dutch for the violence they did them under the cloak of the King's authority, and leaving the town, left all their effects in their ware-houses. This was the matter that caused the great difference that hath made so much noise betwixt those two nations, and which was not determined when we came out of Europe.

After this digression concerning the revolution that had happened in the Isle of Java, we must now pursue our Voyage again. Saturday the eighteenth of August, betwixt five and six o'clock in the evening we came to anchor in the road of Batavia, amidst seventeen or eighteen huge ships belonging to the Dutch East-India company, and a great number of barks which we found there at anchor. This is a very fair and safe road, as may be seen by the cut [illustration].

The civilities of the General of Batavia to the Ambassador

My lord Ambassador had dispatched the night before the Chevalier de Fourbin to go compliment the General of Batavia, and to deliver them the Heer Van Rheeden's letter. He came on board again, just as we were about to drop anchor, and told us that the General had granted all that was demanded of him. He said we might take in fresh water and wood, provide ourselves of all sorts of refreshments, and set our sick men ashore; that the Dutch would give us a pilot to carry us to Siam; and that when we saluted the fort, they would return gun for gun, a thing not hitherto done. It is true, the General made some difficulty as to this last point, saying, that the fort had never returned that salute, neither to the English, Portuguese, nor any other Nation whatsoever, and that it was always thought enough to be re-saluted by the Admiral ship riding in the road. But it being represented to him that there was a great deal of difference betwixt king's ships and other ships, and if the fort had never as yet rendered a salute, it was because they had never seen any king's ships: The General condescended, and promised that in consideration of the King and of my Lord Ambassador, he should for that time, but not as a precedent, order gun for gun to be given. My lord Ambassador was very well satisfied in the sequel with the civilities of the Heer Campiche (for that is the General's name) who very frequently sent the chief of the town to compliment him, and almost daily presented him with all sorts of fresh provisions for his table, and for both the ships' companies.

The Jesuits land at Batavia to make observations

When the Chevalier de Fourbin had thus given the Ambassador an account of his voyage, and assured him that the General would give His Excellency[17] all the marks of respect and esteem which were due to his character; he added that the Jesuits would not be so well received in this town as they had been at the Cape; that the General of Batavia had put a guard upon a Father of their society lately come Tonkin,[18] and that he had been confined to his house for having assisted Catholics who applied themselves to him in their spiritual necessities. Having considered a little what was best for us to do, by the advice of the Ambassador, we took the same course that we had done at the Cape of Good Hope, which was to go visit the General.

The good reception they had from the officers of the Dutch East-India company

Father Fontenay and I arrived at the town about ten of the clock in the morning. The officer who was upon guard at the gate carried us to the chief treasurer, who introduces strangers to the General. After the first compliments we told him who we were, and prayed him to present us to the General, that we might pay him our respects. He promised us audience of His Excellency, (for that's the title commonly given to the General of Batavia) the very same day. But seeing it was now but about ten of the clock, and that no audience was given till towards the evening; we desired to know of him whether or not it would be taken ill if we went to see one of our fathers who came from Tonkin, and was in General Spelmans's garden. He told us that we might do what we pleased without offence, and that he would give us his boat to carry us thither, but that it must be after dinner, because it was already late, and at the same time he urged us to eat with him. Having thanked him for all his civilities, we went into his boat with design to go see Father Fuciti in the place where they had lodged him.

A description of the Garden of the late General Spelman

It is a house standing without the town, but so near the citadel, that it is only parted from it by the river which serves for a ditch, and this river being covered all over with little boats, one may cross it at all times. This house was built by the late General Spelman, that he might take the air there during the excessive heats of summer, which is almost constant at Batavia, and that he might treat the officers of the company, and the

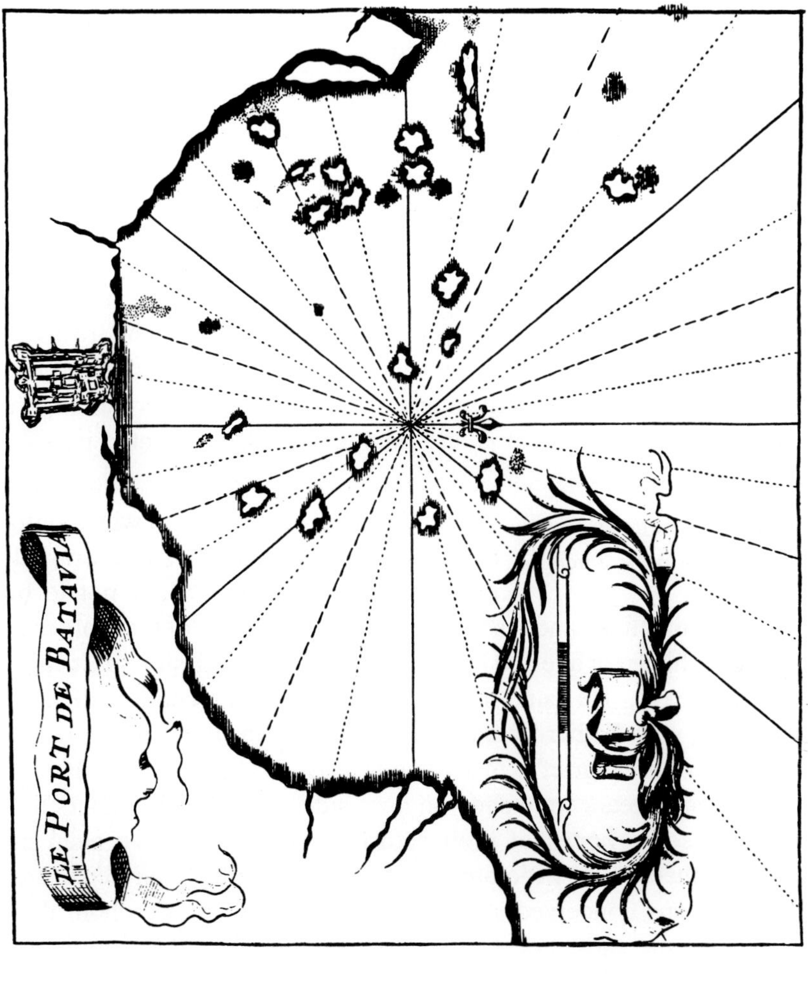

Plate 15. The port of Batavia

ambassadors and envoys of princes or foreign states. It consists in two great galleries open on all hands, which form a double square. The gallery at the end which crosses upon the other is extremely wide, from both of them you enter into halls with several closets, and all this is environed with grass-plots and gardens; on the right hand there is a menagerie full of several sorts of animals, as stags, hinds, wild-goats, antelopes, ostriches, storks, ducks and geese of a singular kind. On the left hand are the gardens and country-houses of the town-people of best quality. Behind it there is a little pavilion consisting of three low rooms and a kitchen, which is separated from the galleries by a large court that reaches on one hand to the ditches of the fort, and on the other as far as the sea. A little river runs under one of these galleries and across the grass-plots, which serves to make ponds where fish are kept. Seeing this building was only made for taking the fresh air, there is no regularity in the whole, tho every party be regular enough. The gardens are full of flowers at all times, but we saw none there that were rare, the trees are orange, lemon and pomegranate trees planted in rows that make lovely walks.

The French Jesuits go to see Father Dominic Fucity

There we found Father Fucity, who having been already informed of our arrival, impatiently expected us. It is not to be expressed how much joy and resolution we felt at the sight of that holy man honourable for his great age and his long labours in the mission of Cochin-China[19] and Tonkin. He came from his church the nine and twentieth of October, 1684, with Father Emanuel Fereira who was the superior of the mission. It was a great grief to many good Christians to see them leave the country, and many tears were shed on both sides. Nay, if the fathers had not left them some hopes of their return, there would have been no comforting of them. Every idolatrous mandarin bewailed their departure, and the Christians conceived so great an aversion to those whom they suspected to be the causes of it , that they would not confess any more, incessantly calling for their first masters and ancient pastors. This we were told by a churchman in the Indies who was a person of good credit, and very well acquainted with affairs of that nature.

The good usage that the Fathers Missioners of Tonkin met with at Batavia

These two fathers arrived at Batavia the twenty third of December, in a Dutch ship that by a storm was forced off of Siam whither they were bound. Father Fucity stayed at Batavia for a passage to Siam, where he was to receive by way of Macao, orders from his superiors, and money to perform his voyage before he returned to Europe; Father Fereira was himself gone for them six weeks before, and in that design went on board a ship of Macao.

The character of Father Fucity, and his Apostolic labours in several Kingdoms

Father Dominico Fucity is a Neapolitan, and left Rome with that great company of Jesuits, whom the famous Father de Rhodes had obtain'd from the Reverend Father General for the Indies. So that he had been almost thirty years in that country, where he hath always laboured as a true apostle, with admirable success and benediction. He lived eight years in Cochin-China, where he baptized above four thousand souls with his own hands, and sixteen whole years in Tonkin, where he hath baptized eighteen thousand. He hath suffered long and irksome imprisonments. He hath been eight days and eight nights with the cangue about his neck which is a great and heavy ladder, and eight or nine months in irons. He hath been condemned to death, and oftener then once upon the brink of martyrdom. His life hath been almost nothing else but a continual martyrdom; he hath made sixteen voyages by sea, and hath been five times in danger of being killed by the infidels. He hath lived ten or eleven years in Tonkin without daring to appear abroad, keeping himself in the daytime hid in a little boat, and in the night-time making his excursions through the towns of the country, visiting the Christians by turns, preaching, catechising, baptising, and administering the sacraments with infinite troubles.

It is not from him that we came to know these things, he is humble and modest, and we observed many great virtues in him during our abode at Batavia and Siam. We were particularly charmed with his mildness towards all people, his reservedness in speaking of those who had persecuted him with greatest violence, with his continual union with God, his tender devotion that makes him melt in tears every time he says mass, or hears it; his patience in suffering all things without complaining, and with his zeal for the salvation of souls. In short, he is a man really apostolical, and would receive eulogies at Rome, whether he is called to justify himself, if his virtues were known there as they are in the Indies.

The earnestness of the Catholics of Batavia to receive the sacraments

When the arrival of those two fathers was known at Batavia, not only the Portuguese who live there, but the Catholics also of other nations that are there, as we were told, in great numbers came daily to see them, were present at their masses on Sundays and holy-days, and confessed to them. Sometime after Father Fereira went away in a Portuguese ship for Macao, whither Father Fucity thought it not fit to accompany him, lest the magistrates of that town might force him to return to Tonkin, with the Ambassadors whom they were about to send thither, because that father is extremely well known and respected there. The zeal of the Catholics made too great a noise at Batavia, and so great was the concourse of people that came flocking to Father Fucity, that the Protestant ministers complained to the General, that a Jesuit performed the public exercise of the Catholic religion in Batavia: that Mohammedanism and idolatrous worship and sacrifice were permitted there, and the ministers don't at all trouble the magistrates with their scruples upon that account. Upon their remonstrances, the General set a sentinel at the Father's door, to hinder Catholics from entering his house, and sent him word that he desired him not to walk abroad in the town, but with a guard to wait upon him.

After a long conference with Father Fuciti, we returned to the treasurers house, thinking that the hour of audience drew nigh. About four of the clock in the afternoon we heard the drums, fifes, and trumpets of the fort, not being far from it. Then the treasurer told us, that now we might go wait upon His Excellency. He took us into his boat, and would needs force us to sit above him. We quickly got to the palace, where we found the Governor's guards a'mustering before him, in a large court. There were four companies of foot and two troops of horse of them, of about an hundred men apiece, all men of good mien, well armed, and clothed in one livery. Their coats were yellow, their breeches red and very wide, and all of them had silk stockings. The horseguards were mounted on Persian horses, which, indeed are not very big, but are light and full of mettle. These horses seem to be hard in the mouth, hang upon the bit, and always toss up their heads; but I believe these faults proceed from their bridles and the neglect of breaking them well.

The General of Batavia receives the Jesuits with much civility and goodness

The muster being over, we went up a pair of stone stairs on the outside of a great hall, where we found guards and the general's pages, all clothed after the same fashion, with this difference only, that the last wear no swords. The treasurer desired us to stay in that hall, until he went and spoke to the General. A moment after, he came back and led us through a gallery into another hall, which was nothing near so big as the former. There we found the General with five or six friends of whom two spoke very good French. We could not have expected greater civilities nor testimonies of friendship than we received from him at this first audience. The joy that appeared in his looks, his caresses and obliging discourses sufficiently convinced us of the sincerity of his heart and actions. He ordered our letters patent for being the King's mathematicians to be read to him, and prayed us to give him an account of the observations we made at the Cape of Good Hope, still praising us, before the gentlemen that attended him.

When he understood that the Heer Van Rheeden had lodged us at the Cape, and how he had received and treated us, he protested he would not be short of him, and that if we had a design to come on shore, he entreated us to lodge with Father Fuciti, to whom from that day forward he gave all sort of liberty for our sakes. He told us that the place was very commodious for making observations in; that on the one hand we had a prospect of the sea, and on the other a vast plain reaching out of sight, and that, in short, if the weather offered fair, and that there was any curious observation to be made, he himself would be present at it.

We made the best answer we could to all his goodness, assuring him that the King should be informed of it, and that my Lord Ambassador would resent it.[20] At length, after a three hours conference, which was only interrupted by tea, sweet-meats and healths to the King, the Royal family, the Ambassador, and our own, which he drank to us, he suffered us with much ado to withdraw. He waited on us to the end of a long gallery which leads into the first hall, and ordered the governor of a province and the treasurer, not to leave us before we were safely returned to General Spelman's garden, where we were to lodge. As we went out of the hall we found a coach, with two pages carrying torches to conduct us to our lodging, what resistance soever we could make, we were necessitated to obey, and it was a new sight to see two Jesuits in the General's coach riding through the capital city of the Indies.

We soon got to our lodging, where Father Fuciti waited for us, and was not a little astonished to see us come home in that equipage. No sooner were we got there, but a plentiful supper was brought us from the General's palace, who during all the time we were at Batavia allowed us a magnificent table for a dozen of guests, where we were served by his officers in fine china and plate, with all neatness, and daintiness, and plenty imaginable.

Next day Father Fucity entreated the Father Superior to carry him on board and present him to my Lord Ambassador, that he might pay his respects unto him, and thank him for his goodness in concerning himself in his liberty. We were all three carried thither in the General's chaloop, which, as he sent us word, he wholly left to us to be made use of as often as we had occasion.

The four Fathers who remained on board were in pain for us; because we could not send them word how we were, and they were apprehensive that some unwelcome accident might have befallen us at Batavia. But they were much surprised when they saw us return in a stately chaloop, with the Dutch flag aboard and all the marks of grandeur that attend the General, except his guards. My lord ambassador to whom we gave an account of all that passed, received Father Fuciti very kindly, and offered him his passage to Siam. Monsieur de Vandiricourt showed him the like civilities; so that it was immediately resolved upon that the father should embark with us and complete the rest of the voyage.

Presently after it behoved us to go ashore again with some instruments to observe with the night following. But the sky was so overcast both night and day all the while we were at Batavia, that we could make but very few observations, and these too did not appear to us to be sure enough to deserve to be communicated to the public.

As soon as we came ashore we went all six to visit the General with Father Fuciti. He received us with the same signs of kindness and good will, as he had done the day before. It is true, he complained a little of the conduct of Father Fuciti, who had been rendered suspect to him because of his zeal in assisting and instructing the Catholics, adding, that he was obliged to see the laws of the East-India Company put in execution; that he believed we would not think his proceeding either ungentle or unjust; that he prayed us to observe measures, and so to carry ourselves in relation to Catholics that he might not be reproached for any testimony of friendship and esteem that he had already expressed towards us, and was ready still to testify upon all occasions. We made answer in Portuguese that His Excellency should be satisfied with our conduct, and that he should never have cause to repent the favours which hitherto he had heaped upon us, and was still willing to honour us with for the future.

Then we fell to discourse on several matters, we talked of news, and particularly of the French king, whose glory and greatness the General seemed to admire. Before he let us go which was pretty late, he showed us several curiosities of Japan, amongst others two human figures of a kind of plaster, extremely well done, and clad in silk after the manner of the Japanese, one of a lord and the other of a lady. He also showed us certain trees whose roots were enclosed within foraminous and very porous stones where they are so insinuated that they receive all their nourishment from the water that is now and then thrown upon them.

Tho we were not so much obliged as we are to Monsieur Campiche General of Batavia, yet we could not but speak well of him: his merit hath raised him by degrees to the highest place of the Indies, which at present he so worthily discharges, after he hath been thrice president of the company of Japan. He is about fifty years of age, somewhat taller then ordinary, an honest, sincere and circumspect man, speaking little, but very judiciously and to purpose. These qualities, accompanied with a mild popular way of carriage, have got him the love of his own country, and the esteem of strangers, both Europeans and Indians. We were told that he had some pictures in his closet, and amongst others, one of Our Saviour praying in the Garden of Olives, with these words written with his own hands, *Anima mea Christus est.*

The days following we went and visited the chief officers of the East-India Company; all of them show'd us great civilities; nay, many of them returned our visit at the company's garden. We were visited also by the Catholics of all sorts and conditions, who desired to receive the sacraments; but that we might not displease the General, nor bring the Catholics into trouble, we appointed such as were able to come on board of us, and confessed the rest so privately, either in their houses at home, or in the place where we were, that no notice was taken of it. Father Fucity especially, took no rest all the while that we were with him. For having upon our coming, got liberty to go about everywhere, he was taken up from morning to night in comforting and confessing here and there all that stood in need of his assistance.

The Catholic religion is the only religion prohibited at Batavia

It is with the Catholic religion in Batavia, and in the Indies subject to the Dutch, as it is in Holland. All sorts, and even idolatry itself, are tolerated, provided they pay a certain tribute to the magistrates. None but the Catholic religion is prohibited;

not that they reckon it the worst of all, but because they look upon it as the most dangerous, and fear that many who do not prefer their interest before their salvation, would embrace it if they knew it.

We were confidently told that some months before; the Portuguese, who are very numerous, had offered a vast sum of money to the East-India company to have leave to build a Catholic church, either in the town or in the suburbs, and that they would engage themselves besides, to pay sixteen thousand crowns a year. This affair having been proposed to the Council of the Indies, was referred to the chief of the company in Holland, but there is no hopes that they will grant this favour to Catholics, for fear, it is said, they should become the masters in Batavia. There are four Protestant churches there, two where they preach every Sunday in Dutch, the one in the fort, and the other in the town. A third where they preach in Portuguese, which is the most common language of the country. And a fourth for the French, who are in pretty considerable number there.

The description of Batavia

As for Batavia, it is the pleasantest town in all the Indies, and would pass for a very handsome place in Europe. The Dutch have built it at their pleasure, with a design to make it the capital city of their empire. The streets are long and broad, all in a straight line, betwixt two walks of trees of the country that are always green; most part of them are even divided into fair smooth ways, and lovely canals, wharfed, which in all seasons are filled by a great river, that at this place discharges itself into the sea.

They have conveyed the water of this river into the ditches of the town and fort, at small charges, because the ground is level and easy be cast up. This wharf is a great ornament to the town, and a great convenience for the inhabitants, who may go abroad and take the air afoot, or by water in boat, which they please. For during the heat, they walk under the shadow of the trees; and the streets are so laid having a descent towards the canal, that the rain-water runs off of them as fast as it falls. The houses are neater still then the streets; the truth is, they are not very magnificent, neither inside

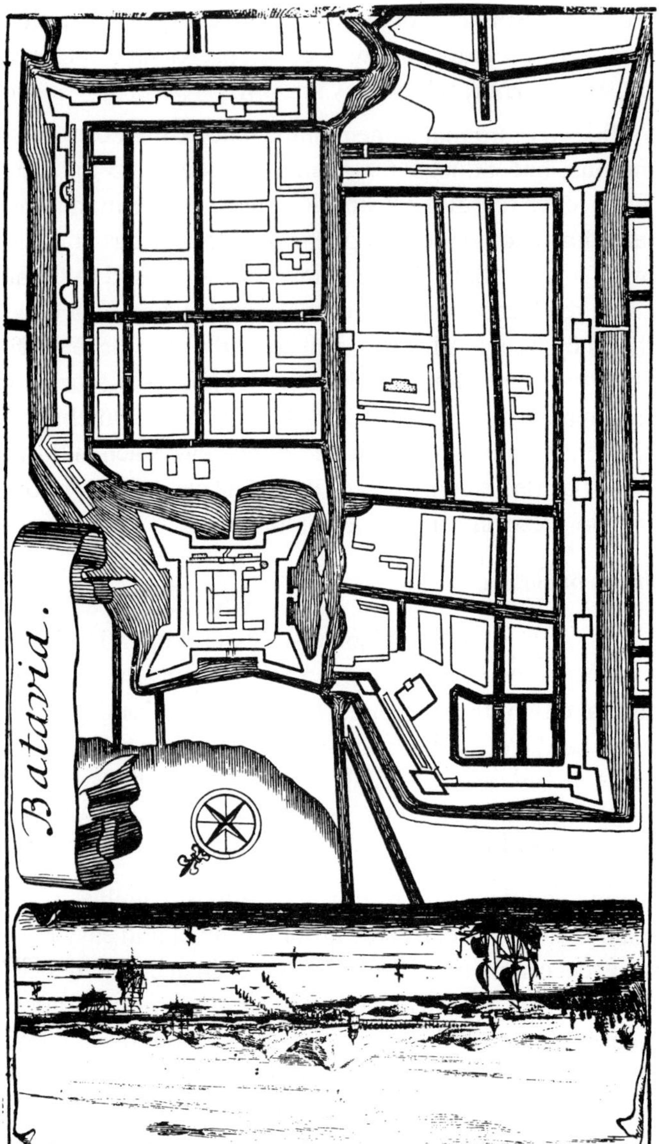

Plate 16. The town of Batavia

nor outside, but they are pretty and commodious. Every thing smiles there, the walls are as white as snow, there is not the least spot to be seen upon them, nor upon the furniture, which is all polished, and shines like looking glasses.

Though Batavia be but six degrees from the line, and by consequence in a very hot climate, yet the houses are built in such a manner, that they have always the cool, by reason of certain little courts contrived in the middle, where for eight or nine months in the year the sun never shines but at noon. It is fortified after the European manner, encompassed with ditches full of water, and in a ground that is all cut by channels, which makes it difficult to besiege it. The citadel hath four bastions faced and mounted with a great number of brass guns. There is a good garrison kept in it, not only to hold it out against Indians and Europeans, and to succour the other places in case of necessity; but also to show the greatness and power of the company to ambassadors and princes, who come thither from all places of the Indies. Batavia is of a very large circumference, and nevertheless extremely full of people of all sorts of nations, of Malays, Moors, Chinese, who pay so much tribute a head, for the free exercise of commerce; of these last there are four or five thousand there, who for the most part fled thither that they might not submit themselves to the Tartars, when these made themselves masters of China. The Chinese being an industrious and skilful people, improve everything at Bätavia, and without their help it would be hard to live conveniently there. They labour the land, there is hardly any other artificers but them, and in a word, they do everything almost. Some of them are very rich, and we were told that one of them died lately, who left behind him a million in coined money.

Having learnt of a Catholic soldier, that these people had their temple and sepulchres abroad in the country, about half a league from Batavia, we pray'd him to conduct us thither that we might see their ceremonies. In that walk we see [saw] the avenues of the town at leisure, they are very broad walks or alleys, that reach out of sight. On each side they are bordered with certain woods always green, which are straighter, and at least as high

Plate 17. The Chinese cemetery

as our tallest trees, beautified with country houses and gardens kept in good order, which belong to the chief townspeople . As we went out of Batavia we found three or four of these walks, all which at their end, met at the chief gate, by which we went out. We took the middlemost, which was our way to the place intended. If the other gates that look into the country have as lovely avenues as this, nothing more pleasant can be imagined.

Within half a league we found the first burying place of the Chinese in a coppice wood, there they had made several small paths, which all led to several sepulchres. There it is where the Chinese of mean quality are buried, and indeed the place is somewhat in disorder, and there is nothing of state in their tombs: A few steps from thence stands the little fort of Jacatra; it has four Bastions, not at all faced, with a sorry ditch. The Dutch keep fifty or sixty men in garrison there. Beyond that fort we entered into a wood, or rather into a large champian[21] full of little hills, covered over with groves and thickets on all sides, which yielded a pretty pleasant prospect, and in that second burying-place the Chinese Bonzes inter the persons of quality of their Nation. Upon the top of one of those little hills I saw an arbour very well made, and a table standing in the middle of it, with benches all round it, where near forty people might commodiously sit. There I saw a great many very little and odd antique idols hanging upon the branches that covered this arbour. They say that the Bonzes make feasts for the dead, and bring them thither for them to eat. Most part of these tombs are so many little mausoleums, very neat and pretty; here is the figure [illustration] of one of the loveliest of them by which you may judge of the rest, for they are all made after the same fashion, with this difference only, that some have dragons instead of lions upon the gate, as you enter into them, and that they are more or fewer steps high, according to their magnificence.

Being come out of the burying-place, we heard the noise of cymbals and little bells, and following the sound, came to a little temple of the Chinese, where their priests were assembled to offer a sacrifice. That temple is built much in the manner of our little churches, both without and within. At the entry there was a pretty big porch open on all hands. There they entertain the Chinese that are present at the sacrifices; there they talk, eat, drink freely, and make no scruple to invite strangers to do so. We would not accept of the betel and areca which they presented us, for fear they might have been offered to Idols. The truth is, under the porch on each side of the temple-door, there was a kind of altar with their steps loaded with pyramids of all sorts of sweet meats, betel and areca in fifty of sixty china dishes as big as plates, which they presented to their idols, before they gave them to their Bonzes, or eat of them themselves. Upon these degrees there were several statues of men and different animals. In the middle of the figures of the men, there was one that represented a Bonze with a very long and black beard, attentively reading in a book which he held very near his eyes, as if he had been short sighted. Near to him there was another doctor with a white beard, and a kind of surplice, who seemed to be speaking in public. As we entered into the temple , we saw seven or eight priests clothed in their sacerdotal habits, pretty like to ours. He who seemed to be the superior was in the middle, and always attended by two or four, who with him performed the same ceremonies. Behind them there were two or three officers, who bowed their bodies down to the ground, when the others made but moderate inclinations, and then [an]other two who had each a little bell in their hand.

In a corner near the door, there was a timbreler beating upon timbrels, to the sound whereof, and of four little bells which two priests who assisted the superior held, all came out in cadence from the altar with a slow and modest pace, making some turns, sometimes following one another, and sometimes putting themselves in a ring, and always singing in a manner that was not unpleasing.

During the sacrifice, two ministers came away from the altar, and lighted pastilles[22] and candles upon all the altars, for besides the chief altar that was at the end of the chapel, there was one also on the left-hand. When they advanced to, or returned from the altars, they made low bows. Now the Chinese seeming to be surprised to see us, we told them that we were priests of the most high God of Heaven and Earth, who were going to China to preach the only true religion. They gave us to understand that they knew there was a great many of our fathers in their country, who were very able doctors, and highly esteemed by the Emperor and great men of the Kingdom. We had a mind to see all to the very last, but being informed that sacrifice was performed for chasing the Devil out of a sick person, and that the ceremony would continue till night; after we had stayed there near an hour, we went our way; much pitying the blindness of these people, and being very desirous to endeavour the conversion of their countrymen.

August the twenty fourth, the Eve of St. Louis, my Lord Ambassador did the General the civility to give him notice, that he would not have him to be surprised, if in the evening he heard guns fired in the road, that it was the custom of the King's ships to honour the festival of St. Louis by such rejoicings. The Ambassador charged another Jesuit and me with that commission, and we went to the palace when the General was at council. So soon as he was told that we waited for him, he came to us, and we made him our compliment in the name of the Ambassador. He was sensibly obliged by that civility, and said that the French showed him greater respect than the English would do in such a case. He asked us if it was the King's birth-day, because then he would take a share in our rejoicings, and testify his respects for that great monarch, by a discharge of all the guns of the fort and ships. But being informed that by that public expression of joy we honoured the festival of St. Louis King of France, whose name the King bore; I am very sorry, Fathers, said he, that I cannot do in honour of St Louis, what, with all my heart I would have done in honour of Louis the Great. When we took our leave of him, he made us a thousand offers of services, and obliged us to promise him that we would not trust our letters to any but him, and that we should do the same when we wrote from China to France, that he would take that commission upon himself, that he might entertain a correspondence with us. We embraced the liberty he gave us, and entrusted him with our letters at our departure. Being come out of the palace we went straight on board to give the Ambassador an account of what we had done, and to confess the Catholics who were to be there next morning. When we were got within three musket shots of the ocean, we saw her fire seventeen, guns, and the *Maligne* thirteen, which were followed by several huzzahs, and some volleys of small shot.

We were informed at Batavia, that it is not now so difficult to enter into China as formerly, and that the Emperor hath a mind to try whether freedom of trade would increase the wealth of his empire or not. It is said the Dutch laid hold on that occasion, and this year sent a solemn embassy with presents to the Emperor of China, that they might obtain the liberty of commerce in his dominions, and that upon the news thereof, the English had sent also one of their ships to Chiucheu; but that they would not let those who were on board come ashore, and that they were obliged to return back again with the loss of their time, fraught[23] and goods.

Sunday in the evening, the five and twentieth of August, all that were ashore had orders forthwith to come on board. Before we embarked we went all seven to the palace, to take our leave of the General, and to thank him for all his civilities. We promised him never to forget his favours, and to pray God that he would reward him in another life. He spoke very obligingly to us, and addressing himself to Father Fucity; I was in good hopes, Father, said he, that I might have fitted you with a passage for Siam in one of our ships; but seeing you will not part from your fathers, I will not be against your design. Once more I entreat you, that you would give me occasion to serve you. Having thanked him a thousand times, we took our leaves with hearts full of gratitude. Next day he sent us his boat to carry us on board, and therein a great quantity of fine biscuit, dry fish, fruit, and other provisions for Father Fucity. He knew very well that we were magnificently treated by Monsieur Devaudricourt at the Ambassador's table, and that we wanted for nothing, but he could not tell if the same favour would be showed to Father Fucity. Before we parted from Batavia we informed ourselves of the Dutch Government in the Indies, and the principal points of it are as follow.

The generalship is the highest office: it gives him who enjoys it a right over everything without exception: it is given for life, but revocable at the Company's pleasure; the General may lay down his place after three years service. The Council of State consists of the General, the Director General, and six counsellors. The plurality of voices carries it in the decision of affairs; but the Generals, who have commonly but two voices pass over that formality, when they'll answer for the success of any affair. The places of counsellors are the rewards of considerable services done to the company. They have a salary of two thousand livres[23] a month, and the General has but twelve thousand livres a year, and the charges of housekeeping defray'd. But seeing he hath all in his power, without being obliged to give an account, it may be said that he has what he pleases. Every counsellor has his province, and the affairs relating to it must be managed by him. The great or supreme council, which is the highest judicature of the country, and judges sovereignly in all causes civil and criminal, consists of a president, a vice president, and two proctors generals. That tribunal may judge and condemn the General himself. The council is that of the sheriffs, who take cognisance of matters concerning the town.

The fourth, which is like a presidial court in France, judges causes of less importance, to the sum of an hundred crowns, without appeal, The Director General holds a second rank; all that concerns trade passes through his hands, and he is obliged to give an account of it. Next to the counsellors of state for the government, are the governors of the provinces, to the number of six, of Coromandel, who resides at Pasicate; of Amboyna, the capital of which is Victoria; of Tarnata, the King whereof hath been obliged to quit his Kingdom to the company, and content himself with a pension of twelve hundred crowns; of Ceylon,[25] who resides at Colombo; and lastly of Malaca. This last government has sometimes governors, and sometimes none at all. The most considerable next to the governors of provinces, are the chief merchants, the commanders of places, and the presidents or heads of factories.

As for war, next to the General, all the command rests upon the Major General. He that has that charge at present is a Frenchman by birth, and is called the Heer St. Martin. That command is afterwards divided amongst the Captains of Batavia, who are colonels when they are abroad out of the town. They have twelve thousand men of regimented forces, and an hundred and fifty ships; there is besides a bailiff or commander of the town of Batavia.

A Dutch ship that ran foul of us

Monday morning the 26th. We put out of the road of Batavia with a fair wind. Betwixt eight and nine o'clock in the evening, it being pretty dark, we made all of a sudden a ship as big as our own, within two musket-shot of us, bearing down upon us before the wind. We presently hailed her and asked who were on board, but it was to no purpose; for nobody made answer. In the mean time the wind being good she was presently up with us. By her way of working it was thought at first she intended to run us on board in the quarter, and perceiving her low sail furled as if she had been to fight, it was not doubted but that in boarding of us she would pour in a whole broadside. Nobody was startled at that surprise, but all seemed ready to do their duty. The clatter that the seamen and soldiers who were upon the watch kept, some running to their arms and others minding the sails, soon awaked those that were asleep; so that in a trice all were upon the deck.

The Ambassador perceiving that this ship had run her bowsprit[26] into our stern, and that no enemy appeared, concluded that they who were onboard had no ill design. He thought it enough to command five and twenty or thirty small shot to be fired amongst them, as a warning to them to be better upon their guard another time. But the other ship having with her bowsprit done some damage to our galleries, got clear of herself, without any seaman appearing onboard.

That adventure occasioned various reasoning. Those of most sense were of the opinion of the Ambassador and Monsieur de Vaudricort, who attributed it to a careless working of the ship. The truth is, if the she had any bad design, she would not have failed to fire her guns, when she laid us on board, and to have poured in a volley of small-shot amongst us. We were informed at Siam by Hollanders that came from Batavia after us, that it was one of their ships coming from Palimbam and that all the men on board were drunk or asleep.

The strait of Banka difficult to be passed because of the want of water

The wind was good, and so that accident did not at all hinder us to pursue our Voyage. It was not long before we got to the entry of the strait of Banka, which is made by an isle so called and the Isle of Sumatra. The banks and shelves that are at the entry of this strait, make it a difficult passage for those that are not acquainted with it. We had a Dutch pilot on board and a very able man, who had several times before passed that strait, and for all that, tho we continually also heaved the head, our ship stuck aground, and so did the frigate too; but the ground being oozy, we were in no danger, and having put out an anchor at a distance in deeper water, we weighed ourselves off again without any prejudice.

The wind continuing fair in a short time we re-passed the line. We felt it a great deal better in this place encompassed with land, then when we passed it the first time out at sea, before we came to the Cape. Calms are not so much to be dreaded here, because of winds that reign there and blow sometime from the land, and sometime from the sea. The safest way of sailing in those calm seas that are as smooth as a mill-pond, is to keep always along the shore, in twelve, fifteen or twenty fathom water, and never go out of sight of land, as we did. Observing this circumspection, you have always the advantage of coming to an anchor when you please, which you will be forced to do very often, because of the currents, that set in to land, and of certain strong gusts and flurries, which commonly blow from the Isle of Sumatra. Some days after we set out from Batavia we were all of a sudden surprised with one of those flurries, which put us into great fear, because all our sails were then abroad; but the diligence that was used in taking of them in, cleared us of the danger.

September 5. We began to make the land of Asia, and the first we made was the point of Malaca. We all felt a secret joy to see those places that had been watered with the sweat of St. Francis Xavier, and to find ourselves in these seas so famous for his voyages and miracles. We publicly and daily invoked the assistance of that great saint after the litanies of the Virgin, on board. We then ranged along the coasts of Jobor, Patane and Paban, whose kings are tributary to the King of Siam; but the Dutch have all the trade of these kingdoms.

September 6. Monsieur de Vanderets D'Hebouville, one of the gentlemen of the Ambassador's retinue, died on board the frigate, in the flower of his age. He was handsome, discreet, and the eldest son of a very ancient and rich family in Normandy. His distemper was a bloody-flux, common enough in the Indies, especially to those who eat too much fruit, as this young gentleman did during the five or six days that he was at Batavia. We had notice of his death by the frigates handling their colours at eight of the clock in the morning, and in the evening we came to know the time of his obsequies, by means of five guns slowly fired one after another.

Funerals at sea are performed with like ceremony. Having sung some prayers, they wrap up the body in a linen cloth, tie a great shot to the feet, and upon a plank to which it is made fast, let it gently drop into the sea. Next day all we that were priests, said a Mass on board of our ship; for the rest of his soul.

At length, September 22, we came in sight of the river of Siam, and next day to an anchor three leagues from the bar, which is at the entry of it. The sight of that Kingdom raised an incredible joy in all of us, after the dangers and fatigues of so tedious a voyage. There had been but little talk till then of the conversion of the King of Siam, which was the cause of the embassy, but at that time it was almost the subject of every discourse. It was known to all that the King had publicly said to my Lord Ambassador that he was in hopes, that by his prudent conduct he would accomplish that great work which was so far advanced. We earnestly begg'd it of God in out prayer, and from our first coming on board, our Father Superior had ordered every one of us to say a Mass weekly for that intention.

So soon as we were come to an anchor, the Ambassador dispatched the Chevalier de Fourbin and Monsieur Vachet with the news of his arrival to the King of Siam and his ministers. The first was to go no higher than Bangkok[27] which is the first place of the Kingdom upon the river, ten leagues from the mouth of it, and the other was to take a *balon*, which is a boat of that country very light, and make all haste to Siam. The Governor of Bangkok by nation a Turk and of the Mohammedan religion, being informed that the Ambassador of the King of France was in the road, prayed Monsieur Vachet to take his repose for the rest of that night, and suffer him to send an express, that he might give the court speedy notice thereof.

The Governor of Bangkok's messenger arrived at Siam next day about noon. The Lord Constance, Minister of State, was acquainted by a letter which he had received that morning from Coromandel, that the most Christian King had named the Chevalier de Chaumont to be his ambassador extraordinary at the court of Siam, and that he had set out from France ever since the month of March with two men of war. Seeing we are often to mention this minister in the sequel of this relation, and that he alone was deputed by the King his master to treat about the affairs of this embassy, it is proper we should make it known who he is.

The Lord Constance is properly called Constantin Phaulkon, and so he writes his name. He is a Grecian by nation born in Cephalonia, his father being a noble Venetian, the son of the Governor of the Island, and his mother a daughter of one of the ancientest families of the country. About the year 1660, when as yet he was but about twelve years of age, he had discretion enough to reflect upon the bad condition into which his parents had reduced the affairs of his family. The thought of that made him take a resolution that could hardly be expected from a child of his years. Not being able to support his quality in his own country, he went on board with an English captain, who was returning into England. His wit and sprightliness, his compliant humour, and agreeable carriage quickly made him be known, and gained him the kindness of some of the lords of court, but despairing of success there, he went to sea with a design to go to the Indies. His purpose was to raise his fortune. His genius put him in the way of it, and if his probity had been less, he might in a short time have got a considerable estate. But he chose rather to pass through all the degrees of seafaring, and to rise by little and little with reputation, than to hasten to be rich all of a sudden by sneaking and unlawful ways.

Having lived some years at Siam, and scraped together a little estate, he resolved to quit the service of the English East-India company, to get a ship of his own, and to trade by himself. He had much ado to get out of Siam, being detained by his friends, and by his effects which he could not as yet get in. At length he put out, but was beaten back again by bad weather, and was cast away twice in the mouth of the river.

Putting out again to sea once more, he was shipwrecked a third time and much more unfortunately, upon the coast of Malabar; he was in danger of having perished there, and could not save of all he had above two thousand crowns. In this sad condition being oppressed with sorrow, weariness and sleep, he had laid himself down upon the shore, when, whether he was asleep or awake, for he hath protested to me oftener than once he could not tell himself, he thought he saw a person full of Majesty, who looking upon him with a smiling eye, most mildly said unto him; "Return, return from whence you came." These words so wrought upon him, that it was impossible for him to sleep all the rest of the night, and his thoughts were wholly taken up about finding a way to return to Siam.

Next day whilst he walked by the seaside, musing upon what he had seen in the night time, and uncertain what to think of it, he saw a man coming towards him dropping wet with a sad and dejected countenance. It was an ambassador of the King of Siam, who upon his return from Persia had been cast away, without saving anything but his life. Since both of them spoke Siamese, they soon acquainted one another with their adventures. The Ambassador discovered himself, and told what extreme necessity he was reduced to. The Lord Constance condoling his misfortune, offered to carry him back to Siam: and with the two thousand crowns that he had saved after his shipwreck, he bought a small barque, clothes for himself and the Ambassador, and victuals for their passage. This so obliging a conduct charmed the Ambassador of Siam, who from that time forward cast about every way how he might testify to him his gratitude.

When they arrived at Siam, and that the Ambassador had given account of his negotiation and shipwreck to [the] Barcalon who is the First Minister of State in the Kingdom, he told him all the good offices which he had received from Monsieur Constance, with so great applause to his merit, that the Minister had a mind to know him. He entertained him in discourse, liked him, and resolved to keep him about him; where he soon gained the esteem and confidence of his master. This Barcalon was a witty man, and well versed in business, but he avoided trouble as much as he could and loved his pleasures. It ravished him that he had found an able, faithful and industrious person on whom he night repose the cares of his place. Nay he often spoke of him to the King; but that which contributed most to beget a good opinion of him in the mind of that prince, was the occasion that I am about to relate.

The King of Siam had a design to send an ambassador into a foreign Kingdom; and seeing he loves magnificence and grandeur, he was willing to spare no cost that he might render it famous by rich and splendid presents. The Moors to whom he usually addressed himself on such occasions, demanded of him prodigious sums of money to set out that embassy in the manner he desired it should be. The Barcalon, to whom the King complained of it, told it to the Lord Constance, who promised him, that if the King would honour him with that commission, he would make much finer presents, and at less charges than what the King offered the Moors. The King being informed of this, sent for him; and charged him with his orders. He obeyed them with so much exactness and good success, that from that time His Majesty conceived a great esteem of his ability. The Moors, in the mean time, taking it ill that they had not the sum which they demanded given them, presented a petition to the King, praying him to order them payment of the money which His Majesty owed them. In that petition they had given a particular account of what they had received, and what they had laid out. So that according to their account he stood indebted to them in a great sum, which, as they said, they wanted. The King would hereupon know the opinion of the Lord Constance, and put the memoirs of the Moors into his hand, so soon as he had examined it, he told the King, that he was cheated, and that His Majesty was so far from owing them anything, that they stood indebted to him in threescore thousand crowns. The Moorish Captain was fain to acknowledge it before the commissioners whom the King deputed to enquire into the business, that they had been mistaken in their accounts.

The Barcalon dying not long after, the King would needs put Monsieur Constance in his place. He declined it, and made answer to his Majesty, that that post would raise him the envy of all the great men, that he most humbly besought him not to raise him higher than he was, for that was all his ambition, being happy enough in that he stood fair in his favours. His modesty, his skill in affairs and diligence in dispatching them, his fidelity in managing the public revenue, and his disinterestedness in refusing both the appointments of his office, and all presents from private people, have more and more increased the King's confidence in him. At present everything passes through his hands, and there is nothing done without him. However his greatness hath not at all changed him, he is easy to be spoken with, mild and affable to all people, always ready to listen to the poor, and to do justice to the meanest of the Kingdom. He is the refuge of the wretched and afflicted; but the great men and officers who do not do their duty, think him severe and morose.

Seeing he left his own country when he was young, and by consequence but little instructed in the Catholic religion, wherein he was bred, it was no hard matter for the English to make him embrace the Protestant religion, which seemed to him to differ little from his own. But having had since some conferences with Father Thomas and Father Maldonat of our company, for whom he still retains a kind friendship, and being convinced in his own judgement of the bad way he had been put into, after full instruction he left it, and abjured his heresy to Father Thomas. Since that time, he hath led a very regular and edifying life, and by his example and credit contributes much to the establishment of the Catholic faith, as will appear by the sequel of this history.

So soon as the King of Siam was informed by his Minister of the honour the King of France did him, by the splendid embassy he sent to him, and was told that the Ambassador was arrived at the mouth of the river, he was overjoyed, and publicly expressed it to all his court. He called his council, and ordered, upon pain of his displeasure, that care should be immediately taken to receive the Ambassador well; that they should show him all the honour that he who represented the person of a great Prince deserved, and that they should not stand upon the ceremonies and customs that were observed in the reception of other ambassadors.

At the same time he named two of the chief lords of his court, the one, first gentleman of his bed-chamber, and the other chief captain of his guards, to go as far as the bar, to congratulate in his name his happy arrival, and to tell him that he impatiently expected the day of his audience and reception. Some hours after, the Lord Constance sent one of his secretaries to compliment His Excellency, and to present him with all sorts of refreshments for himself, his retinue, and both his ships' companies. The Governor of Bangkok had already done the like before; so that in a trice we had plenty of all things.

Since it was His Majesty's intention, that the Ambassador should have an extraordinary reception, the Lord Constance contributed on his part also, to do him the honour that nobody before him had ever received there; not only that he might perform his master's orders, but also that he might testify the profound respect which he had always entertained for the King of France. He went in person to the town of Siam, to pitch upon the lodgings where my Lord Ambassador was to be accommodated; and by his orders, diverse apartments were built hard by for lodging his gentlemen and all his retinue. He caused the Balons of State to be made ready, which were to bring the Ambassador and those which were to follow him; because in the month of September, as it was then, the river of Siam is much out, and all the country about overflow'd. He gave orders that at every five leagues distance, neat houses should be forthwith built on the river side, and very sumptuously furnished; and that as far as Tabangue, an hours journey from Siam, where my Lord Ambassador was to stay, till all things were ready for his reception.

In the mean time, the Bishop of Metellopolis, Vicar Apostolic of a great part of the Indies, came on board, and the Abbot of Lyon with him. They were received with all the marks of esteem and respect that were due to the dignity of the one, and the quality of the other. The Ambassador and Bishop after Mass shut up themselves together, and had a long conference upon the subject of the embassy.

Though we had had the honour to kiss the Bishop'a hands when he came on board, yet our Father Superior judged it convenient, that we should again all six together go and pay our most humble respects to him. This prelate, who is a person of a very sweet and good nature, received us with all testimonies of joy and affection: Nay he offered us his seminary to live in so long as we should be at Siam; telling us, that the house of the company was too small to accommodate us all. And we rendered him our hearty thanks for his goodness.

At that time two great mandarins whom the King of Siam sent to His Excellency, came on board of us in a galley. They were introduced into the Ambassador's cabin, that was spread with a foot-carpet: being come in, they sat down upon the carpet; and then the elder of the two asked my Lord Ambassador in the name of the King his master, news of the King of France, and of all the Royal family, and congratulated his happy arrival. He added, according to the visions of the metempsychosis, wherewith most of the Orientals are infatuated, that he well knew His Excellency had heretofore been employed in great affairs, and that it was above a thousand years since he came to Siam to renew the friendship of the kings who at that time governed the two Kingdoms of France and Siam. The Ambassador having very civilly answered their complements, added with a smile, that he did not remember he had ever been charged with so important a negotiation, and that this was the first voyage he had ever made to Siam. After a short stay, they took leave, assuring the Ambassador, that the King was impatient to see him: and that he had ordered the luckiest day of the year to be pitched upon for his reception. They were served with tea and sweet meats; and one of them, who was a very handsome man, and of a pleasant aspect, drank wine; but the other would not so much as taste it. So they went into their galley again, where they wrote down all they had seen and heard in this congress.

Towards the evening our Father Superior would have me go before with Father Visdelou and Father Bouvet, to take order about our affairs. There offered a very fair occasion by the return of the Bishop and Abbot of Lyon, who were to part next day, and who offered us their *balons*. The Ambassador commanded the Chevalier de Fourbin and the Chevalier du Fay to wait upon the Bishop and Abbot, who went into the chaloop; where we had the honour to accompany them, because their *balons* were not strong enough to come on board.

Pretty late in the evening we got to the mouth of the river, at that place it is but a short league over half a league further up, it is not a quarter of a league over and a little higher, it is not at the broadest place above an hundred and threescore paces or thereabouts over. It has a very fair pretty deep channel. The bar is a bank of ooze lying in the mouth of it, where there is not above thirteen foot water when the tides are at the highest. There is nothing more charming than the sight of that river, the banks on both sides being covered over with trees always green, and beyond them there being nothing but vast plains reaching out of sight covered with rice. It was night when we put ashore at a little lodging where the *balons* of the Bishop of Metellopolis stayed for him. Seeing the country about within a day's journey of Siam, is very low land; it is all overflowed for one half of the year. The rains which fall for several months together swelling the river, cause these great inundations, and that's the thing which makes the country so fertile; were it not for that the rice that grows only in water, and wherewith all the fields are covered, could not supply, as it does, all the Siamese and neighbouring countries with food. This is another convenience of these inundations, that one may go all about in a Balon, even into the fields; which makes so great a number of boats to be in all places, that in the greatest part of the Kingdom there are more *balons* than men. There are some of them very big, covered with houses, which serve to lodge whole families; and several of these being joined together, make a kind of floating villages in those places where they chance to meet.

We continued going up the river all night long, during which we saw a very pleasant sight, and that was an infinite number of fire-flies, wherewith all the trees upon the sides of the river were so covered over, that they appeared like so many great branches set thick with innumerable lights, which the reflection of the water, at that time as smooth as a looking-glass, infinitely multiplied. Whilst we were taken up in viewing of them, all of a sudden we were beset with a prodigious quantity of mosquitoes[28] or maringouins. These are a kind of very troublesome gnat, that stings through people's clothes, and leaves the marks of it a long time behind them. The Siamese who row'd our *balon*, though they were naked, and tugg'd at the oar, made a better shift against them than we; they gave themselves a flap with the hand every time they felt a mosquito, and struck so pat that they never missed them, without losing one single stroke of their oar for all that.

We found a great many monkeys and sapajous upon the river side, which clambered up the trees, and went together in troops. But no pleasanter sight can be seen than the vast numbers of criel herons that swarm upon the trees; at distance one would take them for their blossoms. The white of the birds mingling with the green of the trees, makes the most lovely landscape imaginable. The criel heron is a fowl shaped like a common heron, but far less; it is of a neat proportion of body, and has fair feathers whiter than snow. It hath tops or tufts upon the head, back and belly, wherein its chief beauty consists, and which render it extraordinary.

All the wild birds have most lovely feathers, there are of them of several colours, all yellow, all red, all blue, all green, and that in great numbers. For the Siamese believing the transmigration of souls into other bodies, kill no animals, for fear, as they say, of driving out from thence the souls of their relations, which may very well be lodged there.

We did not make a league of way without meeting with some pagoda, that is to say, a temple of idols. It had always by it a little monastery of *talapoins*,[29] who are the priests and the religious of the country. These *talapoins* live in common, and their houses are so many seminaries, where the children of quality are bred.

So long as children continue there, they wear the habit of *talapoins*, which consists in two pieces of a kind of yellow cotton cloth, whereof the one serves to cover them from the girdle down to the knees, and the other, they use sometimes as a scarf, putting it about their shoulders like a shoulder-belt; and sometimes they wrap it about them like a little cloak. They have their heads and eye-brows shaved as well as their masters, who are persuaded that it would be immodest and sinful to let them grow. Their blindness made us heartily pity them.

Having row'd on all night long, about ten of the clock in the morning we arrived at Bangkok: This is the most important place of the Kingdom, because it defends the passage of the river with a fort that is on the other side. Both are well furnished with brass guns, but ill fortified. Monsieur de la Mare, a French Engineer, whom my Lord Ambassador left at Siam, hath received orders from the King to fortify it regularly, and to make a good place of it. We saw the Governor of it in passing; he is a tall very handsome man, who received us with a great deal of civility. We went afterwards to dine with a French Artisan; for there are no inns in that country. That day we began to use rice instead of bread, and to drink nothing but river water. The rice being only boiled with water, is but an insipid kind of food, and we could, hardly accustom ourselves to it at first, but within a fortnight's time we came to like it as well as bread, which is very scarce and dear there, because the wheat must be brought from Surrat or Japan.

Betwixt Bangkok and Siam, you meet with a great many *aldees* or villages, that almost everywhere border the river. These villages are no more than a great many huts or hovels raised upon high pillars, because of the inundation. They are made of bamboo, which is a tree whose timber is much used in that country. The trunk and great branches serve for making of pillars and joists, and the small branches to make the walls and roof. Near the villages are the bazaars or floating market-places, where the Siamese, who go up or down the river, find their victuals ready dress't; that's to say, fruit, boiled rice, *rack* (which is a kind of strong water made of rice and lime) and some ragouts after the Siamese mode, which a Frenchman could not taste.

Next day, the third of October, we came to Siam. We thought the Bishop of Metellopolis had got before us, and therefore went straight to the seminary, to pay him our dutiful respects at home; but he was not as yet arrived. Whilst we stayed for him, we said Mass, to give God thanks for his protection during all our voyage, which had been exactly seven months long; for we set out from Brest the third of March, and arrived at Siam the third of October.

The Lord Constance receives the Jesuits with extra-ordinary goodness

From thence we went to the house of Father Suarez, the only Jesuit that was then at Siam; Father Maldonat being gone for some time before to Macao, from whence he was to return towards March following. We passed by the French factory, and there saluted the officers of the company. Then we were conducted to the palace which was preparing for my Lord Ambassador; where we met with the Lord Constance, the first, or to say better, the only minister of the Kingdom. We knew before that he was a man of merit, and hath a kindness for us; but we had the experiences of both far beyond our expectation. In that first interview, he gave us many testimonies of goodness, we thanked him for the *balon* which he sent to meet us, and for the chambers that he was pleased to order to be built for us near to Father Suarez, whose was too little to accommodate us with lodgings. He told us that it was a pleasure to him to oblige us; and that he did but his duty, when he built an apartment for his brethren (for so he did us the honour to call us) seeing he could not lodge us in his own house; that moreover he expected more Jesuits, whom he had demanded from the Father General at least a year ago. Then he showed us all the apartments of the Ambassador's palace, which we thought very handsome and neat.

The King of Siam had ordered a stately house to be built for the Ambassador; but seeing it was not as yet finished, and that there was no delay to be made because of the season that pressed his return, Monsieur Constance went himself and pitched upon the fairest and most commodious house of the town, which belonged to a great mandarin, a Persian by Nation, and had it splendidly furnished.

A *description of the palace where the Ambassador lodged at Siam*

In the first story there was two halls of a floor, hung with very lovely fine painted cloth. The first was furnished with chairs with blue velvet, and the other with chairs of red velvet and gold fringes; and the Ambassador's chamber was encompassed with a Japan-screen, of singular beauty; but the divan seemed to us to be the prettiest of all. It was a great ceiled hall, separated from the other apartments by a large court, and built for taking the fresh air during the heats. There was a water work at the entry, a half pace within, with a very rich canopy of state and armed chair, and in the obscurer retreats two closets joining the river, which served for bathing places. Which way soever one cast his eyes, there was nothing to be seen but fine china of all sizes, placed in niches; in a word, everything looked cool and pleasant.

M*r. Constance causes apartments to be built for lodging the Jesuits at Siam*

Having stayed some time there, we took our leave of the Lord Constance, and returned home; where we found Father Suarez staying for us. He received us with extraordinary expressions of joy, and treated us in the best manner his poverty could allow. He is a Portuguese Jesuit threescore and ten years old, and hath lived above thirty years in the Indies, where, by his zeal and capacity, he hath gained the esteem and friendship of all that know him. He straight carried us to see the lodgings that the Lord Constance ordered to be prepared for us. They were building for us upon pilings[30] in the river six little rooms to lodge us in, and a gallery where we might lay our instruments: there were near a hundred workmen employ'd about it, who had two mandarins to oversee them and keep them to their business both day and night. Without that augmentation Father Suarez could not have accommodated us at his house; he had but one chamber and a closet, both so beggarly poor and so ill shut, that the wood-slaves, which are a kind of very venomous lizard, were in all places, behind his trunks and amongst his furniture.

The King of Siam sends a stately balon *to the Ambassador*

Whilst things were thus a preparing the King sent two dignified lords of his court with ten mandarins of the fourth and fifth rank, each with a Balon of State to go wait upon the Ambassador's *balon* to the mouth of the river. It was very magnificent, all over gilt, threescore and twelve foot long, and rowed by seventy handsome men, with oars covered with plates of silver. The chirole, which is a kind of little dome, placed in the middle, was covered with scarlet, and lined with Chinese cloth of gold, having curtains of the same stuff. The balusters were of ivory, the cushions of velvet, and a Persian carpet was spread under foot. This *balon* was accompanied with sixteen more, four of which, adorned also with foot-carpets, and scarlet covers, were for the gentlemen of the Ambassador's retinue, and the other twelve for the rest of his attendants. The Governor of Bangkok joined them with the chief mandarins of the neighbourhood; so that they made about sixty six *balons* when they came to the mouth of the river. These boats are of an extraordinary shape, they are very long and narrow; some of them are as long as galleys, that is to say, an hundred or sixscore foot in length, which at the broadest place are not six foot wide. Their crew consists of an hundred, sixscore, and sometimes an hundred and thirty rowers.

The deputies found a galley at the mouth of the river, which was to carry them on board; it was attended by three others, and six mirous, which are long barks[31] for carrying the baggage. Being come to the Ambassador's ship, they complemented him in the name of the King, telling him that they had orders from His Majesty, to wait upon His Excellency to the city, where the King impatiently expected him, that he might have certain news of the King of France his good friend, and of all the Royal family.

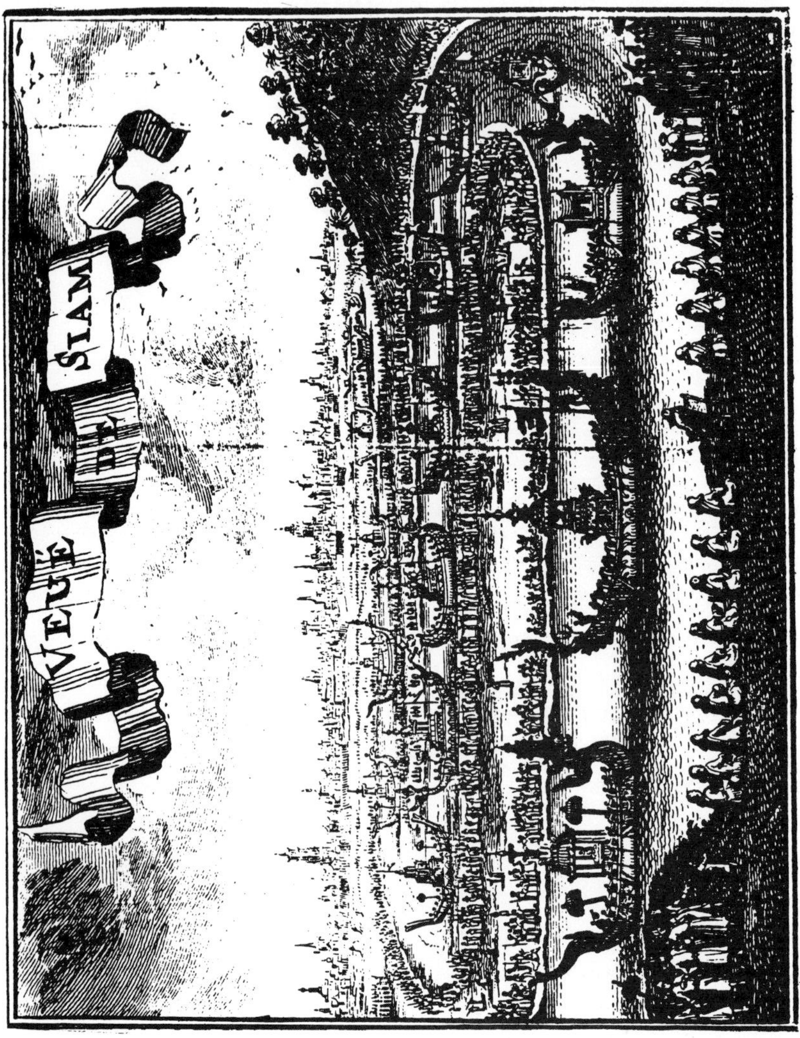

Plate 18. The boats of Siam

Book 4

The Voyage from the Bar of Siam, to the Cities of Siam and Louvo

The Ambassador embarks in the balon *of the King of Siam*

October the 8th. My lord Ambassador being acquainted that the King's *balons* were to come and receive him and all his retinue that day, went into his chaloop with a noise of trumpets, and was saluted by his own ship with fifteen guns. He arrived in good time at the mouth of the river, whither the King's *balons* came. He went into that which was appointed for him with the Bishop of Metellopolis; and was followed by all the rest. That day they advanced but two leagues from the mouth of the river, and the *balons* drawing up round the *Maligne*, which was got up so far, all lay that night in their boats.

Next day they went to Prepadem, where the first resting palace was prepared. Though these little buildings be run up in a weeks time, and made only of reeds and mats, yet they are commodious and pleasant. Since this was the first, and that all the rest were of the same nature, it is fit I should give a description of it.

A description of the houses built on the river's side to receive him

Coming out of the *balon*, we mounted a pair of stairs of six or seven steps, that reached down to the surface of the water, and led into a kind of platform, where after ten or twelve steps, you find two pretty large halls, one on the right hand and the other on the left, which serve the Ambassador's servants for kitchen, lodging and all. Beyond that there were two rooms on one side the Ambassador's chamber, and on the other a chapel. The corridor or platform butted upon a hall which the Portuguese call *Sala da presensa*. On the right as you entered it, there was a half pace covered with a Persian carpet, a large canopy of state of a stuff made of gold and silk, with a gilt chair underneath and crimson velvet cushions with gold galloon. Over against it there was a cupboard covered with a carpet of lovely China-work cloth of gold, and in the middle of the hall a long table for threescore persons. All these apartments were neatly furnished, and seeing the heats are excessive in that country, they were hung only with very fine Indian tapestry, and the floors were covered with extraordinary fine mats. The floor of the Ambassador's chamber was covered with a large Persian carpet, and the rising with a very rich stuff.

In all these palaces of repose there were seven officers of the King's household, of whom the first were gentlemen of the King's bed-chamber, and the seventh, captain of the life-guards with some soldiers who kept guard day and night, and went several rounds about the house to prevent noise and disorder. The first six and those whom they commanded, took care that nothing was wanting to the magnificence of the table and neatness of the apartments.

As soon as the Ambassador stepped ashore at Prepadem, he was complimented by the Governor of Bangkok and Piplis, who had waited for him there, since the day before. After dinner he embarked again, with the same court and attendance and went to Bangkok. Half a league from the town two Olouans, mandarins of the third order, of whom the last was, as it were, general of the galleys, came in the King's name to receive him, and so to wait upon him to the capital city. It was five o' clock before he arrived at Bangkok. An English ship lying at anchor under the fort, saluted His Excellency with one and twenty guns, and the town that was over against it, with one and thirty. As he went ashore, he was received by a great number of mandarins drawn up in two ranks, having the Governor of Bangkok and Piplis at the head of them, and he was conducted to the lodging that had been prepared for him in the town. The streets through which he past were perfumed with aquila which is a very precious wood, and of a rare smell. So soon as he was come into his palace, the fort which had not as yet saluted him, discharged all its artillery. Next morning after breakfast His Excellency was conducted back to his *balon* with the same ceremonies. As he put off, the fort which was on the same side, saluted him with one and twenty guns, the other fort fired twenty nine; and the English ships twenty one, and it was the Lord Constance's recommendation that made the ship show that civility to the Lord Ambassador.

The same honours were performed to him in all places where he went ashore, and the King daily sent mandarins of the chiefest quality to salute him on his part, who being all ordered to stay with him till he came to a place called the Tabangue, his court in attendance was thereby rendered very numerous. A quarter of a League from thence, he found the presidents of all the nations that are at Siam. The English came with eight *balons*, and then the Chinese and Moors. When the nations had made severally their compliments, they all together waited upon him to his lodging, then took leave. The governors of places who had received him at the entry into their governments, waited upon him also so far. It is an extraordinary honour, and had never before been rendered to any ambassador.

It was the King of Siam's pleasure, that the Ambassador of the King of France, should be treated with marks of distinction from all others, and even from those of the Emperor of China, who all over the East is reckoned the greatest monarch of the Universe.

How the King of Siam receives the ambassadors of neighbouring princes

The ambassadors of the King of Cochin-China, Tonkin, Golconda, Malaya, and Laos, are received in a court covered with a carpet. The great men of the Kingdom are prostrate in two halls on the two sides, and the other mandarins of inferior quality, are prostrate in the court.

The Ambassador is with all his retinue in another more remote court, where he waits till he be called to audience by the King's order.

The King within the prefixed time, with sound of trumpets, drums and other musical instruments, that are used in the courts of eastern princes, appears at a kind of tribune or window, raised six foot higher than the first court. Then the Chief Minister having demanded the King's orders, sends for the Ambassador, by an officer of his chamber of more or less quality, according as he intends to honour the King his master. When the door of the court is opened, the Ambassador appears prostrate with the interpreters of his nation, and the gentleman who commonly serves on such occasions as master of the ceremonies. All together perform before His Majesty the *zombaye*, which is a profound inclination of the body; and then come creeping along upon hands and knees, till they come to the middle of the court; then raising themselves thrice on their knees, with their hand joined upon their head, they bow down and knock their forehead as often against the ground. When that is done, they advance, creeping as before till they come to a pair of stairs betwixt the two halls where the great men are prostrate, and there having made the zombaye, the Ambassador waits till the King does him the honour to speak to him. Before he receives audience, he ought to send the presents and letter to the Minister, who having fully examined them in council, causes them to be laid upon a table betwixt the King and the Ambassador. Betwixt that table and the Ambassador, there is still a mandarin to receive the King's orders, when it pleases His Majesty to send the betel, which at the end of the audience he presents to the Ambassador.

At the court of Siam there are mandarins appointed to take care of the affairs of the several nations. To these private men apply themselves to have their petitions presented to the King, and to obtain audience of him. They wait upon the ambassadors of the Kingdoms, whose affairs concern their province, and therefore are called mandarins of the nations or captains of the port.

In public audiences these mandarins are betwixt the Ambassador and Chief Minister, to carry the word from the one to the other. The King speaks first, and bids his Minister ask the Ambassador how long it is since he parted from the King his master, if he and all the Royal family were in health when he left him; the Ambassador makes what answer he has to give by his interpreter, not immediately to the King, but to the Captain of his nation, and this man repeats it to the Barcalon, who tells it to the King. He is then questioned in the same manner as to the chief points of his embassy, and so soon as he hath made his answer, they bring him betel and a vest by the King's orders, who thereupon immediately retires without any other ceremony, but the sound of trumpets and other instruments, in the same manner as he entered.

How the ambassadors of independent kings are received at Siam

But for the ambassadors of independent kings, as of the King of Persia, the Great Mogul, of the Emperors of China and Japan, he uses them in this manner. The great mandarins of the first and second order, lie prostrate in a lane according to their rank, at the foot of the King's throne, and the other mandarins are prostrate in the two low halls on the sides which we have mentioned already. The Ambassador is to come with his interpreter to a place assigned him near the palace, where he stays till the chief master of the ceremonies, comes and introduces him to his audience.

As he enters the palace, he sits down upon the ground, and lays his hands upon his head, which is a mark of the profound respect he pays to His Majesty. Then he rises again, and advances betwixt the two halls, where the mandarins of the third, fourth and fifth order, lie prostrate with great silence; when he comes to the foot of the stairs that lead into the hall of audience; he kneels, crawling along upon his hands until he comes into the hall, and in that posture appears before the King, who is upon his throne raised ten or twelve foot high, upon a very broad half space, where the great mandarins lie prostrate. He stops at the side of the half space, above thirty foot from the throne. In the space betwixt, there is a table carrying a great golden basin, where the presents which he hath brought are, and the letter of the King his master open, having been already read by the Barcalon. When he is come to his place, he continues there without rising up. The Chief Minister's lieutenant takes the Prince's letter that is upon the table, and reads it aloud to the King. When the letter is read, His Majesty asks the Ambassador news of the King his master's health, and of all the Royal family. The King speaks to the Barcalon, the Barcalon repeats it to the Captain of the nation, and the Captain to the interpreter, who explains it to the Ambassador. He again makes answer to his interpreter, and from him it passes through the same hands to the King. In short, His Majesty having in this manner put some questions, and heard the answers, orders betel and a vest to be presented to the Ambassador, and so withdraws with sound of Trumpets.

The Chevalier de Chaumont being informed of those ways of receiving ambassadors below the character which he bore, sent for the chief mandarins, who accompanied him by order from the King their master, and told them that he would be glad [if] the King of Siam would name some lord of his court to adjust the ceremonies of his entry and audience, that so nothing might pass but what suited the grandeur and friendship of both kings. The Mandarins made answer to His Excellency, that they should acquaint the Barcalon, who would have the honour to speak of it to His Majesty.

The King of Siam orders the Lord Constance to adjust with the Ambassador the ceremonies of his reception

They failed not to do it, and the King immediately named the Lord Constance, with orders to go forthwith to the Ambassador, and concert with him the manner how he was to be received in the capital city and palace. His Majesty hath already said publicly, that he would not have the ancient ceremonies observed as to him, which were used at the reception of the Ambassadors of the Mogul, Persia, and China, and that he consented that the Ambassador of France should enter his palace with sword by his side, and that he should sit at his audience, which had never been before granted to any ambassador.

The Lord Constance thought himself much honoured by that commission, and came to wait on His Excellency. After their first complements

M. de Chaumont spoke of the King's conversion as the chief subject of his embassy. The Lord Constance seemed astonished at it, and told the Ambassador, that it was the thing in the world which he most desired, but that there was no appearance of effecting it; that the King was extremely addicted to the religion of his ancestors, and that he would be strangely startled at an overture for which he was not at all prepared; that he adjured the Ambassador not to speak of that affair, which without doubt, would cause disorder in the present junctures, and could produce no good. The Ambassador made answer, that he would consider of it, but that he could hardly suppress the most considerable, and almost sole reason of his voyage.

Then they treated about the manner how the Ambassador's gentlemen should be present at the audience, for they would have had them either not to come at all, or that they should be in a posture of profound humility.

My lord Ambassador was positive that they should enter with him into the hall of audience, and stay there as long as he did. It was to no purpose for the Lord Constance to tell him that it was a new thing, and never practised at the Court of Siam, and that the King would hardly condescend to that; that the Ambassadors of the Kings of Tonkin and Cochin-China themselves came only creeping to the hall-stairs, and appeared prostrate before the King. My lord Ambassador stood his ground, adding, that he could not go to audience but upon that condition; that to compound the matter, he was willing to consent that his gentlemen should not stand in the King's presence; that they should enter the hall before His Majesty appeared there, and that they should be sitting upon the carpet when he should appear upon his throne. The Minister thought these proposals reasonable; but seeing he knew how nice the King would be upon that point, he prayed the Ambassador to give him time to speak of it to His Majesty; whereupon, after a long conference they parted full of esteem and friendship for one another. The Lord Constance managed that affair so well, that the King granted the Ambassador all that he desired; and so there was no more now to be done, but to complete the preparatives of the entry.

The several nations at Siam come and compliment the Ambassador

Two days after, all the eastern nations that live at Siam, would needs show the high esteem which they hath conceived of the King of France. About three and forty of different countries of the Indies, joined together to make their ceremonies more splendid, and came in a vast number of *balons*, variously decked to complement the Ambassador. Next day, four great Balons of State came by orders from the Lord Constance, each manned with fourscore rowers, and we had never seen the like. The two first were shaped like sea-horses, they were all over gilt, and to see them coming at a distance upon the river, one would have taken them to be alive. Two officers of the Kings guards were in them, to receive the presents of the King of France. So soon as they were loaded, they put out with great silence, and took their station in the middle of the channel. All the while that they lay there, there was not the least noise to be heard upon the shore, and no *balon* was then suffered to come up or down the river, lest they might fail in the respect that is due to the Balons of State, and to the presents they carried.

The day before that which was appointed for the Ambassador's entry into the city of Siam, and for his first audience, the King sent two princes of his court to attend him next day: The first was called Oya Prassedet, and the other Peya Taph de Cha. This last was cousin-german to the King of Cambodia,[32] and Oya Prassedet was the chief and protector of all the *talapoins* of the Kingdom, having power to judge, and sentence them to be punished when they deserve it, which is one of the chief and most important offices of the State.

They brought with them sixteen Balons of State, with other six for the guards, and they were followed by forty mandarins of the third, fourth, and fifth order, all in their *balons* of ceremony, appointed to wait upon that which was to carry the Ambassador, and was one of the finest that belonged to the King. They began to set out upon the river about eight of the clock in the morning. The *balons* of the mandarins of inferior quality, to the number of forty, went first by pairs, and keeping a due distance from one another: After them came ten or twelve mandarins of the second and third rank, who had come all the way from Bangkok, and the last were followed by the two princes, whom the King had sent the evening before. After a competent interval appeared the four *balons*, where-into they had put the King's presents, and then that which carried his letter separated from all the rest by a considerable space; for before the Ambassador parted from the tabangue, it behoved him to conform to the custom of these people, to take the King's letter with great respect, and put it into the hands of the Abbot de Choisi, who was to carry it to the *balon* solely appointed for it. My lord Ambassador came next, in a magnificent *balon*, all shining and covered over with gold. On his right and left-hand he had six galleys of the guards, in which were the trumpets, drums, and other instruments that go before the King when he goes abroad publicly. He was followed by four of the King's *balons*, where his gentlemen and servants were; after them came so vast and confused a number of great and small *balons* of all the nations, that they covered the Menam, which is the name of the river, and in the Siamese language, signifies the mother of waters. That long train of Balons of State which advanced in good order to the number of an hundred and fifty, and a crowd of others covered over all the river as far as one's sight could reach, and made a pleasant show. The shouts that the watermen made, according to the custom of the Siamese, as if they had been going to charge an enemy, brought crowds of people to both sides of the river to be spectators of that august ceremony.

None but the Portuguese absented themselves, except three or four who are officers in the King of Siam's forces. By that they pretend to be even with the French, who two years before had not assisted at the entry of the Ambassador of Portugal. Only Father Suarez, for all his great age and infirmities came and pay'd his respects to my Lord Ambassador. This good old man expressed his joy by all the means he could, and made his bells to ring when the Ambassador past by our church.

The Dutch factory which is on the other side of the river, and one of their ships riding at anchor hard by saluted the Ambassador with all their guns:

the city of Siam did the same, when he passed by the first bastion, and the French company made their ship, which was splendid in pennants and streamers, fire all its guns twice when the Ambassador passed by it, going and coming from his audience.

The Lord Constance receives the Ambassador at the River-side

Having coasted along part of the town walls, he came to the landing-place, which was a quarter of a league from the palace. The Lord Constance was there to give orders, and to receive the Ambassador, and so soon as he had intelligence that the *balon* drew nigh, he mounted his elephant, and put himself at the head of twenty elephants of war more, who were drawn up on the river side. When my Lord Ambassador landed he alighted from off his elephant, and having made a deep bow to the *balon* that carried the King's letter, he advanced to meet His Excellency, with whom he exchanged many civilities.

The respect shown to the King's letter

My lord Ambassador went afterward to take the King's letter out of the *balon* where it was put, but he found that the mandarin had already brought it ashore with the gilt pyramid wherein it was. This poor mandarin committed a great fault, when he thought that he did very well; he was punished for it upon the spot, and had his head pricked, as an earnest of a severer chastisement. For in embassies of the East, there is another guess [great] respect showed to the letters which princes send, than to their Ambassadors. The letter they look upon as the Royal word, whereof the Ambassador is no more but the carrier. The Ambassador then took the letter and gave it to the Abbot of Choisi, who went with great reverence and laid it upon a gilt chariot, which was to carry it enclosed within a high pyramid to the palace gate.

The Ambassador is carried to the palace

After that ceremony was over, the Ambassador sat down in a great gilt chair, raised upon a half space covered with a rich velvet carpet. In that manner he was carried upon ten men's shoulders, environed with mandarins, who walked afoot, except two who were carried by his sides upon lower chairs. The Abbot de Choisi followed him, carried in a chair painted red, and adorned with ivory, and the gentlemen rode upon horses that were prepared for them. This march was somewhat singular, it began by twenty elephants of war, that filed off first amidst a double lane of pikes and muskets drawn up along a great street, that reached from the water-side to the palace: next came the guards and officers of the governor of the town, and many mandarins on horseback. The Lord Constance marched last upon an elephant, and went immediately before the chariot that carried the King's letter, to which the people sitting on the ground, made the zombaye so soon as it began to appear. After the chariot came the Ambassador's three trumpeters on horseback, with their magnificent liveries, and the Ambassador seemed to be raised upon a throne. He was clothed in a rich flowered silk of a fire-colour, embroidered with gold, that looked very splendid. The Abbot de Choisi followed after in a surplice and camail, carried in an open chair. Then marched the gentlemen on horse-back, all glittering with gold and silver, and followed by pages, footmen, and a great many menial servants, all very neatly clothed. The march was brought up by an incredible multitude of people keeping profound silence.

A Description of the palace of the King of Siam

The palace of the King of Siam is of a vast extent, but in the architecture there is nothing that is regular nor like to our building. It consists of spacious courts encompassed with walls and containing some piles of building; on one side are the apartments of the King's officers, and on the other a great number of pavilions, where the elephants are. There are a great many pagodas in it also, both great and small, which though irregular, make still an object pleasing enough to the eye. When we came to the first gate of the palace all alighted, and my Lord Ambassador went and took the letter out of the triumphant chariot, and gave it to the Abbot de Choisi.

In this manner we entered into the first court of the palace, where on one side were fifty elephants of war harnessed with gold, and on the other two regiments of guards, to the number of eight hundred men drawn up in batalia. From thence we advanced into the second court, where were eight elephants of war more, and a troop of threescore more on horseback; they were armed with lances, and had a very good mien. In the third court were sixty elephants, with harness richer than the first, and two thousand men under their arms. Upon entering into the fourth court, which had one half the pavement covered with mats, we found two hundred soldiers who carried more sabres adorned with gold and tambag, called by the Portuguese, *Os bracos pintados,* because their arms are painted red. These soldiers are the rowers of the King's *balon*, and as it were, the guards of the channel. In two halls more forward there were five hundred Persians of the King's guard sitting on the ground cross-legg'd because in the King's palace no man is suffered to be upon his legs, unless he be going, and all the Siamese soldiers were squatted upon the tail, holding their arms betwixt their joined hands.

A description of the throne of the King of Siam

The fifth court into which we entered, was covered with fine mats, on which lay prostrate all the mandarins of the third, fourth, and fifth order, and at a little distance those of the second order were in the same posture upon Persian carpets. having passed amongst all the mandarins, and crossed so many courts, we came at length to the foot of a pair of stairs, where on the right-hand were two elephants covered all over with gold, and on the left, six Persian horses, part of whole saddles and stirrups were of massive gold, and their harness set with pearls, diamonds, rubies and emeralds. My Lord Ambassador stopped there, and the gentlemen going up to the hall of audience, where the King was not come as yet, sat down upon Persian carpets over against the throne, at twenty paces distance as it had been agreed upon. This throne, to speak properly, is no more but a large window raised seven or eight foot higher than the half space, and answering to the middle of the hall. On the right and left-hand were two great parasols of cloth of gold, consisting of seven or eight stories, whose staves were of beaten gold, and so high that they almost touched the ceiling. The Bishop of Metellopolis, the Abbot of Lyon, and Monsieur Vachet, sat in the hall in the same manner as the gentlemen did, near the seat which was prepared for the Ambassador. In that hall the princes, ministers and mandarins of the first order lay prostrate, to the right and left, according to their rank and quality.

There are three sorts of princes at the court of Siam; the first are the princes of the blood royal of Cambodia, and other Kingdoms that are tributary to the King of Siam. The second are the princes of Laos. Chiamay, and Banca, who have been taken in the wars, and some others that have voluntarily put themselves under the King's protection. The third are those whom the King has raised to the degree of princes; every one of them had before them great cups of gold and silver, which are the badges of their dignity, and they lay prostrate with profound silence, expecting the coming of the King. Sometime after all were thus placed, a great noise of trumpets, drums and many other instruments was heard, and then the throne was opened, and the King appeared sitting on it. But he was to be seen only to the girdle, the rest being hid by the front of the window. All the prostrate mandarins rose up upon their knees, and having their hands joined over their heads, made profound inclinations of body, and knocked their foreheads against the ground: The King wore a tiara all shining with precious stones. It is a long cap ending in a point like a pyramid, encompassed with three rings of gold, at some distance from one another. On his fingers he wore a great many large diamonds that cast a great lustre, his vest was red on a ground of gold, and over that he hath a gauze of gold with buttons of big diamonds: all these ornaments, together with a brisk air, full of life, and always smiling, made him look with a great deal of gracefulness and majesty.

The Ambassador enters the hall of audience

No sooner was the Ambassador advertised by the noise of the instruments that the King was come, but he entered the hall, followed by the Abbot de Choisi and the Lord Constance. Having advanced four steps, and looking upon the King, as if that had been the first time he had perceived him; he made a bow to the ground, a second he made in the middle of he hall, and a third when he was come near to the seat that was prepared for him. The King answered every bow he made by an inclination of body, which he accompanied with a serene and smiling countenance. Then my Lord Ambassador began his compliments in this manner, and having uttered the first words, sat down and put on his hat.

The harangue of the French ambassador to the King of Siam

SIR,

The King my master, at present so famous in the world by his great victories, and the peace he hath so often given his enemies at the head of his armies, hath commanded me to wait upon Your Majesty, and to assure you of the particular esteem he hath conceived for your person: He knows, Sir, your august qualities, the wisdom of your government, the magnificence of your court, the greatness of your dominions, and what particularly you were willing that he should know by your ambassadors, the esteem you have for him, confirmed by that constant protection which you give his subjects, especially the Bishops who are by me, and who are the Ministers of the true God.

He is very sensible of the many illustrious effects of the esteem you have for him; and he resolves, Sir, to correspond with it to the utmost of his power. In that design he is ready to treat with Your Majesty, to send you of his subjects to entertain and increase commerce, to give you all the testimonies of a sincere friendship, and to begin betwixt the two crowns a union that may remain as strict to posterity, as your territories are separated from his by those vast seas that disjoin them. But nothing will more confirm him in that resolution, nor unite you more closely together, than to live in the sentiments of the same belief.

And it is that particularly, Sir, which the King my master, a Prince so wise and sharp sighted, that he hath always given good counsel to the Kings that are his allies, hath commanded me to represent to you on his part. He adjures you by the interest, which as being one of your most sincere friends, he takes in your real glory, to consider that sovereign majesty wherewith you are invested upon earth, cannot he derived from any but the true God, that's to say, from an omnipotent, eternal, and infinite God, such as Christians acknowledge him to be, who alone makes kings to reign and rules the fortune of all people.

To submit your grandeur to this God who governs Heaven and Earth, is much more rational, Sir, than to refer them to the other deities that are worshipped in the East, whose impotence, your Majesty, who hath so much light and penetration, cannot but easily see.

But it will be made far more palpable to you, Sir, if you'll be pleased for some time, to give a hearing to the Bishops and other missionaries that are here. It will be the welcomest news that I can carry to my master, Sir, that Your Majesty being convinced of the truth, takes pains to be instructed in the Christian religion. This will raise in him a greater esteem and admiration for Your Majesty, and make his subjects more eager to come into your dominions; and in a word, Sir, will complete your glory, seeing by that means, Your Majesty, having so prosperously reigned upon earth, makes sure of an eternal reign in the Heavens.

In what manner the Ambassador presented the King's letter to the King of Siam

The Bishop told the Lord Constance in Portuguese the sense of his excellencies compliment, and that Minister explained it to the King in Siamese, keeping in the meanwhile in a very respectful posture, as the other princes and lords did, who still continued prostrate in the hall at his side, but a little lower. It would be no easy matter to describe the joy and gladness which the King of Siam expressed on that occasion and during the whole day.

It was a surprise to the Ambassador, when he entered the hall, to see the King so high above him, and he seemed somewhat troubled that he had not been told of it. When his compliment was made, the next thing he was to do in course, was to advance and present the King his master's letter to the King of Siam. It was agreed upon with the Lord Constance, that to show greater respect to the King's letter, the Ambassador should take it from the Abbot de Choisi, who for that end should stand by his side during his speech, and hold the letter in a golden cup with a very long foot. But the Ambassador perceiving the King so high above him, that to reach up to him he must have taken the cup by the lower part of the foot, and raised his arm very high, thought that distance suited not with his dignity, and that he ought to present the letter nearer hand. Having a little considered, he thought it was his best course to hold the cup by the bowl, and to stretch his arm but half out. The King perceiving the reason why he acted so, rose up smiling, and stooping with his body over the throne, met him half way to receive the letter: He then put it upon his head which was a mark of extraordinary honour and esteem that he was willing to show to the great king that sent it. After that he made answer to the Ambassador, that he was extremely obliged to his most Christian majesty for the honour he did him, and that he had no greater desire than to entertain an eternal peace and amity with His Majesty. He than asked him about that prince's health, whom he always called his good friend, and about the health of all the Royal family, and expressed his gladness that His Excellency and all his retinue were arrived in good health.

The Ambassador presents the Abbot of Choisi and the gentlemen of his retinue to the King of Siam

The Ambassador having thanked His Majesty for all his favours, presented to him the Abbot of Choisi as a person of merit, and the gentlemen of his retinue, saying that they were all officers in the King's Fleet; that most of them had been on several occasions engaged against the enemies of the State, and therein signalized their valour. The King listened to him with a great deal of satisfaction, and then turned the discourse upon the ambassadors, whom he had sent into France, of whom he had no news. He enlarged a pretty while upon the praises of the King, seeming overjoyed to hear what the Ambassador told him of his greatness, wisdom, conquests, and of the peace which he had given to Europe. In fine, he did tell the Ambassador, that if he stood in need of anything in his Kingdom for himself and followers, he should address himself to his Barcalon, whom he had expressly charged to satisfy him in all things. So the first audience ended with much satisfaction on both sides.

The Ambassador sees the white elephant in his apartment

When the Ambassador came out of the hall, the Lord Constance carried him to see the white elephant which is so highly esteemed in the Indies, and which hath been the cause of so many wars. He is but little, and so old, that he is wrinkly all over. Several mandarins are appointed to take care of him, and he is only served in gold, at least the two basins that were set before him were of beaten gold of an extraordinary size and thickness. His apartment is stately, and the ceiling of the pavilion where he stands very neatly gilt. It being now late, the Ambassador came out of the Royal palace, and in the same pomp and order that he came to his audience went to the house that was prepared for him.

Some time after the Bishop was sent for by orders from the King, to translate the King of France his letter into the Siamese language, which being done, it made a great impression on the mind of that Prince. These are the terms wherein it was conceived.

The French King's letter to the King of Siam

Most high, most excellent, and most magnanimous Prince, our most dear and good friend, God augment your glory with a happy end. I have learnt to my trouble, the loss of the Ambassadors which you sent to Us in the year 1681, and we have been informed by the Fathers Missionaries who are returned from Siam, and by the letters which our Ministers have received from him to whom you entrust the principal care of your affairs, how earnestly you desire our Royal friendship. To correspond therewith, we have chosen the Chevalier de Chaumont for Our Ambassador to you, who will inform you more particularly of Our intentions, as to everything that may contribute to the settling of a solid and lasting friendship betwixt us. In the mean time we should be extremely glad to find occasions of expressing to you the gratitude wherewith we have learnt that you continue your protection to the Bishops and other Apostolic Emissaries, who labour to instruct your subjects in the Christian Religion; and the particular esteem we have for you, makes us ardently desire, that you would yourself condescend to hear them, and learn of them the true maxims and sacred mysteries of so holy a law, wherein one has the knowledge of the true God, who alone can, after a long and glorious reign over your subjects here, make you eternally happy hereafter.

We have entrusted our Ambassador with some presents of some of the most curious things of Our Kingdom, which he will present to you as a mark of Our esteem, and he will also tell you what it is We may desire for the benefit of the trade of Our subjects. Whereupon we pray God that he would augment your greatness with a most happy end.

Given at our castle of Versailles the one and twentieth day of January 1685.

Your most dear and
good friend,
LOUIS

COLBERT

The Ambassador visits the Bishop of Metellopolis

After the Ambassador had audience of the King, he rendered his first visit to the Bishop of Metellopolis at the seminary. This prelate is Apostolic Vicar in the greatest part of the Indies submitted to apostolical vicars. He hath been labouring for a long time with much assiduity and zeal, in the conversion of the Siamese, whose language he hath carefully studied. We received from him our approbations in writing, and when he sent us them he signified to us that we might exercise our functions in the Indies as well as in Europe. He resides commonly at the seminary ever since he hath been weakened by long sickness, it is one of the prettiest houses in the whole town or country about Siam; consisting of a large double house, built after the French way and two stories high, where twenty people may be conveniently lodged. The rooms are large and high, some of them lying towards the garden, and the rest towards a church, which the King of Siam orders to be built hard by, and is not as yet finished. It will be very large, and if they had been so careful at first as to have made a regular design of it, it might have passed for a pretty church even in Europe.

The King of Siam sends a present to the Ambassador

It is a custom established at the court of Siam, to give a vest to all who have the honour of being introduced into the King's presence, and it is always brought to the ambassadors at the end of the audience when they present them the betel. The King being informed that the French made no use of betel, and that perhaps a suit of clothes made at Siam would not suit them, he would not have it given them at that time, but some days after he sent His Excellency twenty pieces of very rich stuff with flowers of gold, and as much silk stuff for linings. He made a like present to the gentlemen of his retinue, that they might make lighter clothes, (these are the Kings own words) and so suffer with less inconvenience the great heats of climate to which they were not accustomed.

The Ambassador ordered money to be thrown out at the windows to those who brought him the present

When the Ambassador received the King's present, he caused a great deal of money to be thrown out at the windows, to the servants of the Mandarins who brought it, and to the people who were gathered together there in great crowds. This made much noise in the city of Siam, and surprised all the people who had never before seen that kind of magnificence. There was no other talk for a long time but of that rich shower of gold and silver, which fell in the court of the Ambassador of France. That piece of seasonable liberality much increased the esteem which the great men and people had conceived of the French Nation.

So soon as the Ambassador was settled in the city of Siam, the Lord Constance who lived before in the field of the Japanese, came to a fair house that he has near the Ambassador's palace, and lodged there; nay all the while that we were at Siam he kept open table for the French, and upon their account to all the other nations. His house was very well furnished, and instead of tapestry which would be intolerable at Siam because of the heat, all round the divan there was a great Japan-screen, of a surprising height and beauty. He kept always two tables for twelve people apiece, where all things were very delicate and in very great plenty. There we had all sorts of wine, Spanish, Rhenish, French, Cephalonian and Persian. We were served in great silver dishes, and the cupboard was furnished with most lovely gold and silver plate of Japan rarely well wrought, with a great many large dishes of the same metal and workmanship.

The King of Siam sends his presents to the Pagodas with much pomp

The rumour that was then spread abroad that the King was about to go in great state and make a present to his Pagoda, raised the curiosity of the French gentlemen, to be spectators of the pomp. One of the Mandarins who was always in the house, to prevent disorders, and to take heed that nothing were wanting, took them to a place where they might conveniently see that show. The streets through which the King was to go were paled in with red lattice breast-high, and strewed with flowers in several places. The King came not abroad that day, nevertheless his present was carried to the Pagoda with great ceremony. First came a man upon an elephant playing upon timbrels, with two trumpeters on horseback before him, several mandarins on horseback also marching two and two came after, and then a great number of foot-soldiers of those who are called *Painted Arms* advanced in good order. They were followed by fifteen elephants, of which seven or eight carried parasols of three stories with gilt chairs, wherein sat as many mandarins who were charged with presents of the King. After these elephants came the mandarins of the first and second order who were known by the silver and gold rings that went about their round caps made in shape of a pyramid.

Ambassadors have never more than two audiences at the court of Siam, one first when they come, and the other of leave when they depart. Nay many times they have but one allowed them, and all their affairs are to be treated with the Barcalon, who gives the King an account of them. But His Majesty as a mark of particular distinction to this Embassy, sent the Ambassador word, that as often as he had a mind to have audience, he was ready and willing to give it him. Indeed, eight or ten days after the Audience of Entry, the Ambassador had another; it was private, and the gentlemen were not admitted to it. The Ambassador took none with him but the Bishop of Metellopolis; the Abbot de Choisi and the Abbot de Lyon, the rest stayed in the first Court of the Palace, where upon the side of a canal under the shade of trees there was a long table of twenty four covers placed, with two side tables furnished with most lovely gold and silver plate of Japan and several sweet boxes, wherein the precious wood of aquila was not spared.

The King treats the Ambassador in his palace magnificently

The audience being ended they sat down to table, and continued at it almost four hours. There were above an hundred and fifty dishes served up, and infinite number of ragouts, not to speak of sweet meats, of which commonly they make two courses. Wine they had of five or six sorts; everything was magnificent and delicate, and it was the King's pleasure that the greatest men of his Kingdom should that day serve the French at table, to show the greater honour to the Ambassador, and render that Regal more agreeable.

About that time they began to examine the conduct of the two Mandarins whom the Barcalon sent to France with Monsieur Vachet. The complaints that were made of them had reached the Kings ears, who was offended at their proceedings. The Ambassador spoke in favour of them, and the eldest came off for a months imprisonment, and some other small punishment. But it is not as yet known what the other will suffer, tho it be certain that had it not been for so powerful an intercession, he had lost his head.

The Ambassador could not at first send the presents which he brought to the Barcalon, who enjoys the highest place in the Kingdom of Siam. It behoved him to delay some time to have them viewed, and what was spoiled by the air and sea, refitted. When everything was in good condition, Monsieur Vachet went to his house and presented them to him, and two days after the Ambassador paid him a visit.

Seeing there are no coaches at Siam, he was carried in a very neat chair which he brought with him from France. The Bishop took one like to those which the superiors of the *talapoins* use; the Abbot de Choisi was carried in a palanquin, and the gentlemen went on horseback. The Barcalon's lodgings were above a large quarter of league from the Ambassador's palace, tho there be but three streets betwixt them, but they are extremely long, all paved with brick and bordered on each side with low houses, behind which there are trees that cast a shade into the streets, and which make pleasant walks when the heat is over. The Barcalon's house is large, but built of wood, as most of the houses of Siam are, with this difference that it hath three roofs one over another, which are the badge of his dignity. It was then surrounded with water by reason of the inundation, and the entry into it was over a bridge which landed upon a terrace. A great many mandarins made a lane at the entry into the bridge, and all alighted except the Ambassador, who was carried over to the terrace, from whence he entered into the hall where the Ambassador gives audience. He came to receive the Ambassador at the hall-door, and conducted him to the end of it, where he made him sit down in an armed chair opposite to his own. The Bishop and Abbot de Choisi had also chairs brought them to sit in by the Ambassador; and the gentlemen stood at his back. The conversation lasted not long; all the discourse was about matters indifferent, and so the Ambassador returned in the same manner as he went.

The Ambassador visits the most famous Pagoda of Siam

The Ambassador had been told so much of the Pagoda of the Palace, and of the idols that are in it, that he had a great mind to see them; and seeing in everything they were ready to please him, a proper day was pitched upon, when they might be all shown to him at leisure. About eight o'clock in the morning he was conducted to the palace, where the Lord Constance expected him. Having crossed over eight or nine courts, we came at length to the richest and most celebrated Pagoda of the Kingdom, it is covered with calin, which is a kind of a very white metal betwixt tin and lead, with three roofs one over another. At the door of it, there is on the one hand a cow, and on the other a most hideous monster. This pagoda is pretty long, but very narrow, and when one is within it, there is nothing to be seen but gold. The pillars, walls, ceiling and all the figures are so well gilt, that all seem to be covered with plates of gold. The building is pretty like to our churches, and supported by thick pillars. Advancing forwards within it you find a kind of altar upon which there are three or four figures of beaten gold near about the height of a man; some of them stand, and others are sitting cross-legged after the manner of the Siamese. Beyond that there is a kind of quire, where they keep the richest and most precious pagoda or idol of the Kingdom, for that is a name given indifferently to the temple, or the idol that is within it. That statue is standing and the head of it reaches up to the roof. It is about five and forty foot high and seven or eight broad; but what is most surprising, it is all of gold. Of the bigness it is, the mass of it must needs contain above an hundred picks of that metal, and be worth at least twelve millions six hundred thousand livres.

A pick weighs an hundred and twenty five pound weight

They say that this prodigious colossus was cast in the same place where it stands, and that afterwards they built the temple over it. It cannot be comprehended, where those people otherwise poor enough could find so much gold; but it must needs touch one to the quick to see one single idol richer than all the tabernacles of the Churches of Europe. At the sides of it there are several others less but of gold also and enriched with precious stones. However this is not the best built temple of Siam. It is true there are none that have any figures of so great value, but there are several that have greater proportion, and beauty and one amongst others, which I must here give a description of.

A description of one of the fairest temples of Siam

About an hundred paces south of the palace there is a great park walled in, in the middle whereof stands a vast and high fabric built cross-ways in the manner of our churches, having over it five solid gilt domes of stone or brick, and of extraordinary architecture, the dome in the middle is far bigger than the rest, which are on the extremities and at the ends of the cross. This building rests upon several bases or pedestals, which are raised one over another, tapering and growing narrower towards the top. The way up to it on the four sides is only by narrow and steep stairs of betwixt thirty and forty steps three hands broad apiece and all covered with gilt, calin or tin like the roof. The bottom of the great stair-case is adorned on both sides with above twenty statues bigger than the life, some whereof are of brass, and the rest of calin and all gilt, but representing but sorrily the persons and animals for whom they have been made. This great pile of building is encompassed with forty four great pyramids of different form and well wrought, ranked orderly upon different platforms. On the lowest platform stand the four greatest at the four corners of it upon large bases. These pyramids end at the top in a long very slender cone, extremely well gilt, and supporting a needle or arrow of iron, that pierces through several crystal balls of an unequal bigness. The body of those great pyramids as well as of the rest, is of a kind of architecture that comes pretty near ours; but it has too much sculpture upon it, and wanting both the simplicity and proportions of ours, it comes short of its beauty, at least in the eyes of those that are not accustomed to it. If we have time we may give a more perfect idea of that architecture upon the second platform, which is a little above the first, there are six and thirty other pyramids somewhat less than the former: making a square round the pagoda, nine on each side. They are of two different figures, some taper into a point as the former did, and the rest are made round like a bell on the top, after the manner of the domes which crown the building; they are so mingled that there are not two together of the same form. Over these in the third platform, are other four pyramids on the four corners of it, which terminate in a point. They are less indeed than the first, but bigger than the second. All the fabric and pyramids are enclosed in a kind of square cloister, above sixscore common paces in length, about an hundred in breadth, and fifteen foot high. All the galleries of the cloister are open towards the pagoda; the ceiling thereof is not ugly; for it is all painted and gilt after the Moorish way. Within the galleries along the outer wall which is all close ranges along pedestal breast high, on which stand above four hundred statues, rarely well gilt, and placed in most excellent order. Though they be only of brick gilt, yet they appear to be very well shaped, but they are so like one another, that if they were not unequal in bigness, one would think that they had been all cast in the same mould. Amongst these figures we reckoned twelve of gigantic stature, one in the middle of each gallery, and two at each angle. These figures, because of their height are sitting upon flat bases cross-leg'd, after the manner of the country and of all the Orientals. We had the curiosity to measure one of their legs, the thumb of it was as big as an ordinary arm, and the rest of the body proportionally big and tall. Besides these which are of the first magnitude, there are about an hundred others that are as it were demi-giants, having the leg from the extremity of the foot to the knee four foot long. In short between the first and second, we reckoned above three hundred, of which none are less than the life, and these stand upright. I mention not a great many other little pagodas no bigger than puppets, which are mingled among the rest.

We never saw a fabric [edifice] no, not in France, where symmetry is better observed, either for the body of the building, or the ornaments about it, than in this pagoda. The cloister of it is flanked on the outside on each hand with sixteen great solid pyramids, rounded at the top in form of a

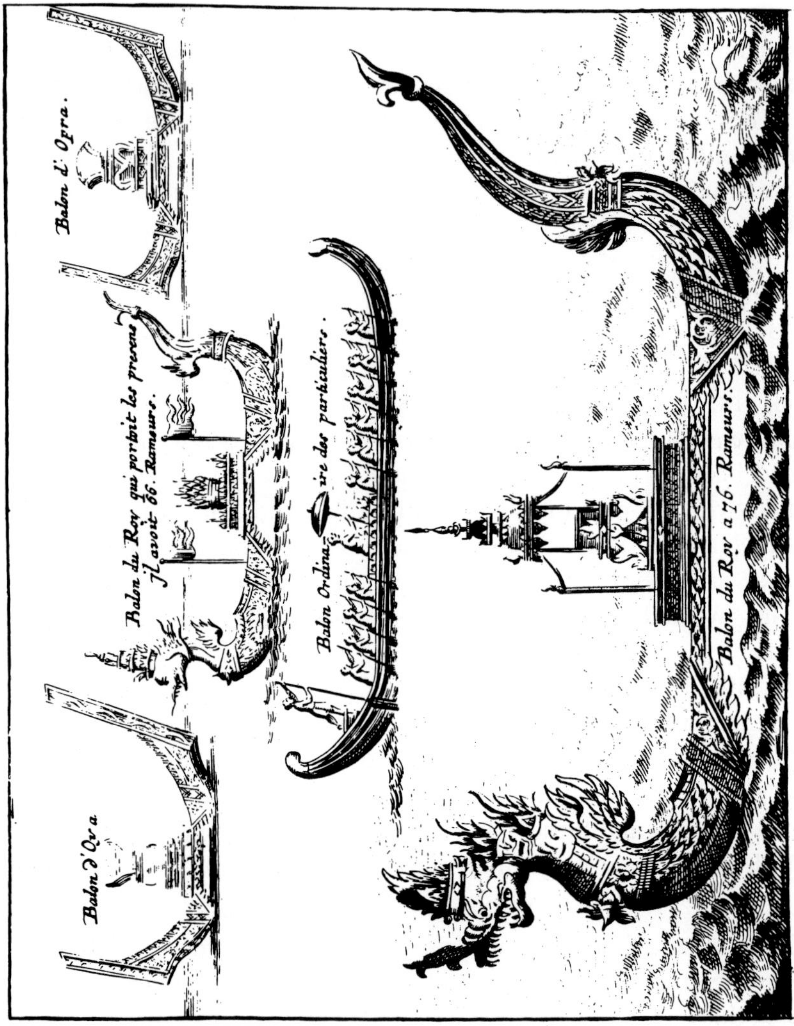

Plate 19. The varieties of *balons*

dome, above forty foot high, and above twelve foot square, placed in a line like a row of great pillars, in the middle whereof there are larger niches filled with gilt pagodas. We were so long taken up with the sight of these things that we had not time to consider several other temples close by the post within the same compass of walls. They judge of the nobility of families at Siam by the number of roofs that cover their houses. This hath five one over another, and the King's apartment hath seven.

Rejoicing performed at Siam for the coronation of the Kings of England and Portugal

Some days after we were arrived at Siam, there were two solemn services performed in the Church which we have in the field of the Portuguese, the one for the late Queen of Portugal, and the other for the late King Don Alphonso. Father Suarez a Dominican Friar made the funeral sermons. After that the festivals of the coronation of Don Pedro King of Portugal, who reigns at present, was celebrated in the Church of the Dominicans, where one of their fathers preached. The Lord Constance was at the charges of the obsequies and festivals. He would also have had a solemn service performed for the late King of England, if he had had certain intelligence that he died a Catholic. He only expressed his joy at the coronation of the Duke of York by illuminations and fire-works, which for their novelties pleased the French very much. There were long horns out of which were streams of fire that spouted up to a height like water-works, and lasted a long while, these festivals were accompanied with great feasting, to which the chief of all the nations of Europe, to wit, the French, English, Portuguese and Dutch were invited. My lord Ambassador could not excuse himself from being present at two feasts, which were made for the coronation of the Kings of England and Portugal. We were obliged to be there too, the Lord Constance having come and taken us with him in his own *balon.* The health's of all the Kings and Royal families were drunk there, with the noise of many great guns.

After these rejoicings came several divertissements; the first was a kind of a Chinese comedy, divided into acts, various bold and antic postures, and some pretty surprising feats of agility of body served for interludes. Unless on the one side the Chinese were acting their comedy, the Laos who are a people that border on that Kingdom to the north, gave the Ambassador on the other side the diversion of an Indian puppet show, which differ not much from ours. Betwixt the Chinese and the Laos there was a troop of Siamese men and women, cast into a ring, who danced after a pretty odd manner, that's to say, with their hands as well as feet, making as many figures with the one as they did with the other. The voices of some men and women, who sang a little in the nose, joined to the noise they made with their hands, regulated all the cadence.

After these plays tumblers appeared, who mounted to the top of high bamboos planted on the one end like masts, and about fourscore or an hundred foot high; they stood on the top of them on one foot, and holding the other in the air, then placing their head where their foot had stood, they railed their feet upright, standing upon their head. At length having hung by the chin that rested only on the top of the bamboos, their hands and the rest of their body hanging in the air, they came down a long ladder standing upright, turning their body about every step of the ladders with incredible swiftness and agility. Another placed upon a kind of litter or portable couch seven or eight daggers with the points upwards, sat down, and then lay along upon them, without hurting his body which was stark naked; he afterwards made a very heavy man stand upright upon his belly, and none of the points which touched his naked skin pierced him. These diversions were followed by several concerts that were performed by musicians of divers nations. There was nothing extraordinary, neither in the music nor voices; yet the novelty and diversity of them, made them pleasant enough not to prove tedious the first time. The Siamese, Malays, Pegus and Laos, gave a trial of their harmony by turns, striving to surpass one another. Their instruments much resemble ours, but are very imperfect: there was one that seemed extraordinary to us, it was mounted with a dozen of little bells hanging by it, which being gently struck upon with little sticks, rendered a most harmonious sound. In fine the scene concluded with another

Chinese comedy, which began a little to cloy the spectators, who were already weary. We were fain to be present at all these shows. The Lord Constance having obliged us to stay them out to the end; and the Ambassador pressing us not to leave him.

The King of Siam goes abroad publicly to visit a pagoda

The eight and twentieth of October being Sunday, we had notice that the King was to go abroad to do his devotions, as his custom was, at a famous pagoda upon the side of the river, three leagues from the town, and at the same time to render a visit to the Sancra, who is chief of the religion, and of all the *talapoins* of the Kingdom, and much respected by that Prince. He was accustomed on that occasion heretofore, to do the ceremony of cutting the waters, that's to say, to strike the river with his dagger at the time of the greatest inundation, and to command the waters to retire: but this Prince having found by many years experience, that the waters increased sometimes, for all they were ordered to abate, hath left off that ridiculous ceremony, and thought it enough this year by going as in triumph to the pagoda, to show the zeal he has for his religion. That this magnificence might be seen by the Ambassador, who in secret bewailed the blindness of that Prince, there was a gallery purposely prepared on the side of the river for him and his whole family. The Lord Constance who was there to explain the order of all the procession, would have us also to be present. This was the order and pomp of this show.

Three and twenty Mandarins of the lowest order of the Palace appeared first, every one in a Balon of State, with a red chirole. These *balons* advanced in file on two lines, and went long the side of the river. They were followed by fifty other *balons* of His Majesty's officers, who were all sitting in their chiroles, some of them being all over gilt, and the rest only on the sides. The *balons* hath from thirty to sixty oars apiece, taking up a very large space, by reason of the order they went in. After these came twenty *balons* more, bigger than the former, in the middle of which there was a very high seat, all gilt and spiring into a pyramid; these were

Plate 20. The *balon* of the king

Plate 21. A gentleman's *balon*

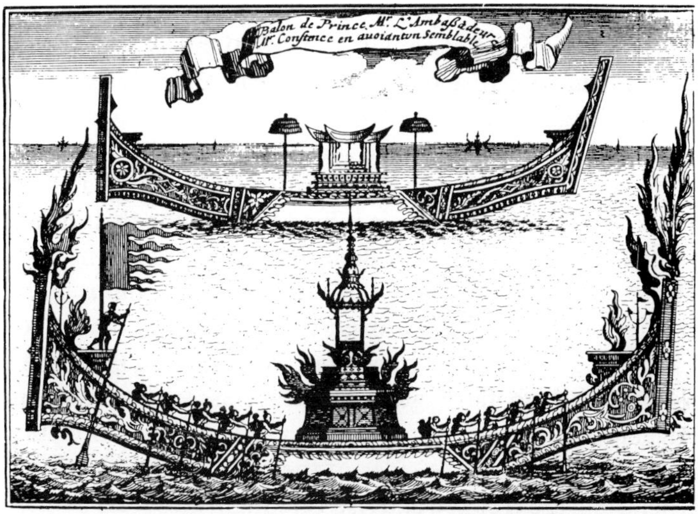

Plate 22. The *balon* of H.H. the Ambassador

the *balons* of guards, as they call them, of which some hath fourscore rowers and gilt oars, and the other four hath only oars streaked with gold. Next after that long train of balons, the King appeared in his, raised upon a throne of pyramidal figure and extraordinary well gilt. He was clothed in a rich cloth of gold set with precious stones: He wore a white cap ending in a point, encompassed with a ring of gold all flowered, and set thick with precious stones. The King's *balon* was gilt as low as the water, and rowed by sixscore water-men, who wore upon their heads a kind of toque covered with plates of gold, and on their stomach, stomachers adorned in the same manner. The King's standard bearer all glittering with gold stood behind towards the stern, with the Banner Royal of cloth of gold on a red ground; and four great Mandarins lay prostrate at the four corners of the throne. The Balon was attended by three others of the same form, that were every whit as stately, but the toques and breast-plates of the rowers were not so rich.

The King intending that my Lord Ambassador should see him, passed near to him , advancing but slowly that he might have time to consider him. The Ambassador rose up out of his seat, and made three profound bows to the King; all the rest who sat upon a carpet made him low inclinations of body. The Siamese that were upon the sides of the river sitting on the ground, so soon as they saw the King at a great distance, got upon their knees, and putting their joined hands upon their heads, in that posture touched the ground with their forehead, and left not off making the zombaye, till the King was out of sight. Twenty *balons* with chiroles and oars streaked with gold followed the King's, and other sixteen half painted and half gilt, brought up the rear. We reckoned in all one hundred and fifty-nine, of which the biggest were near sixscore foot long, and hardly six foot over at the broadest place. I have inserted [illustration] the bigness of the most extraordinary, the sides of them are even with the water, and the ends bend and are crooked and rise very high; most part of these *balons* have the figure of sea horses, dragons, and other sorts of animals. Nothing but the poop and prow are gilt, the rest hardly appearing above water; some of them are beautified with several figures made of pieces of mother of pearl wherewith they are inlaid.

After that the King had said his prayers at the pagoda, and there made his presents, he went to one of his palaces hard by, and in the evening returned to the town, according to his custom. Upon his return he took pleasure to make a match at rowing, and proposed a reward to those that should get first to the palace, from whence he set out in the morning. All the afternoon was spent in drawing up the *balons* into squadrons, and to match one against another; whilst matters were thus ordering the Ambassador came to see the show. He was conducted by the Lord Constance, who also invited us, and sent us a *balon* to carry us along with him. The King would needs be one of the antagonists, but seeing his *balon* was manned with more rowers, and those all choice men, he quickly got the better on't and victoriously entered the town, long before the rest. We placed ourselves near the Ambassador, that we might see the King. As he passed along by our *balon* we saw him very near, and he looked upon us in such a manner, as made us conclude, that the Lord Constance had already spoken of us to him. It was pleasant to see with what rapidity these *balons* every way proper for cleaving the water, mounted up the river in emulation one of another, and none of the rowers in the space of three leagues took so much as one minutes rest. They shouted either for joy or grief, according as they gained or lost the advantage. All the city and people about came running to see this show. They drew up in their *balons* by the shore, as in two lines which reached three leagues off of the city; so that having seen and considered that confluence of people that went down and came up the river, we judged that there could not be less then about twenty thousand *balons*, and above two hundred thousand souls; the other French reckoned a great many more, and confidently averred that there were above six hundred thousand souls of them. When the King passed by upon the river all the windows and doors of the houses were shut, and the portholes of the ships too. All commanded to go out, that so nobody might be in a higher place than the King.

The King's Progress from Siam to Louvo

Eight days after, the King with the Princess, and all his wives, went abroad again in a progress to Louvo. This is a town fifteen or twenty leagues to the Northward of Siam, where he spends nine or ten months of the year, because he is more at liberty there, and is not obliged to be shut up a he is at Siam, that he may keep his subjects in obedience and respect.

The Lord Constance, who having seen our patents for being the most Christian King's mathematicians, was resolved to procure us a private audience at Louvo, would have us go thither with our instruments and intimated to us, that the King was desirous to entertain us at court, until we should embark for Macao. He sent us two great *balons* for our baggage, and another of four and twenty oars to carry us. We parted the fifteenth of November about one of the clock in the afternoon, and went in the retinue of my Lord Ambassador.

The funeral of a great Talapoin

About two leagues from the town upon a vast plain covered with water, and reaching out of sight, we met with a new spectacle; and that was the obsequies of a famous Talapoin, chief of the religion of the Peguans. His body was laid in a coffin of aromatic wood. The coffin was mounted upon a funeral pile, round which were four great pillars of gilt wood, which carried an high pyramid of several stories. This kind of burning chapel was accompanied with several little pretty high and square towers made of wood, and covered with pasteboard very rudely painted, with a great many paper figures. All this was surrounded with an enclosure built square, upon which several other towers were placed at competent distances. Four of them were as high as the pyramid in the middle, and stood in the four corners; and on each side of that great square there were two other towers less than the former. They were all full of fireworks, and we saw many flying fuzes come out of them. The four great towers placed at the four corners of the great square, were joined together by little wooden houses, painted with several antic figures of dragons, apes, devils with horns on their heads, etc. Betwixt these hovels there were at competent distances certain openings contrived in form of a portal to let Balons in and out. The *talapoins* of Pegu, to a vast number, in their *balons*, took up almost the whole space that was betwixt the funeral pile and the great square enclosure. They all looked with a grave and modest countenance, now and then singing, and sometimes keeping profound silence. An infinite number of people, men and women indifferently come after them, and assisted at this funeral pomp.

So new and unexpected a scene made my Lord Ambassador stop for some time, and us with him, that we might view the ceremonies of that stately funeral. However, we saw nothing but mimical dances, and certain ridiculous farces, acted by the Peguans and Siamese under sheds of bamboo that were open on all hands. They acted the postures of men possessed, with hideous masks upon their faces. Seeing this funeral pomp was to last till night, and that we had four or five leagues to go before we could come to the place of lodging, we saw only the beginning of it, and some fire-works. The honours of this nature given to the dead amongst the Siamese, makes them strongly addicted to their religion. The *talapoins*, who are very interested doctors, teach that the more expense is made in the obsequies of a dead man, the more advantageously his soul is lodged in the body of some Prince, or some other considerable animal. In that belief the Siamese many times undo themselves by making magnificent funerals.

We came in very good time to the house where we were to lie; it was in all things like to those little palaces which were erected for my Lord Ambassador upon the river. It may be said of this country, that there cannot be a more pleasant prospect than it affords. When we were upon the canal cut through the fields to shorten the way from Siam to Louvo, we saw plains reaching out of sight full of rice, and when we entered into the river, the green trees and villages wherewith it was bordered, refreshed our sight with an agreeable variety.

Before we left that place, the Ambassador had a mind to see one of the King's palaces that was hard by. We only saw the outside of it, because the house-keeper had orders to suffer none to enter it. It seems to be a very little and narrow palace, encompassed on the outside with a little low gallery in form of a cloister, but very irregular in its architecture, the pedestals being full as high as the pilasters. Round that gallery runs a low balcony encompassed with rails and balusters of stone breast-high.

The description of a palace of the King of Siam, built after the European manner

About an hundred paces from that palace, we saw another much bigger, and far more regular. On the outside there are great pilasters at an equal distance from one another, which savour very much of art. It stands in a great square above an hundred and fifty or sixty paces in length. On the four sides there are four very high piles of buildings in form of galleries, and covered with a double roof made round above like an arch. These galleries on the outside ambassadors and envoys of princes or foreign states. It consists in two great galleries open on all hands, which form a double square. The gallery at the end which crosses upon the other is extremely wide, from both of them you enter into halls with several closets, and all this is environed with grass-plots and gardens; on the right hand there is a menagerie full of several sorts of animals, as stags, hinds, wild-goats, antelopes, ostriches, storks, ducks and geese of a singular kind. On the left hand are the gardens and country-houses of the town-people of best quality. Behind it there is a little pavilion consisting of three low rooms and a kitchen, which is separated from the galleries by a large court that reaches on one hand to the ditches of the fort, and on the other as far as the sea. A little river runs under one of these galleries and across the grass-plots, which serves to make ponds where fish are kept. Seeing this building was only made for taking the fresh air, there is no regularity in the whole, tho every party be regular enough. The gardens are full of flowers at all times, but we saw none there that were rare, the trees are orange, lemon and pomegranate trees planted in rows that make lovely walks.

The French Jesuits go to see Father Dominic Fucity

There we found Father Fucity, who having been already informed of our arrival, impatiently expected us. It is not to be expressed how much joy and resolution we felt at the sight of that holy man honourable for his great age and his long labours in the mission of Cochin-China[19] and Tonkin. He came from his church the nine and twentieth of October, 1684, with Father Emanuel Fereira who was the superior of the mission. It was a great grief to many good Christians to see them leave the country, and many tears were shed on both sides. Nay, if the fathers had not left them some hopes of their return, there would have been no comforting of them. Every idolatrous mandarin bewailed their departure, and the Christians conceived so great an aversion to those whom they suspected to be the causes of it , that they would not confess any more, incessantly calling for their first masters and ancient pastors. This we were told by a churchman in the Indies who was a person of good credit, and very well acquainted with affairs of that nature.

In the mean time we considered the garden and outside of the palace. It has a most excellent situation, being seated by the river side upon a smooth and even eminence, and is of a large compass. We saw nothing remarkable but two great separated piles of building, and the roofs all shining with gold. In this they are singular, that they are covered with yellow varnished tiles, which glitter like gold when the sun shines upon them; we were told that every one of these tiles cost about ten groats. Without the palace we saw a lion presented by the French company to the King: It seemed to be bigger, handsomer and stronger than those at Vincennes, but his hair is not altogether so yellow.

The audience lasted almost two hours. Whilst they discoursed of several things, the King took occasion to tell the Ambassador, that he was informed six Jesuits were come with him; that they were the French King's mathematicians, whom His Majesty sent to make observations in the Indies, and to labour in the perfection of arts; and that he should be glad to see those learned men. The Ambassador let not slip the occasion of doing us that good office, and spoke many things in our favour. The King was not then so high above the Ambassador as he was at the first audience. He wore upon his head a white painted cap, encompassed below with a circle of diamonds. He was clothed in a straight coat purled with gold, having over it a large vest of a very fine and transparent stuff. He had some large diamonds on his fingers, but they were ill cut and ill set. As he has more wit than your Oriental Princes commonly have, he said many things very wittily to the glory of the most Christian King, and obligingly for the Ambassador. He added, that he prayed the God of Heaven to give him a more speedy and successful voyage homeward than he had in coming abroad.

In the evening the Lord Constance invited abroad the Ambassador with all his attendants, to take the air, all severally mounted upon elephants, they that ride them sit on the middle of their back in a kind of very wide chair environed with small gilt rails, but without a back, whilst two officers that serve the elephant, one upon his neck, and another on his rump, govern him with a great iron hook, as may be seen by the figure [illustration]. It is to be observed, that these beasts have their domestic servants as persons of quality have: the least have fifteen men that wait upon them quarterly, and others have twenty, twenty five, thirty and forty, according to their rank; but the white elephant has an hundred. The Lord Constance told me that the King hath at least twenty thousand in his whole Kingdom, not to reckon the wild that are among the woods and mountains. Sometimes they'll take fifty, sixty, nay eighty of them at one single bout of hunting.

The elephants have five toes in each foot

The gentlemen of the Academy Royal of Sciences recommended it to us to examine whether or not all elephants had claws in their feet; we saw not so much as one but that had five on each foot, at the end of five great toes; but their toes are so short, that they hardly peep out of the fleshy lump. We observed that their ears are nothing near so big as they are commonly painted, and are less by a half than they are made to be in the cut [illustration] that was given us of one. Some we have seen who hath teeth of extraordinary beauty and length; they reach above four foot out of the mouth of some of them, and at certain distances are adorned with rings of gold, silver and copper. In one of the King's country-houses, upon the river side, about a league from Siam, I saw a little white elephant, which they design shall be the successor of him that is in the Palace, who, as they say, is near three hundred years old. This little elephant is somewhat bigger than an ox, hath many mandarins in his service; and for his sake there is great respect showed to his mother and aunt that are kept with him. The King of Cambodia presented him to the King of Siam about two or three years since, when he sent to demand assistance from him against one of his subjects that had revolted, and was supported by the King of Cochinchina.

A description of Louvo

The town of Louvo stands most pleasantly, and in a most wholesome air; the compass of it is pretty large, and it is become very populous since the King had been pleased to live much there: He designs to fortify it, and Monsieur de la Mare, an able engineer, whom the Ambassador left at Siam, had already drawn the plan of the fortifications that are to be made, to render it a strong and regular place. It is seated upon a height which discovers all the country about, is not commanded by any place, and on one side is washed by a great river that runs at the foot of it. It is true, that river is not at all considerable but during the time of the inundation. But seeing the inundation and rains last seven or eight months, on that side which besides is very steep, the town cannot be besieged. The other sides are either marshes which may be easily overflowed, or rising grounds in form of an amphitheatre, which are designed to be taken into the town, and which will serve for deep ditches and terraced ramparts, proof against all artillery. They'll set about the fortifications of Louvo as soon as Bangkok is fortified, which is a place of greater importance, and, as it were, the key of the Kingdom of Siam. These works will soon be completed, because an infinite number of workmen will be employed, and the ground is easy to be cast up.

The King of Siam gives a private audience to the French Jesuits

November the two and twentieth we had notice sent us, that the King would give us a private audience the same day. About four of the clock in the afternoon the Lord Constance carried us to the Palace, and made us pass three courts, where we saw several mandarins lying prostrate on each side. As we entered the inner court, we found a large carpet, where that minister made us sit down. We had no habit of ceremony, nor did they oblige us to be barefooted, which was a great work of distinction. So soon as we were sat down, the King, who was going abroad to see a fight of elephants, wherewith he thought fit to entertain the Ambassador, mounted his elephant magnificently harnessed, which waited for him at the gate of his apartment; and having perceived us at ten or twelve steps distance from him, he came up to us. Our Father Superior had prepared a compliment to thank him for the honour he did us in admitting us into his presence, as it had been concerted with the Lord Constance; but that minister perceiving the King in haste to be gone, spoke for us. The King eyeing us one after another attentively, and with a smiling and gracious countenance, told us, how being informed that the King of France had sent us all six into China upon a great design, he had desired to see us, that he might tell us by word of mouth, that if we stood in need of anything in his Kingdom, either for the service of the King our master, or for ourselves in particular, we should address ourselves to his Minister, whom he had ordered to furnish us with all we wanted. We had no time to make answer to that favour any otherwise than by humble thanks and profound inclinations. We only let him know that we should acquaint the King our master with the obligations that he had put upon us.

The King went his way, and having passed through this court into another, amidst a lane of mandarins prostrate before him in great silence, with their foreheads against the ground, he found at the first gate of the palace the chief of the companies of the European merchants bare-footed, on their knees, and leaning upon their elbows, to whom he gave a short audience. The Lord Constance having told us that it would be fit we should write the compliment that was to be made to the King, and then present it to His Majesty, Father Fontenay, who foresaw that circumspection would not be unnecessary; because perhaps he might not have time to read it, presented it to the King, who ordered the Lord Constance to take it. It was both in the Siamese language and the French, and conceived in these terms.

The Jesuits harangue presented to the King

SIR,

We have left the greatest King that France ever had, but have had the happiness in coming hither, to find again in Your Majesty the qualities of that Prince. That greatness of soul which so generously inclines you to assist your allies, the courage wherewith you repress your Enemies, the advantages you have lately got over them, that extraordinary submission of your subjects, that magnificence wherein you show yourself to them, these famous embassies which you receive from the remotest parts of the world, that protection you give to strangers, that particular affection you express toward the ministers of the Gospel, that goodness which you so bountifully make also appear towards us; all these things, Sir, are convincing arguments that you are a magnanimous, victorious, politic and equitable King, and as fame and the acclamations of your subjects publish it, the greatest Prince that ever sway'd the sceptre of Siam.

The sciences, Sir, that we make profession of, are esteemed all over Europe. Our King does so encourage them, that for their use, he has erected stately observatories, and for their sake given his august name to our companies college where they are taught. We have studied to improve them from our youth upwards, especially astronomy, which best agrees with our inclinations because it raises our minds to the frequent contemplation of Heaven, the habitation of the blessed, and the country we only aspire unto. His Most Christian Majesty knowing that it is our profession to make use of human sciences, that by means of them we may bring men to the knowledge and love of the true God; and being persuaded that the mathematics have been our particular study, has chosen us to go to China in quality of mathematicians: so that it is a charge laid upon us to join our endeavours with those whom he keeps at home by himself in the improvement of arts and sciences. For the more easy accomplishment of so great a design, our great Monarch hath given us letters patents, which recommend us to all the Princes of the Earth; in consideration whereof, Your Majesty heaps honour upon us by admitting us into your presence.

It is impossible for us, Sir, to make any suitable returns for so great favours; but since we cannot do it as we ought to do, we hope Your Majesty will suffer us to do it the best way we can. We are the servants of the true God, and the subjects of a great Monarch. As the subjects of so great a King, we will inform him of the favours Your Majesty hath showed us, and as servants of the true God, we

> will make our earnest prayers to him, that he would in all things prosper your reign, and so enlighten Your Majesty with his divine truths, that after so glorious a reign upon earth, you may come to the possession of the glories of Heaven.

Some days after the Lord Constance discoursed His Majesty about a project which he had a long time in his thoughts, of bringing to Siam twelve Jesuit mathematicians, whom he hath already demanded of our reverend Father General, and about the design of building an observatory in imitation of Paris and Peking.[33] He made His Majesty sensible of the glory and profit that would thereby redound to him, and the advantage that his subjects would reap from it; who would be taught the finest arts and sciences of Europe. His Majesty much approved that project, and bid the Lord Constance tell us, that he would have an observatory built in his Kingdom, which he would bestow upon the fathers of the company of Jesus, whom he much esteemed, and whom he would protect and favour in all things that lay in his power. Whereupon the Lord Constance thought it fit that some of us should return to France to press that affair, which seemed to him to be of extreme consequence for religion. He mentioned it one day to the Father Superior when we were all three together. We joyfully consented to it; and the commission falling upon me, I had orders presently to prepare for my return. It grieved me to the heart then, to see myself for a long time removed to so great a distance from China, which I had longed after for so many years.

The Lord Constance who is no less ready to embrace the occasions of advancing the glory of God, than of procuring advantages to his master, communicated to us another view, which he thought might contribute much to the conversion of the Siamese. He pretends that if once their esteem and affection can be gained by zeal, meekness and learning, it will be no difficult matter to dispose them to hearken to instruction: that he thoroughly knew the temper of that nation, and no man better; why Christianity hath made no greater progress at Siam after so many years endeavours of having it planted there; that besides the observatory, there must be another house of Jesuits, where they should as much as lay in their power lead the austere and retired life of the *talapoins*, that they should take their habit, visit them often, and endeavour to convert some of them to the Christian religion; that in short, it was well known how that conduct had succeeded with the Portuguese Jesuits who are at Madura towards Bengal.

The truth is, we have learnt from several places, and very lately too at Siam from a French missionary who had been at St. Thomas two months before, that these fathers had lived several years amongst those people, and applied themselves with care and pains to their conversion without any considerable fruit. One of them, who had been made superior of that mission, having long implored assistance from Heaven, and reflecting on the reverence that those people had for the Brahmins, who are their priests and religious, thought that if he did take the habit of the Brahmins and lived after their manner, he might gain credit amongst them, and win them over to Jesus Christ. He communicated that design to his superiors, who proposed it to the congregation *de propaganda fide*. It was considered of at Rome, and it being represented to the Cardinals that the habits the Brahmins wore were no mark of religion, but of nobility and eminent quality, they permitted that father and some other Jesuits who approved his judgement, to try that last way for the conversion of those people.

Having so taken the badge of the Brahmins, they began to live as they did; and since that time these apostolic men have been seen walking upon the burning hot sand bare-footed and bareheaded, and continually exposed to the heat of the sun, which is extraordinary there, because the Brahmins wear no stockings nor shoes, and never cover their head; living on nothing but herbs, and spending three or four days without eating, under a tree, or on the high way, waiting till some Indian affected with such surprising austerity, should come and hear them. God hath so much blessed their zeal and mortification, that they have converted above threescore thousand Indians, and the people come flocking in so great numbers to be instructed, that they value not all the hardship and trouble they have endured.

The same Churchman added, that he had seen one of those fathers, whose feet had been all chapped with the burning sand, which getting afterwards into the wounds, put him to extreme pain, and raised strange swellings. Upon what he told us of these missions, we earnestly desired to see a more ample relation of them, being persuaded that we should therein meet with rare examples of zeal, and great ground of edification.

Book 5

Of our Return from Siam

When it was resolved upon, that I should return to France, the Lord Constance redoubled the testimonies of friendship, wherewith he had till then honour'd me, telling me that he wished he might frequently discourse [with] me in private. Next day I went to see him, according as he had enjoined me at parting. I found him taken up in preparing presents for those who had had the greatest hand in the favour which the King had done us of sending us to China; and making us draw near to see them, these are but very mean presents, said he, for so great lords. But you shall tell them, Father, that I came to know of it but very late, and after I had given away all the finest and most curious things I had. For besides the presents which he sent to France, and that he had given to the French who were at Siam, he had sent some very considerable to Portugal, by the three Ambassadors whom the King of Siam had dispatched to Lisbon, sometime before we arrived there. Nor is it, said he, a present that I would have them take as from me, but as from one of your brothers, to thank them for the goodness they have for you, and the protection they honour you with. We could make no answer to such obliging expressions, but by our most humble thanks; but he would not hear us, interrupting and adjuring us not to speak to him in that strain, that being our brother, he was persuaded he did no more but his duty.

The same day that we had audience, the King was to treat the Ambassador with a fight of elephants, and His Majesty had already commanded six to be made ready for us, that we might follow him to the field of battle, which was out of town. The Lord Constance gave us a mandarin to be our guide, and as we came out of the Palace we found six elephants with their gilt chairs, and very neat cushions. Every one got up on the back of his own in this manner. The Pastor (for so they call the man that sits on the elephant's neck to govern him) made the elephant kneel, who afterward lay half down on one side, so that one could put his foot upon one of his fore-legs, which he thrust out, and then upon his belly; after that, the beast rising a little up again, gave one time to sit down conveniently in the chair which he carried on his back; one may also make use of a ladder, as some do, to get upon the elephants back. It is for the convenience of strangers, who are not accustomed to elephants, that they put chairs on their backs. The natives of the country, whatsoever their quality be, unless it be the King, ride on the neck and conduct them themselves, except when they go to war, for then, besides two pastors, who get up one upon the neck, and the other on the rump, the Mandarin armed with a lance, or a kind of javelin, sits on the elephants back, as I my self have seen it at a hunting of elephants, whither the mandarins go armed as to a battle. I observed also that the King, who was in a kind of throne, started up upon his legs when the wild elephants would have forced their way through on his side, and got upon the neck of his to stop them.

We followed the King then into a large plain, about an hundred paces from the town. The King, mounted on an elephant, had my Lord Ambassador on his right hand at fifteen or twenty steps distance, the Lord Constance on his left hand, and all round a great many Mandarins prostrate at the feet of his elephant out of respect. We presently heard some trumpets which make a very harsh and inarticulate sound; then the two elephants which were to fight roared and made a most horrid noise: They were tied by the hind-feet with great ropes, held by several men, that they might be drawn off, in case the shock proved too hard. They let them approach in such a manner, that their teeth crossed, and yet they could not hurt one another. They say that sometimes they'll encounter so fiercely, that breaking one another's teeth by their efforts, the splinters of them will fly about: these fought but with little violence, they encountered but four or five times, and then were parted, and the engagement was so short, that it was thought the King had only appointed it that he might have occasion in a more agreeable manner, to make a present to Monsieur de Vaudricourt, who had brought the two Siamese Mandarins, and was to carry the Ambassadors to France; for at the end of the show, His Majesty drew near him, and with his own hand, gave him a shable with a handle of beaten gold, and a tortoise shell scabbard, adorned with five plates of gold, with a great filigree gold chain also, to serve for a shoulder-belt, and a vest of cloth of gold, with gold buttons: He told him that he put that scimitar[34] into his hands, that he might securely conduct his ambassadors, and therewith protect the King his master against his enemies. The King of Siam never gives that kind of shable but to his generals of armies, when they are setting out upon a warlike expedition. He made such another present to Monsieur de Joyeux Captain of the frigate, but not so magnificent.

Some days after, the Lord Constance sent rich presents to the Ambassador, the Abbot de Choisi, Monsieur de Vaudricourt, Monsieur de Joyeux, and to every one of the gentlemen of the Ambassador's retinue. These were Japan plate, wrought agates, a great many fine china dishes of all sizes, China-night gowns, right bezoar-stones, the ginseng root that is worth eight times its weight in silver, the odoriferous wood of aquila, so much esteemed in the Indies, and excellent tea in great quantity. These presents seemed to be of so considerable a value, that for some time it was thought by many that they had been sent by the King.

We spent most of the days we stayed at Louvo in shows. The fight we just now mentioned, was followed by another of elephants against a tiger; we were obliged to be there as well as the rest, and mounted on elephants. We made use of no other beast to ride on, that we might not scandalise the *talapoins*, who say that it is prohibited to them to ride on horse-back.

About a quarter of a league from the town, they had raised a high palisade of bamboo, about an hundred paces square. Three elephants appointed to fight the tiger, were got into the middle of the lists. They had a kind of large breast-plate, which covered their head and part of their trunk.

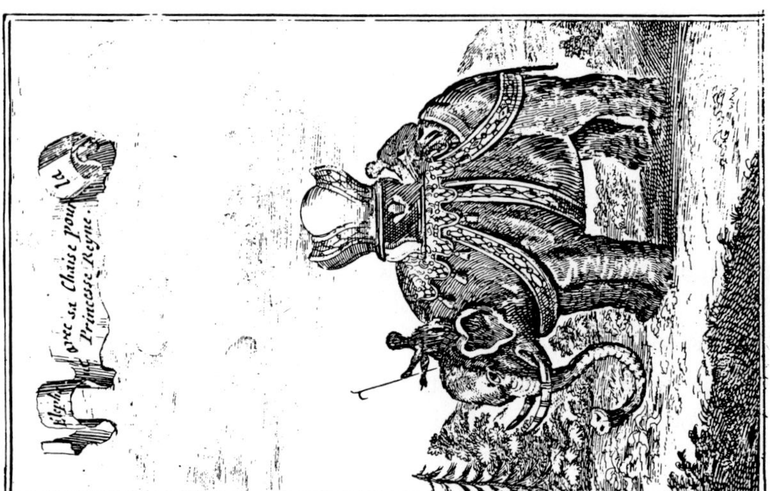

Plate 23. The princess' howdah

Plate 24. The howdah provided for foreigners

Plate 25. The king mounts his elephant

So soon as we were come, out of a lodge that was in a low place, they brought a tiger, of a shape and colour which seemed strange to the French that were spectators. For besides that, he was much taller, grosser, and more lumpish than those that we had seen in France; his skin was not spotted in that fashion, but instead of spots scattered here and there without order, it hath long broad streaks that encompassed it like rings. These streaks beginning at the back joined under the belly, and continuing to the end of the tail, made thereupon white and black rings, which were set very thick, and covered it all over. The head and limbs of the beast hath nothing extraordinary, save that they were longer and bigger than those of common tigers, though this was but a young tiger, and not yet come to his full growth, for the Lord Constance told us that there were some in the Kingdom three times bigger than that, and that being a hunting one day with the King, he saw one at a very near distance that was as big as a mule. They have little ones in that country also, like those they bring from Africa to Europe, and they showed us one of them at Louvo the same day.

They did not let slip the tiger that was to fight at first, but held him tied by two ropes, so that not having liberty to shoot himself out, the first elephant that came near him, gave him two or three blows with his trunk on the back. This shock was so rude that it laid the tiger for some time all along upon the ground, and without motion, as if he had been dead. Nevertheless, so soon as he was untied, though the first bout had quelled much of his fury, he made a terrible cry, and would have thrown himself upon the elephants trunk, but the elephant turning it cunningly inwards, secured it by his teeth, which he presently presented to the tiger, and therewith struck him so pat, that he tossed him up to a great height, in the air. This so stun'd the beast, that he durst no more approach the elephant, but taking several turns about the yard, he sometimes sprang at those whom he saw in the galleries. Then three elephants were let loose against him, who mauled him so by turns, that once more he counterfeited to be dead, and afterward made all the shifts he could to avoid them. They would certainly have killed him, had not the Ambassador begg'd his pardon of the Lord Constance, who put an end to the combat.

Next day towards the evening, we went to the Palace with my Lord Ambassador; there we saw an illumination, which is yearly made at the beginning of the year: It consisted of eighteen hundred or two thousand lights, some whereof were places in little windows purposely made in the walls that environ the Palace, and the rest in lanterns,[35] in a pretty singular order. Above all we admired some certain large china lanterns like to globes, which are made of one single piece of transparent horn as clear as glass, and some others of a kind of china glass made of rice. These illuminations were accompanied with the noise of drums, fifes and trumpets. All the while that the King was present at this show, the Princess gave the like to the court ladies in another part of the palace.

When the King was gone, we had time to consider all things at a near distance. The Lord Constance show'd us the Elephant Prince, who is of an extraordinary height and beauty; we were told that they called him by that name, because he came into the world the same day that the present king was born. He made us also observe near to the King's apartment, a pavilion where they keep the elephant that is upon guard, it is one of those that are in the palace, and are relieved by turns, being always kept in a readiness, if the King should chance to want them by day or by night. Having often mentioned elephants, and the different manner, they are harnessed according to the qualities of those that mount them, it hath been thought fit to give the reader the following cuts [illustrations] of the several sorts of them. These illuminations lasted several days; all the while we were in the palace to observe them, a great many mandarins of the first and second order, lay prostrate upon the ground before the King in two different halls, making to him the zombaye, which is the most reverential mark of adoration.

Much about the same time the Moors made great illuminations for eight days together, in honour of their prophet Mohammed and his son, whose funerals they celebrated. They began to solemnise the festival the evening before about four of the clock at night, by a kind of procession, wherein there were above two thousand souls. There they carried the figure of the tombs of those two impostors, with many symbols of a pretty neat representation, amongst others, certain great cages covered with painted cloth, and carried by men that marched and continually turned in cadence to the sound of drums and timbrels. The quick and regular motion of these huge machines which we saw at a distance, without perceiving those that carried them, occasioned an agreeable surprise.

The Moors make a feast to celebrate the memory of their prophet

At the head of this great confluence of people, some grooms led three or four horses in rich trappings, and a great many people carrying several lanterns at the end of long poles, lighted all the procession and sang in divers quires after a very odd manner. With the same zeal they continued this festival for several nights together till five of the clock in the morning. It is hardly to be conceived how these porters of machines, that incessantly turned, could perform that exercise for fifteen or sixteen hours together, nor how the singers that raised their voices as high as was possible for them, could sing so long. The rest of the procession looked modest enough, some marched before the singers, who surrounded coffins carried upon eight men's shoulders, and the rest were mingled in the crowd with them. There were a great many Siamese men and women, young and old there, who have embraced the Mohammedan religion. For since the Moors have got footing in the Kingdom, they have drawn over a great many people to their religion, which is an argument that they are not so addicted to their superstitions, but that they can forsake them, when our missionaries have had patience and zeal enough to instruct them in our mysteries. It is true, that nation is a great lover of shows and splendid ceremonies, and by that means it is that the Moors, who celebrate all their festivals with a great deal of magnificence, have perverted many of them to the sect of Mohammed.

These shows made us heartily condole the misfortune of those poor infidels, and we often discoursed of the fruit that so many able men as are in Europe, and particularly in France, might reap amongst them, if they had as much zeal as learning.

The King who took pleasure to give the Ambassador new diversions daily, would have him to see the manner of taking and taming elephants. This being a thing unknown in Europe, and we having been witnesses of it, the reader, I hope, will be glad to find here an example and exact description of the same.

The way of taking and taming elephants

About a quarter of a league from Louvo there is a kind of an amphitheatre, of a large and long square figure, encompassed with high walls and terraces, where the spectators are placed. Along these walls within runs a palisade of thick pillars fastened in the ground at a foot distance one from another, behind which the huntsmen retreat when they are pursued by the fretted elephants. There is a very large opening made towards the country, and opposite to it, on the side of the town one less, which leads into a narrow alley through which an elephant can hardly pass, and that alley ends in a large manage, where they completely tame him at length.

When the day appointed for this hunting is come, huntsmen go into the woods, mounted on she-elephants which are trained to the game, and cover themselves with leaves of trees that they may not be seen by the wild elephants. When they are got pretty forward in the forest, where they think some elephant may be, they make the female give some neighs that are proper to attract the males, who presently answer by dreadful roaring. Then the huntsmen perceiving them at a vast distance return back again, and gently lead the females towards the amphitheatre we mentioned: the wild elephants never fail to follow them; he whom we saw tamed entered with them, and so soon as he was there the bar was shut; the females kept on their way cross the amphitheatre, and at one another's tails past along the little alley that was at the other end: The wild elephant which had followed them to that place, stopping at the entry of the narrow pass, all manner of ways were used to make engagement, they made the females who were beyond the alley, cry; some Siamese provoked him by clapping their hands and crying out, others pricked him with long sharp pointed poles, and when they were pursued by him, slipped betwixt the pillars and hid themselves behind the palisades which the elephant could not break through: at length having pursued several of the huntsmen he made at one single man with a great deal of fury. The man run into the alley and the elephant after him; but so soon as he was within, he was taken, for the man having made his escape, they let fall purposely too portcullises[36] one before and the other behind the elephant, so that it being out of his power to go forwards or backwards or to turn himself, he struggled prodigiously and made terrible cries. They endeavoured to pacify him by throwing buckets full of water upon his body, rubbing him with leaves, pouring oil upon his ears, and they brought tame elephants both males and females to him who caressed him with their trunks. In the mean time they fastened ropes under his belly and to his hind-feet, that so they might pull him out from thence, and they persisted in throwing water upon his trunk and body to cool him. At length they brought to him one of those tame elephants that are accustomed to instruct the new-comers. An officer was mounted upon him who made him go forwards and backwards, to show the wild elephant that there was no danger, and that he might come out. So at length they opened the gate to him and he followed the other to the end of the alley. So soon as he was there they fastened an elephant to each side of him, another went before and pulled him by a rope into the way that they would have him take, whilst a fourth made him go forwards by thumping him with his head behind, until he came to a kind of manage where they tied him to a great pillar made for that purpose, which turns like the capstan of a ship. They left him there till next day that he might spend his anger; but whilst he tormented himself about that pillar, a Brahmin (that is to say one of the Indian priests who are numerous in Siam) clothed in white and mounted on another elephant drew nigh, and turning gently about this which was tied, sprinkled him with a certain water consecrated after their manner, which he carried in a vessel of gold. They believe that that ceremony makes the elephant lose his natural fierceness, and fits him for to serve the King. The day following he begins to go with the rest, and in a fortnight's time is fully tamed.

Amidst all those diversions the Ambassador was wholly taken up about the subject of his embassy, which was the conversion of the King; but perceiving that he had no solid nor positive answer as to that, he resolved to draw up a short memoir, which he intended should be presented to the King by the Lord Constance. He spoke of it to that minister, who in a long conference they had together dissuaded him from pressing the King upon that point; but the Ambassador very prudently still persisted in his opinion, and prayed the Lord Constance to present that writing to His Majesty, wherein he besought him to give him a positive answer that might be acceptable to the King his master. The Lord Constance having received the memoir from the Ambassador, went to the palace in the evening, and there prostrating himself at the King's feet, made him a discourse full of that Asiatic eloquence that was so much esteemed in ancient Greece. Here you have a true translation of the very words he used.

The Harangue of the Lord Constance to the King of Siam

Sir,

The Ambassador of France hath put into my hands a memoir which contains certain propositions whereof he has to give an account to the King his master; but before I read it to Your Majesty, suffer me, Sir, if you please, to lay before you the principal motive that engaged the most Christian King to send you so solemn an embassy. That so wise a Prince, your good friend, Sir, knowing the greatness of your soul and the generosity of Your Majesty's Royal heart by the Ambassadors and magnificent presents which you designed for him, without other interest than perceiving that Your Majesty's ministers hath sent to the ministers of his Kingdom two Mandarins with considerable presents to congratulate the birth of the grand-son of their great King, worthy of a perpetual posterity, which may eternally represent to France the image of his admirable virtues, and secure the happiness of his people. That great Monarch, Sir, being surprised by so disinterested a procedure, resolved to answer those obliging cares, and to do so, devised a means worthy of himself and suitable to the dignity of Your Majesty; for to present you with riches; it is in your Kingdom, Sir, that strangers came in search of wealth, to offer you his forces? He knew very well that Your Majesty is dreaded by all your neighbours, and in a condition to punish them if they should offer to break the peace which by their prayers they have obtained from you. Could he have thought of bestowing lands and provinces upon the sovereign of so many Kings, and the master of so great a number of Kingdoms, as make almost the fourth part of Asia; neither could it enter into his thoughts to send hither his subjects only upon the account of trade, because that would be a common interest to his people and Your Majesty's subjects. So that it would have been hard for him to have hit upon the right course, had he not reflected that he might offer to Your Majesty somewhat infinitely more considerable, and which, was congruous to the dignity of two so great Kings. Having considered what it was that hath raised him to that high pitch of glory where at present he is seated, what hath made him take so many towns, subdue so many provinces, and gain so many victories, what to this present hath made the happiness of his people, and what hath brought him from the extremities of the Earth so many ambassadors of Kings and Princes who court his friendship, what, in fine, hath obliged Your Majesty to prevent this incomparable Prince by so splendid an Embassy which you sent to him; having, I say, attentively considered all those great things, that King so wise and perspicacious, found that the God whom he adores was the sole author of them, and that he owed them to the intercession of the Holy Mother of the Saviour of the world, under whose protection he hath consecrated his person and Kingdom to the true God. That view and the extreme desire he hath to communicate to Your Majesty all those great advantages, hath made him resolve to propose to you, Sir, the same means that have procured him so much glory and happiness, and which are no other than the knowledge and worship of the true God, which is only to be found in the Christian religion. He offers Your Majesty then, by his Ambassador adjuring you and your whole Kingdom to embrace and follow it.

That Prince, Sir, is more admirable still by his wisdom, judgement, and prudence, than by his conquests and victories. Your Majesty knows his generosity and Royal friendship, you cannot make a better choice than to follow the wise counsels of so great a King your good friend. For my part, Sir, I never begg'd anything of the great God for Your Majesty, but that grace, and I would be ready to lay down a thousand lives that I might obtain it of the divine bounty. May it please Your Majesty to consider that by that action, you will crown all the great and illustrious exploits of your reign, you will eternize your memory, and procure to your self immortal honour and glory in the next world.

Ah, Sir, I adjure Your Majesty not to send back the Ambassador of so great a King his master, for establishing and rendering your alliances and Royal amities inviolable; at least if Your Majesty hath entertained any good thought, or if you find the least inclination to embrace that party, that you would make it known. It is the most acceptable news that he can carry to the King his master. Now if Your Majesty hath resolved not to condescend to what I have had the honour to represent to you, or that you cannot give a favourable answer to the Ambassador, I beg of you to excuse me from carrying your Royal answer, which cannot but be displeasing to the great God whom I adore. You ought not to think it strange that I speak to you in this manner; whosoever is not faithful to his God, cannot be so to his Prince, and Your Majesty ought not to do me the honour to suffer me in your service, if I entertained other sentiments.

The King of Siam answers the Lord Constance

The King heard the discourse of the Lord Constance without interrupting him, and having a little pondered with himself, as one whose mind was taken up with great thoughts, he answered him upon the spot in these terms.

'Fear not that I will force your conscience. But who hath made the King of France my good friend believe that I entertained any such sentiments?'

'Ah, Sir, who can doubt,' replied the Lord Constance, 'but that Your Majesty has those great thoughts, when they consider the protection you give to missionaries, the charity you give to the fathers of China. It is upon that, Sir, that the King of France grounds his persuasion that Your Majesty hath an inclination towards Christianity.'

'But when you told the Ambassador,' added the King, 'the reasons that make me continue in the religion of my ancestors, what answer had you from him?'

'The Ambassador of France,' replied the Lord Constance, found your reasons to be very weighty, but seeing the propositions he made you in the name of the King his master was sincere and disinterested, and that great Monarch had no other prospect but Your Majesty's good, he did not think that any of the reasons which I told him ought to hinder him from obeying his masters commands, especially when he understood that the Ambassador of Persia was arrived in the Kingdom of Siam, and that he brought Your Majesty the Koran[37] to the end you night follow it. In that view the Ambassador of France thought himself obliged to offer Your Majesty the Christian religion, and to adjure you to embrace it.'

'Is it true, answered the King, 'that the Ambassador of Persia brings me the Koran?'

'It is so reported,' reply'd the Lord Constance, to which the King forthwith made answer.

I wish with all my heart the Ambassador of France were here to see what reception the Ambassador of Persia should have from me. Certainly if I had no religion at all I would never choose the Mohammedan.

But to answer the Ambassador of France,' continued the King, 'you shall tell him from me, I think my self extremely obliged to the King of France his master, finding in his memoirs the marks of his most Christian Majesty's Royal friendship, and since the honour that great Prince hath done me is already made public all over the East, I cannot sufficiently acknowledge his civility; but that I am not in the least acquainted: that I refer my self to the wisdom of the most Christian King, that he himself may judge of the importance and difficulty which occur in so nice a matter as the change of a religion received and followed throughout my whole Kingdom without interruption during the space of two thousand two hundred twenty nine years.'

The motives that keep the King of Siam firm in his religion

After all, it is strange to me that the King of France my good friend should so much concern himself in an affair that relates to God, wherein it would seem God does not at all interest himself, but leaves it wholly to our discretion. For would not the true God that made Heaven and Earth, and all things that are therein, and hath given them so different natures and inclinations, when he gave to men like bodies and souls, if he had pleased have also inspired into them the same sentiments for the religion they ought to follow, and for the worship that was most acceptable to him, and make all nations live and die in the same laws? That order amongst men and that unity in religion depending absolutely on divine providence, who could as easily introduce it into the world, as the diversity of sects that in all times have been established in it; ought not one to think that the true God takes as great pleasure to be honoured by different worships and ceremonies, as to be glorified by a prodigious number of creatures that praise him every one in their own way? Would that beauty and variety which we admire in the order of nature, be less admirable in the supernatural order, or less beseeming the wisdom of God? However it be, continued His Majesty, since we know that God is the absolute master of the world, and that we are persuaded that nothing comes to pass contrary to his will, I wholly resign my person and dominions into the arms of the divine mercy and providence, and with all my heart obtest his eternal wisdom to dispose thereof according to his good will and pleasure.

So that I most expressly command you to tell that ambassador that I shall omit nothing that lies in my power, to cherish the Royal friendship of the most Christian King, and instead of complying with the means that he hath proposed to me, I shall take such care during time that God grants me life, that hereafter my successors and subjects, shall on all occasions testify as well as I, the grateful acknowledgement and high esteem which they ought to have for the Royal person of his most Christian Majesty, and for all his successors.

This was the answer of the King of Siam in the same terms that he delivered it to his minister, and as he gave it in writing to my Lord Ambassador. The wit of the Prince sufficiently appears by that reasoning who without any knowledge of the sciences of Europe, hath alleged with so much force and perspicuity the most plausible reasons of the Pagan philosophy against the only true religion. They who know the uprightness of that Prince cannot doubt but that he sincerely said what he thought, and what seemed to him most rational.

The Lord Constance's reply to the King of Siam's objections about changing of religion

The King having said so, was silent for some time, and then eyeing the Lord Constance: 'What do you think,' added he, 'the Ambassador will answer to these reasons which I command you to give him in writing?'

'I shall not fail Sir,' answered the Lord Constance, 'to obey Your Majesty's orders; but I cannot tell what the Ambassador of France will answer to what you have now said to me, which seems to be of very great weight and consequence. Sure I am, he must needs be surprised at the high wisdom and wonderful perspicuity that he'll perceive thereby in Your Majesty.

'However I fancy he may answer, that it is true all the beings which God hath created glorified him every one after its way; but that there is this difference betwixt man and beasts, that when God created these, he gave them different properties and particular instincts, to know what is good for them and pursue it without any reflection, to discern their evil, and avoid it without any ratiocination. So the stag flies from the lion, and tiger the first time he sees them, the chickens new hatched dread the kite and flee under the wings of the hen, without any other instruction but what they have received from nature. But in the creation of man God hath endowed him with a mind and reason to distinguish the good from the evil, and divine providence hath thought it fit that in pursuing and loving the good which is proper for him, with reference to his ultimate end which is to know and love God, man should from the divine bounty merit an eternal reward.

'The truth is, it is as easy for man to make use of his hands, eyes, and feet, in the commission of evil as in doing of good, if his prudence enlightened by the wisdom of God directed him not to pursue the ways of real grandeur, which are not to be found but in the Christian religion, wherein man finds the means of serving God as rest pleases his divine goodness. But all men follow not so holy and so rational notices. It is just so as with Your Majesty's officers, who are not all equally addicted to your Interests, as you but too well know, tho all of them call themselves your subjects, and account it an honour to be employed in your service. So all men serve God, it is true; but in a very different manner. Some like beasts follow their passions and irregular appetites and live in the religion they have been brought up in, without examining it. But others perceiving so great a difference betwixt themselves and beasts raise themselves above their senses, and by means of their reason, which God fails not to enlighten endeavour to know their creator, and the true worship which he would have men render unto him, without any interest but that of pleasing him, and to this sincere search of the truth, God Almighty hath annexed mans' salvation. Hence it is that negligence in not being instructed, and weakness in not following that we judge the best, will render us guilty in the sight of God who is the sovereign judge of all flesh.'

This answer from a man of no studies, who from ten years of age had been applied to trade and commerce, wrought a great surprise in me, when he did me the honour to acquaint me with it. I confessed to him, without any fear of flattery, that a divine consummated in the study of religion, would have been hard put to it to have answered better. The King was smitten with the discourse of the Lord Constance, and if any knowing man, who is acceptable to him, hath the happiness to insinuate into his favour, and procure his esteem, it is not to be despaired but that he may be brought to know and embrace the truth: and if once he come to know it, seeing he is the absolute master of his people, who adore him, all the nations who are under his dominion, will humbly follow his example.

A *Character of King Narai of Siam*

The King of Siam who reigns at present is about fifty five years of age. He is without contradiction, the greatest Prince that ever governed that state. He is somewhat under the middle stature, but straight and well shaped. He hath an engaging air, a sweet and obliging carriage, especially to strangers. And amongst them particularly to the French. He is active and brisk, an enemy of idleness and laziness which seems to be so delightful to the princes of the East, and which they look upon as the greatest prerogative of their crown. This Prince, on the contrary, is always either in the woods a'hunting of elephants, or in his Palace minding the affairs of his Kingdom. He is no lover of war, because it ruins his people whom he tenderly loves; but when his subjects revolt, or that neighbouring Princes offer him the least affront, or transgress the bounds of the respect that's due to him; there is no king in the East that takes a more conspicuous revenge, nor appears more passionate for glory.

Some great men of his Kingdom having rebelled, and having been openly supported by the forces of three kings, whose territories environ the Kingdom of Siam. He attacked those Princes so briskly, that they were obliged to abandon the rebels to his wrath. He would know everything, and having a pregnant and piercing wit, he easily is master of what he has a mind to learn. He is magnificent, generous, and as true a friend as can be imagined. These are the great qualities which acquire him the deference of his neighbours, the fear of his enemies, the esteem and respect of his subjects that's nothing short of adoration. He hath never been given to those vices which are so common to the Princes of the East, nay he hath severely punished the most considerable Mandarins, and principal officers of the crown, for being too much addicted to their pleasures: So that the most invincible obstacle to the conversion of idolatrous Princes, is not to be found in him, I mean the immoderate love of women.

By the sharpness of his wit, he hath discovered the erroneousness of the religion of his ancestors. And he does not believe an annihilated God, according to the popular opinion, or as some of their doctors say, a God, who weary of governing the Heavens, plunges himself to repose, and for ever buries himself in the forgetfulness of what passes in the world, nor a thousand other superstitions preached by the *talapoins*, who are the preachers and priests of the Kingdom. On the contrary, he believes that God is eternal, that his providence continually governs the world and disposes of all things. To the same immortal God he often makes his prayers, and implores his assistance with most profound reverence at least twice a day, for two hours time, in the morning after he is up, and at night before he goes to rest. The Pope having sent him two pictures, one of our Saviour, and the other of the Blessed Virgin, he hath a singular veneration for them, and as a sign thereof, hath placed them in a very high place of his chamber far above him; and never speaks of them but with honour and respect.

The Embassy which the King sent to him, if it hath not determined him to embrace Christianity, had at least, made him reflect and consider. As he has an extraordinary esteem for the wisdom of the most Christian King, so when the Lord Constance explained to him the sole reason that moved that great Monarch to send the Ambassador to him, he seemed affected therewith, and it is known that he hath many times reflected thereupon since. These are considerations that should excite those who may read these memoirs, to pray to God for the conversion of that Prince, which would be attended with the conversion of an innumerable multitude of people, and which without doubt would gain to our holy law the neighbouring Princes, who admire the conduct and parts of the King of Siam.

There lie great obligations upon us to that Monarch, for all the marks of esteem and goodwill wherewith he was pleased to honour us, and we are glad we have the occasion of publishing the same; from the time that the Lord Constance made him sensible of our ways and the prospects that put us upon acting, that Prince favoured us upon all occasions, notwithstanding the bad impressions that some endeavoured to give him of Jesuits. The Lord Constance omitted not to set off to him to the best advantage the extraordinary goodness that the King of France hath for our company, and that's the thing that contributed most to make us merit his favours. It is an example of great influence upon the mind of the King of Siam; and so indeed, he hath by obliging cares intimated to us that he will imitate it, and hath often assured us of his Royal protection, and that we should never fail of a safe refuge in his Kingdom.

We began to make observations at Louvo

So soon as we arrived at Louvo we began to make observations, and especially such as might be needful to us for observing exactly the eclipse of the moon, which was to happen on the eleventh of December. We could not till then make use of our instruments for these operations; because all the while we were at Siam, the city and country about were so overflown, that we had no place to fix them upon. Nay and the house too where we lodged being only of wood, the least motion made it so shake, that our Pendulums and Quadrants were thereby wholly disordered.

Observation about the variation of the needle

December the sixth and seventh we observed by the astronomical ring of Mr. Butterfield, that the variation of the needle was two degrees twenty minutes towards the West. This observation was constantly alike during those two days.

The ninth of the same month by the heights taken of the same border of the sun, morning and evening the true hour of noon by the Pendulum with seconds, was 12 h.5.3.

Plate 26. The king observes the eclipse of the sun at the palace of Louvo

The variation of the needle by the Parallatick Engine of the *Sieur Chapotot* was observed.

One time	16.min. only	}	
Another	31.min.	}	Towards the West.
Another	35.min.	}	
Another	38.min.	}	

That variation was found by taking several times morning and evening the height of the sun, and every time observing the azimuth, the needle still continuing upon the line of the south and north.

The King of Siam observes with the Jesuits an Eclipse of the moon in his Palace

In the last audience that His Majesty gave the Ambassador, he told him that he would take it well that we made the observation of the first eclipse in his presence. Some days after he commanded the Lord Constance to acquaint us with the honour he intended to put upon us. For that effect they pitched upon a Royal house called Thlee-poussonne, a short league from Louvo eastwards, not far from the forest where the King was a'hunting of elephants. The lord Constance carried us to view the place two days before the eclipse, that's to say the ninth of December. A more convenient place could not have been chosen, we saw the Heavens on all hands, and had room enough to place our instruments. Having put all things in order we came back to Louvo.

Next day December the tenth, by the elevations of the same border of the Sun, taken in the morning betwixt nine and ten o'clock, and in the evening betwixt two and three, the true hour of noon by the same Pendulum with seconds was. 12. h. 2. 31.

The variation of the needle by the Parallatick Engine.

One time	28 min.	}	
Another	33 min.	}	Towards the West.
Another	21 min.	}	

In the sequel we shall examine whether or no the needle of the astronomical ring decline too much towards the West, as it is very probable; for if so, then something is to be deducted from the variation of the Cape of Good Hope, which we found to be eleven degrees and a half towards the West, and the pilots with their compasses only nine degrees.

The King of Siam invites the Ambassador to an elephant hunting

The same day the King invited my Lord Ambassador, to come and see the illuminations that were made for the hunting of elephants. It was His Majesty's pleasure that we also should be there, and did us the honour about four in the afternoon to send us six elephants with the Barcalon's Lieutenant to be our guide. We sent to Thlee-poussaonne our telescope and a spiral pendulum that went very right and was set by the sun. For we were to observe the eclipse there according to the orders. The King's method of the hunting was in the manner that I am now about to relate.

A description of that hunting

About forty six or forty seven thousand men had surrounded and made an enclosure in the woods and upon the mountains of a long square, whereof the two great sides might very well be ten leagues a piece, and the other two, each three leagues. All that vast extent was bordered by two rows of fires, which ranged all round upon two lines at four or five steps distance once from another. These fires are kept burning all night long with the wood of the forest, and stand seven or eight foot high in the air, being supported by little square platforms raised upon four stakes, which was the cause that they would be all seen at once and very far off too. It seemed to me in the dark the finest sight and loveliest illumination that ever I saw. Great lanterns placed at convenient distances made the distinction of quarters, which were commanded by different heads, with a certain number of elephants of war and hunts-men armed like soldiers. Ever now and then they fired some small field pieces, that by that noise and the fires they might frighten the elephants, that should attempt to force their passage through as they had done some days before, because that circumspection had not been used. There was a very steep mountain within the precincts of the hunting; but that being looked upon to be inaccessible to those creatures, they had the time before neglected to secure it by fires, guards and artillery. However ten or twelve of them escaped that way, and for that purpose made use of a very surprising expedient; fastening themselves by their trunks to one of the trees that were upon the side of that very steep mountain, they made a skip to the root of the next, and in the same manner clambered from tree to tree with incredible efforts, until they got to the top of the mountain, from whence they saved themselves in the woods. What had happened at that time, was the cause that nothing was neglected at this bout, that so none might any more escape.

The King of Siam demands the Chevalier de Fourbin from the Ambassador

The King upon his return from hunting , found the French drawn up in a line at the entry into the forest, and mounted on elephants. He eyed them very much, and took pleasure to see men of so good means. He had just given audience to the Ambassador, which had been pretty long. About the end of it, he sent for the Chevalier de Fourbin, an old officer, who had gained reputation on many occasions. The Lord Constance had prayed the Ambassador to leave him at Siam with the King his master . Nay His Majesty himself thought fit to demand him of the Ambassador, and made him a present of a very lovely shable, as a mark that he received him into his service. He added to the present besides, a vest of a flowered stuff, with gold buttons. In the meantime it was late, and the King was gone home; however we alighted in a pleasant place, where a splendid collation of all sorts of sweet-meats and fruit was prepared for us. My lord Ambassador drank the King of Siam's health in a large cup of beaten gold which he had presented to him. The lid and salver of it were of the same metal. This place was presently encompassed with elephants of war and fires, to secure us from tigers and other wild beasts, that were enclosed within the precincts. Afterward the Ambassador took his way back to Louvo, and the Lord Constance conducting us straight to the castle of Thlee-poussonne, where the King was already come to be present at the observation of the Eclipse.

The Jesuits prepare to observe in the King 's presence at Theepossone

About nine of the clock we came to the side of the canal, which leads to the castle, and there we found one of the King's *balons*, which had waited for us a long while. This canal is very broad, and above a league in length. It was lighted on both sides with an infinite number of such fires as were mentioned before, which all together in the obscurity of the night rendered a very charming prospect. When we were got within half a quarter of a league of the castle, our water-men, who till then had pulled hard and made much noise in rowing, began to row so easily, that we hardly heard the noise of their oars. They told us, that we must either hold our peace, or speak very low. The truth is when we landed, all was so quiet, though there were a great many soldiers and Mandarins thereabouts, that we thought we were in some remote solitude. The reverence they have for the King's person, makes them observe that profound silence in all places where he is. We presently fitted several telescopes upon some props that had been raised to support them. It did not require much time to adjust our instruments; so that we took boat again an hour after, and went to spend part of the night in the house of the Lord Constance, which is almost an hundred paces from the Palace.

When we were to step ashore at the foot of the wall which is on the other side of the canal, there was danger of being pricked by a kind of caltrop; for there were a great many iron chains laid in length at half a foot distance from one another, and these take up the wall. They are armed with a double row of thick iron spikes; they are every night, without fail, stretched round the castle, and serve to hinder any approaching to it. At our coming ashore, the Lord Constance gave us very timely notice to take heed to ourselves, having observed that one of our Fathers was about to step on land. He sent for the officer of the guard, and ordered him to take up those caltrops which hindered our coming ashore. Having then got as near the walls as we could, we walked in a little path two foot broad, which is left free, for making the rounds in the night time, and about eleven o clock at night we arrived at the house of the Lord Constance.

They begin the observation of the eclipse before the King

Having rested three or four hours there, we re-embarked and went to the gallery where the observation was to be made. It was then near three of the clock in the morning. So soon as we were come, we put all things in readiness: we had already showed His Majesty, by the Lord Constance's mediation; a great figure of an Eclipse, wherein one might see the moon entering by little and little under the shadow, with the immersion of the spots, and His Majesty seemed to be pleased with it. We prepared a very good telescope for him five foot long, in the window of a room that looked into the gallery where we were. The Penumbra being pretty far advanced, notice was sent to the King, who immediately came to that window. We were sitting upon Persian carpets, some at the telescopes, others at the pendulum, and others were to write down the time of the observation. We saluted His Majesty with a profound inclination of body, and then began to observe,

After midnight,	Hou.	Min.	Sec.
The beginning of the Penumbra,	02	53	00
The Penumbra thicker,	03	02	00
The Penumbra very thick,	00	12	00
The doubtful begin of the Ecl.	00	15	08
The certain beginning,	00	19	00
Riccioli,	00	19	45
The beginning of Grimaldi,	00	21	34
The end of Grimaldi,	00	22	36
Kepler,	00	29	32
Gassendi,	00	32	36
Heraclides.	00	36	40

	Hou.	Min.	Sec.
The beginning of Capricorn,	00	37	10
The middle of Capricorn,	00	39	00
The beginning of Plato,	03	48	25
The Middle of Plato,	00	49	05
The end of Plato,	00	49	24
Menelaus,	00	58	45
St. Denis,	00	59	49
Plinius,	04	02	11
Promontorium acutum,	00	07	40
The beginning of Mare Chrysium,	00	14	30
The middle of Mare Chrysium,	00	17	45
The end of Mare Chrysium,	00	19	18
The total Immersion.	00	22	45

The King puts several questions of astronomy to the Jesuits

The King expressed a particular satisfaction, seeing all the spots of the moon in the telescope, and especially perceiving that the type or map that was made at the observatory of Paris, agreed so well with it. He put several questions to us during the Eclipse; as for instance, why did the moon appear revers'd in the telescope? Why was the part of the moon eclipsed, still to be seen? What o'clock was it at Paris? For what could observations made by concert in remote countries be useful? Etc. Whilst we satisfied all his questions, one of the chief officers of his house brought us upon a large silver basin,[38] six cassocks and as many cloaks of flowered satin, wherewith the King presented us in a most obliging manner. He had a mind to look in a telescope twelve foot long, which Father Fontenay made use of; and we presently carried it to him. He suffered us rise and stand in his presence, and would look in the telescope after us; for we must needs set it to its point when we presented it to him. They who know what reverence and respect the Kings of Siam expect from those who are in their presence, have spoken of that favour to us, as of a very rare thing.

His Majesty would then know which of the fathers was to return to France; and being told that it was I, he told me very obligingly, that seeing he was sending ambassadors to France, who were not well acquainted with the customs and manners of Europe, he trusted much to the good counsels that I should give them, and especially the good offices that I would render them by means of our friends; that he had ordered them to demand of the King of France twelve mathematicians of our society, and for that end to address themselves to Father de la Chaize, that he might second their demand; in short, that he made no doubt but that I would also in particular do what lay in my power in managing of that affair. At the same time the Lord high Chamberlain, in His Majesty's presence presented me with two lovely Crucifixes in a large gold basin. The Christ was of massive gold, the cross of tambag, which is made of mixture of seven parts of gold, and three parts more of a metal as precious as gold it self, the foot was of silver. His Majesty told me, that the biggest was designed for Father la Chaize the King's confessor, whose merit and fidelity in the service of his master, he knew by the character that the Lord Constance had given of him. Then he fell a'praising the zeal and disinterestedness of his own minister, whom he always called our brother; telling us, that he had received most signal services from him on all occasions that ever presented. After that His Majesty commanded me to tell the Father Confessor, when in his name I presented him that that crucifix, that he could not render him more acceptable service, nor more useful to his State, than in obtaining for him twelve mathematicians from the King; that I might assure them, that before their arrival, there would be an observatory, a house and a church for them at Louvo as well as at Siam. At the same time he enjoined the Lord Constance to get them forthwith built, and with assistance of the Fathers to choose places for them in the two towns I have been speaking of. As for the other crucifix, I freely give it you, said he, with a most gracious look, that it may serve you for a faithful companion during all your voyage. Let me hear news from you as oft as you can; and above all things, endeavour to return back again with the first opportunity. I beseech Divine providence, that takes care of the conduct of the Universe, to give you a prosperous voyage. At length, having recommended to my care what he then had enjoined me, and what he was told by others from him, he again wished me a speedy return, and so went away, expressing the pleasure and satisfaction that he had received during the two hours that he had done us the honour to be present at our observations. Nobody was near his person all the while he was with us, but the Lord Constance, the Lord Chamberlain, and a gentleman of his bed-chamber. So many favours to which it behoved us to answer upon the spot, hindered us from observing the immersion of several spots. After the King was gone, the Lord Constance stayed alone with us, and having well remarked the circle of the shadow, and Mare Chrysium in the telescope, he observed together with us the rest of the phases until the total immersion.

From thence we returned to the house of the Lord Constance, where we expected the emergence of the moon, which appeared above a quarter of an hour before sun-rising, that is to say, at six o'clock and six minutes, the beginning of the emergence was at 6 h. 1 m. 11 sec. or rather, at 6 h. 9 m and to that observation it was concluded we must hold: It is true, the vapours of the horizon hindered us a little. The moon was still to be seen near the horizon at 6 h. 22 m. 0 sec. but soon after she set, and the sun rose. The pendulum was set at one o'clock afternoon, and from three o'clock in the afternoon the day before had lost but three minutes and three seconds. The hours set down in the observation are according to the clock not rectified. Thus the hours on noon by the great pendulum, observed the ninth and tenth of December, 1685, and the loss of the little one in respect of the great, according to which it was set the tenth of March, at three o'clock in the afternoon, show that the little pendulum at 4 h. 22 m. 45. sec. after midnight, next day went too slow by a minute, and that the true hour was 4 h. 23 m. 45 sec.

I have communicated these observations to the members of the Academy Royal of Sciences, and it was found that the total immersion having been observed the eleventh of that instant,

	Hou.	Min.	Sec.
At Louvo,	04	23	45
At Paris by Mr. Cassins,	09	49	30
The difference of merid.	06	34	15

At 6 h. 9 m. the same little pendulum went too slow 1 m. 25 Sec. the hour then was 6 h. 10 m. 25 Sec. at that time the emergence began, as it appeared at Louvo. The same emergence was observed at the observatory of Paris by Monsieur Cassins.

	Hou.	Min.	Sec.
The difference of Meridians,	11	36	18
	06	34	07

	Deg.	Min.
So that the diff of longit will be	98	32
The longitude of Paris being	22	30
Then that of Louvo will be	121	02

By the observations of the Lunar Eclipse, February 21. 1682, the longitude of Siam was found to be of 121 degrees, which exactly agrees with these new observations.

It is a strange thing that there should be modern maps that put the longitude of Siam in the 145 degree, whereas the great map of the observatory made long before these observations, gives it 122 degrees, within a degree or little more of these observations.

A Brahmin astrologer, who was at Louvo, had foretold this eclipse to a quarter of an hour almost; but he was mightily mistaken as to the duration of it, saying that the emergence would not appear above the horizon till after the sun was up. Some days before, we had a conference with the Brahmin; but since we understood not the Siamese language, we could not learn anything of the manner how he calculates eclipses. He proposed to us some questions about the sun and stars, which were easily answered, as for instance, in what sign the sun was? How many fixed stars we reckoned, etc. He asked us, if what we had read in some Chinese books, was true, that there always appeared a fixed and very sparkling star perpendicularly over the palace of the Emperor of China at Peking? We told him it was a fable; and it was no hard matter to make him of the same mind. He was not of the opinion of the Siamese *talapoins*, who imagine and teach, that when the moon is eclipsed, a dragon devours her, and casts her up again. When it is objected to them, how it comes to pass then that we know and foretell the very moment of the eclipse, how great it will be, how long it is to last; how comes it to pass that sometimes there is but part of the moon eclipsed, and sometimes all of it? They dryly answer, that this dragon has his meals regulated, that we know the time of them, and the measure likewise of his appetite, which is sometimes greater and sometimes less. One had as good say nothing at all, as to offer to prove that those all are chimerical notions; for they wilfully persist in their illusion. To conclude this matter, I shall here subjoin the letter which the Lord Constance wrote to Father de la Chaize, wherein that minister had been pleased to give him an account of what passed at the last audience which the King gave us upon occasion of the eclipse; it hath been translated out of the Portuguese.

Most Reverend Father,

I cannot express to Your Most Reverend Paternity the joy that I have felt this year, and I hope you will not take it ill, if I give you a particular account of the grounds and causes of it. The first was the arrival of his most Christian Majesty's ambassador at this court, which hath furnished me the occasion that I so passionately desired of rendering to that Prince in the person of his ambassador all the services I am capable of. The second was the great and pious matters which that ambassador came here to manage; and lastly, the coming of six of my brethren, whom the most Christian King hath sent into these parts on so noble a design, these enterprises, worthy of so great a Monarch, have ravished into admiration all the Princes of the East, and have wrought in them an ardent desire of soliciting the friendship of so wise and generous a King. But the King my master hath been more affected with these things, than all the other Princes of the Indies besides. Though before anything of these mutual expressions of friendship, the King my master had conceived a high esteem and particular amity for his most Christian Majesty, I dare assure Your Paternity, that since the time I have had the honour to serve him, he hath never seemed better pleased then in hearing the relations of the conquests, victories and other grandeurs that always attend his most Christian Majesty. I will not enlarge any more upon that, because it would be impossible for me or any else who has the honour to know the King, my master, to express how sensible he is of anything that regards the glory of the most Christian King, whom he most particularly loves and esteems. Besides, that which completes my joys in this juncture, is, that I hereby find an occasion of demanding the good correspondente of Your Paternity, for whom I shall ever entertain the esteem I ought. Wherefore I adjure you most heartily, to let me know your intentions, and to assist me with your good counsels, and you will find me ready to do anything, especially when the glory of God, or the interests of the most Christian King are concerned. These reasons have obliged me in the name of the King my master, to demand Father Trachard of the Reverend Superior to return into France, and I have entrusted him with certain affairs, which he is to communicate to your paternity.

I have presented the Father Superior and my other brethren who are come with him, to the King my master. His Majesty did me the honour to receive them with extraordinary marks of affection. He hath also honoured them with his presence, having nobody near him but four of his chief Mandarins, when they observed the eclipse which happened the eleventh of the month of December. During all that time, His

Majesty was not four foot distant from the Fathers who sat, making use of their instruments, and acting with as great freedom as if they had been in the observatory of Paris. Nay, the King had the goodness to call the Father Superior to him, and to order him to set his telescope, to the end His Majesty might the more easily observe; taking the instrument out of the Father's hand, as if he had been his familiar friend. During that observation, he did the fathers the honour to bestow upon each of them a cassock and cloak of China damask; and for Father Trachard, who will present you this letter, he added a golden crucifix, that he might give him a faithful companion for his voyage (these are the King's own words) charging the same Father to present another much bigger to your paternity, with his particular desires that you would procure from the most Christian King twelve Fathers mathematicians of the Society, who will be received here with much joy. The King my master, having already ordered the Father Superior to choose a place at Louvo, and another at Siam, there to build churches, observatories, and houses that may be proper for them; he charged me at the same time to take a course that all these things should be ready to receive the Fathers upon their arrival. If the six Fathers mathematicians and my brethren have been able to do such brave things in two months time, what would not fifty or more be able to do in the space of twenty years?

I have given the Ambassador of the King my master some curiosities of this country, to be presented in my name to Your Paternity. I pray you to accept of them, and it shall be to me a new occasion of joy to all things that depend on me. I commend my self to Your Holy Sacrifices, and am, with all due respect and friendship,

Most Reverend Father,
Your most Humble,
and obedient
Servant and Brother,
CONSTANTINE PHAULKON.

The way of catching elephants

After the King had observed the eclipse with us in the manner I have related, he invited us to participate in the diversion which that day he gave in the forest, for taking the elephants which were there kept enclosed. We made ready to set out about seven of the clock: then we were told that my Lord Ambassador was set out, and that the King was coming out of his palace. Presently after the Ambassador arrived on horse-back with all his retinue; the Bishop of Metellopolis, the Abbot de Lyon, and Monsieur Vachet attended him. No sooner had all alighted from their horses, and mounted the elephants that were prepared for us, but the King appeared attended by a great number of Mandarins mounted on elephants of war. We followed, and entered about a league into the wood, as far as the enclosure where the wild elephants were. It was a square park of about three or four hundred geometrical paces, paled in by great stakes, however large openings were left at convenient distances, and within there were fourteen elephants of all sizes. So soon as the company came, they made a ring of about an hundred elephants of war posted round the park, to hinder the wild ones from breaking through the palisade; we were behind this ring, and near to the King. Twelve of the strongest of the tame elephants were sent in within the precincts of the park, every one of them carrying two men with great ropes and running nooses, where of the ends were made fast to the elephants they rode upon. They presently made up to the elephants they had a mind to catch, who finding himself pursued, offered at the barrier to break through and make his escape; but all the way was blocked up by elephants of war, by whom they were forced back within the enclosure again, and as they ran to and again within that space, the huntsmen, who were mounted on tame elephants, threw their nooses so exactly upon the places where the beasts were to set their foot, that they never failed catching of them. Indeed, they were all taken in the space of an hour.

They afterwards tied every wild elephant, and on each side of him put a tame one, which were to be left a fortnight with him, that by their means he might be daunted.

Amongst that herd of wild elephants, there were two or three very young and little ones. The King said he would send one of them to the Duke of Burgundy; but considering that the Duke of Anjou might be emulous and take exceptions thereat, he added that he would also send him one less, that so there might be no jealousy nor dispute betwixt them.

When the hunting was over, the King told the Ambassador, that they had never had better sport in so short a time, that therefore they ought to give good thanks. He then prayed him to leave with him Monsieur de la Mare. The Ambassador presented him to him, and His Majesty presently made the Lord Constance give him a vest of cloth of silver with gold buttons. Monsieur de la Mare is a very able engineer, and a very honest man: He hath long served both by sea and land having from his youth applied himself to the mathematicals, wherein he hath made great progress. He is very skilful in navigation, fortification, and geometry: on that occasion all the gentlemen took their leave of the King, who wished them a happy voyage, and expressed himself with condescending civility towards them.

The Ambassador takes his audience of leave of His Majesty of Siam

The King returned to Thlee-poussonne, and the Ambassador to Louvo. The King came there also in the evening, that next day he might give the Ambassador his audience of leave. December the twelfth, about eight of the clock in the morning, an Oya who is a Mandarin of the first rank, came with a pompous train to wait upon the Ambassador from his house to audience: the ceremonies were much the same that were observed the day of his entry and first audience, save that the Ambassador's gentlemen followed him no farther than into the second court of the Palace. The audience was not long. The King having charged the Ambassador with his compliments for the most Christian King, and all the Royal family, made him a present of a great piece of golden plate, which in the Siamese language is called Telom, and in Portuguese, Bolseta, and is the badge of a great Oya and Prince. None at the court of Siam but only the Prince of Cambodia is allowed to have the like. The Lord Constance told the Ambassador from the King, that

His Majesty would willingly have completed the ceremony which is observed on such occasions, but that he omitted it because of some things, which perhaps would not be agreeable to the Europeans. His Majesty ordered a crucifix, such as he had given me the day before, to be presented to the Abbot de Lyon, and another to Monsieur Vachet, whom he sent to France to accompany his ambassadors. As they came from the audience, a table was prepared with above fifty covers, in a neat hall, in the middle of a grass plot, encompassed with water-works; all were served in large dishes of plate, and the plenty of dishes was no less considerable, than the ragouts were delicious. No kind of wine was wanting , and the sweet-meats of China and Japan were highly esteemed above anything that was there. The Ambassador and lord Constance would needs have us to be present at the treat. When that splendid entertainment was over, the Ambassador embarked for Siam, being accompanied by a great many mandarins of all the orders. I stayed with the Lord Constance till next day, and when I was to part from our fathers, it troubled me extremely to leave them. The Father Superior and other two would needs go along with me, and wait upon my Lord Ambassador on shipboard.

Our water-men rowed all night long, and December the fourteenth, about seven o'clock in the morning, we arrived at the Ambassador's house in Siam. His servants were employed in putting on board the China and other furniture of his Palace, which the King had presented him with. Before I left the city, I had a long discourse with Father Suarez and Father Fucity. These Fathers have learnt to suffer without complaining, and as to that point they have a niceness of conscience that makes them observe measures, that the strictest morality could not always comply with. They only hinted to me that they had been surprised, that the Jesuits of the Indies should be accused of taking money (as it is practised in parishes) for administering, baptism, saying mass, etc. Seeing an infinite number of people could bear witness to the contrary, and they protested to me before God that never anything had been done, that might in the least alter the rule of our institution. I had long desired an opportunity of being cleared as to a matter of fact that had made a noise, but I had forgot to do it till then. I asked them if it was true, that a certain minister of Batavia, called Ferreira, was an apostate Jesuit, as it was given out. They made me answer, that he had never been neither of our company, nor of any other religious society, which he had acknowledged to several persons, and to Father Fucity himself at Batavia; that perhaps the thing that had given occasion to the report, was the conformity in name which he had with a Jesuit, who is also called Ferreira, and who hath been formerly mentioned, from whence ground had been taken to confound the two into one person. Would to God that the original of such kind of reports were only to be attributed to a bare mistake; for how many such have been of late years published in certain libels that have flown about in Holland? Distance of place hath in this favoured the malicious, and the natural inclination or interest that men have to give credit to that that's evil, has been the cause that some have believed it. Having viewed things at nearer distance, I have with humble submission adored providence, that suffers men sometimes to lash out and speak the worst of those, of whom, had they been just, they might have said the best. They ought to consider that very far from injuring those whom they would decry, they only exercise their patience, keep them humble, and hinder them from receiving in this world a weak recompense for the labours which deserve a more solid reward in Heaven, which is a great kindness to them; whereas all reflects upon religion, which is exposed to the censure of heretics, and the contempt of Infidels.

Departure from Siam

We parted from Siam the fourteenth of December, about four or five o'clock in the evening. The Lord Constance who would wait upon the Ambassador as far as the bar, followed him in a stately and princely *balon*, which the King sometime since had obliged him to take, and just such another as that which carried the Ambassador. The train consisted of twenty Balons of State, which went as low as the Tabangue, where he was received the day of his entry. As soon as they arrived there, they drew up and made a lane, according to their quality, that the Ambassador's *balon* might pass betwixt them, and so the Mandarins who were on board of them took their leave and returned. We came to Bangkok about four o'clock in the morning, where the Lord Constance prayed the Ambassador to stay till next day, that he might view the fort-ifications of the citadel, and give his judgement of them. Whilst we were at Bangkok, a frigate of the King of Siam passed that way, carrying the letter which His Majesty wrote to the King of France. The letter was in a gold box shaped like a cone, and this box was put up in another bigger silver box, which also was enclosed within a third of Japan wood varnished, wrapped up in a piece of rich silk stuff flowered with gold. All this was in a gilt pyramid placed aloft on the stern of the frigate, with many parasols to cover it. When the frigate passed by with its convoy of Balons of State, the governors of places that lie upon the river, made a discharge of all their artillery, and every one of them waited upon the letter as far as their government reached, receiving it from one another with the same honours and ceremonies.

The King of Siam's letter is carried on board the Oyseau

Sunday, December the sixteenth, the Ambassador arrived at the bar, and the same day about seven of the clock at night went on board the Oyseau. As I had been all along in the *balon* of the Lord Constance, so he would have me to go on board of one of his frigates at the mouth of the river, and stay with him there two days to dispatch some business. There he gave me a letter to the King, which I have had the honour to present to His Majesty. We afterwards weighed and came to an anchor again near the Ambassador's ship, to do him the honour that he had never done to any before. The King of Siam's ambassadors, who were not as yet come on board the Oyseau, desired the Ambassador to send them the long-boat to carry on board their master's letter. They went and fetched it from the frigate, and when they were come to the ship's side, the second ambassador put the pyramid wherein it was upon his shoulders, and so came on board, no body daring to touch it. It was placed upon aloft on the stern with the parasols, and one and twenty guns were fired at the ceremony. Nevertheless the Ambassadors were prevailed upon to carry it into their cabin, because being so placed, it would hinder the working of the ship. The Ambassador and lord Constance visited one another on board their ships, with the usual salutes; and the last time that the Lord Constance came on board the Oysean to take his leave of the Ambassador, they gave one another great marks of mutual friendship, and parted with grief. Our three fathers who were come so far, returned with the Lord Constance and Bishop of Metellopolis, leaving me troubled and pensive, but I endeavoured to moderate my sorrow by the hopes of seeing them again within a few years. When all were gone into the chaloop, the Lord Constance called me and gave me a chaplet made of the costly wood of Calomba, but the cross and great beads were of tambag. Then the chaloop put off, and we saluted her with thirteen guns for the last farewell.

We were ready to set sail, and stayed for nothing now but Monsieur Vachet, and the Ambassador's secretary; they had fallen down with the rest to the mouth of the river, but for three days time nobody could tell what was become of them. This put a stop to our voyage, and we were just going to weigh anchor when we saw them coming with two or three Mandarins of the retinue of the Ambassadors of Siam. The currents had carried away the galley they were on board of with so much violence, that they could not resist it, nor come up with us sooner; several others were to have embarked with us; but the season already far spent, suffered us not to stay for them, so that we put under sail.

Departure from the bar of Siam

And parted from the bar of Siam with a good wind the two and twentieth of December. The Lord Constance had sent us on board all sorts of fresh provisions in so great abundance, that we were fain to pray him to send no more, and even to leave some of them. We came to Bantam the tenth of January, after we had run aground in the strait of Banca through the fault of the Dutch pilot, whom we took in at Batavia. Nobody can well tell what whimsy made him cast anchor, which put us in danger of being cast away; for had not the ground been so away as it was, the anchor we drooped would have bulged the ship that ran foul of it; and it was some trouble to get her off. A Dutch ship that came after, had more wit than to follow us, and so was not stranded as we were.

So soon as we came to an anchor before Bantam, the Ambassador sent M. de Cibois, Lieutenant of the ship to make a complement to the Governor, not doubting but that he would come off with better grace than he did the time before, and the rather, that he was not ignorant of the civilities that the General of Batavia had shown the Ambassador; but we were mistaken. Monsieur Cibois could not speak to the Governor, who, they said, was sick, and bid the Governor of the fort tell him, that they would send on board fresh provisions. This promise amounted to no more but the sending of two or three bullocks, with an excuse that there was no more to be had. In the evening came a man, who pretended to be sent from the Governor, and demanded money for the bullocks, which it was thought the Governor had presented to my Lord Ambassador. That messenger was used as he deserved, and had an answer given him to carry to the Governor, suitable to such a clownish and uncivil behaviour. So next day we made sail towards the Cape of Good Hope.

We had the best luck imaginable in passing the strait of the sound, which is a very difficult passage to shoot, because of contrary winds that commonly reign there in that season. But God was graciously pleased to send us most excellent weather, which in a few hours put us out of all danger. We had a more particular instance of his divine providence three days after: Our pilots had a mind to keep thirty or forty leagues to the southward of the Isle Mony, and thought they had steered their course accordingly, when about break of day Monsieur de Vaudricourt, made land at three or four leagues distance from us, we had certainly run foul of it, had it blown a little fresher in the night-time. This land is so low that it is not to be known but by the breaks [breakers]. We were obliged to bear away to the leeward, and leave it to the south, contrary to our first design. During the whole voyage, we had as fair weather as heart could wish, until we were off of the Isle of Bourbon, February the thirteenth, where we met with one of the most violent gusts of wind that the old officers, as they said, had ever seen. It lasted three days, and having carried away the frigate's main sail, separated her from us much about the same place that we lost her when we were outward bound, and we had no more sight of her, till that day we came to an anchor at the Cape of Good Hope, whither she had got two days before us.

News from an English ship outward bound

March the tenth, we made a sail bound towards the Indies: As we drew nearer we knew her to be an English ship by her colours. My lord Ambassador being willing to hear news from Europe, sent Monsieur Cibois and his secretary, who spoke very good English, to the Captain. They brought back word that ship had been five months out of England, and that she was bound straight for Tonkin, without touching any where; that all was quiet in Europe; that the King of England had defeated the rebels, and made the Duke of Monmouth, who commanded them, prisoner, who was shortly after beheaded; that many of his followers had suffered death, and other tasted of his Britannic Majesty's mercy.

These were very acceptable news to us, and especially when they told us that the English ship had made the Cape the day before about seven leagues off. We then found that we were much nearer in than we imagined, and next day casting out the lead, we found ourselves about seven o'clock in the morning, upon the bank of the needles, in ninety fathoms water, and about noon we made the Cape of the needles. The wind was then fair, and we made the best use of it all night long, so that next day we made the Cape of Good Hope about eight leagues off. About three in the afternoon we came to the mouth of the bay; but the wind blowing too high for putting in, we came to an anchor betwixt Isle Robin and the main land, near the frigate.

The day following, March the thirteenth, the wind being abated, we came to an anchor in the bay, amongst seven great Dutch ships that made up the East-India fleet that was to return to Europe, so soon as three or four ships more, which they daily expected, were come to the Cape. The Ambassador sent a compliment to the Governor of the fort, who received it as kindly as the time before, when we passed that way. We saluted the fort with seven guns, and they returned us gun for gun. Whilst we were taking in water, and providing other necessary provisions, I went to pay a visit to the Governor, who had asked news of the six Jesuits whom he had seen the year before. He made me many offers of services, offering me a friend's house, if I would stay ashore, because the observatory, which was pulled down to be built again with greater magnificence, was not yet finished. Being informed that I was to return to the Indies with several other Jesuits, he added very obligingly, that all should be ready against our arrival, and invited me and all my companions before hand, to come and refresh ourselves there. After all these civilities, he made me a present of four lovely tiger's skins, and of a little tame beast which he had taken in his last expedition; by the hair and size of it, it resembles a squirrel, and had much the shape of one, when he gave it me, he told me it was the implacable enemy of serpents, and was at cruel wars with them.

It was then vintage time, which was very far advanced, we ate of the grapes of Africa that are plentiful, and have a rare good taste. The white wine is very delicate, and if the Dutch knew as well how to cultivate vines, as to make colonies and pursue trade, they might have excellent wines there of the other colour.

The Governor told me that he was just returned from a great journey he had made up into the country northward, where he had discovered many Nations, who have some form of government, and well ordered economy, as may be seen in the description of the Cape of Good Hope.

Putting out from the bay of the Cape

Having taken on board provisions, and our sick men, who were recovered by the land-air, we put out of the bay the twenty sixth of March. We steered our course towards the Ascension Island. This isle lies in eight degrees south latitude, and seven degrees fifteen minutes longitude. There is so great plenty of tortoises or turtle to be had there, that in a night or two as many may be caught as will satisfy to feed a whole ship's company, consisting of four hundred men, for a fortnights time. These tortoises are of an extraordinary bigness, and in the evening after sunset, when they come ashore to lay their eggs, men turn as many of them as they intend to take, upon their backs, for the seashore is full of them, and in that condition they leave them till next day, when they come and carry them on board in boats. We made that isle, which appears at a great distance by a high hill, the nineteenth of April, about four of the clock in the afternoon, we had a good wind, and we should have lost time if we had put into the road, and therefore the Ambassador would not stop there.

We passed the line at the first meridian

We passed the line at the first meridian, the seven and twentieth of April, and from that time forward, till the last of May, we had very easy winds, but then met with a strong contrary wind. Next day towards the evening, we were much surprised to make the Isle of Corvo on head of us, which is the most northern Isle of the Azores. Our pilots thought we had been near an hundred leagues beyond those islands. I have read in many journals, and learnt from several able seamen, that men are many times out in that course, and that they never fail to make the Azores, when they think they have passed them. That is a sign that in those places the currents set westward with great rapidity. So that men should sail with much circumspection upon their return from Africa, that they may not fall into so considerable a mistake, which may prove to be of fatal consequence.

June the eleventh, it blew so fierce a storm, that we were forced to furl all our sails, and to lay a-try under one course. That gust lasted not long, and we stood away eastward. One day, as we were sailing with all sails drawing, and were in hopes soon to make the land of Ushan, because we were already got into the soundings, a seaman upon the watch cried out, that we were about to run upon a rock. It was late, and the darkness of the night increased our fear, occasioned by so present a danger; but it was over in a trice, when instead of that pretended rock, we found a great fishing boat at an anchor. Had not we tacked in the very nick of time, we had been foul of her. The poor men on board were so alarmed, that they still kept crying with all their force, that we would take pity of them, though we were already at a pretty good distance from them.

Next day we met a boat, that assured us we were but eight leagues from Ushan. This news rejoiced all the ship's company, which was increased next day by the sight of that island. When we made it, we clapped on all the sail we could, that we might stand in to the Iroise, but it being again tide, and the wind failing us, we were forced to come to an anchor betwixt the black stones and the main land in five and twenty fathoms water on sandy ground. Next day, the eighteenth of June, we came to an anchor in the road of Brest. There we sang *Te Deum*, to thank God for so prosperous a voyage, with a noise of all the guns of both ships, and afterwards we went ashore.

Book 6

The Manners and Religion of the Siamese

I will say nothing but what I have seen my self, or what I have learned from the Lord Constance and some other very intelligent persons, that I may not impose upon the public by false or uncertain reports. This wise advice I had from that minister all the while I had the honour to be with him, who gave me to understand that some men had given abroad memoirs of a great many things that are not much to be trusted. So I shall speak nothing of Tonkin and Cochin-China, because of three persons who lived there many years, and whom is anything else I should readily believe, with much ado two could agree together about a great many questions that were put to them in relation to those places. For as to the Orientals, all know that they tell things not really as they are, but as they fancy you could wish they were; wherefore they little care to contradict one another, as to matter of fact they have declared, provided they comply with the inclinations of him that puts the question to them; so that if they be taken in any contradiction, it does not at all trouble them to be told of it. What pleased you yesterday, will they say unconcernedly, displeases you today, and that makes us speak today in another manner then we spake yesterday. I shall not so much enlarge upon the customs and government of the Siamese as upon their religion, which I have taken great care to be informed of, and have learnt many particulars relating thereunto, which, as I think, will be very acceptable to the curious. I owe almost all of them to a Siamese churchman who came to France with the Ambassadors of the King of Siam.

The situation of the Kingdom of Siam

The Kingdom of Siam reaches from the point of Malaca to the Kingdoms of Pegu and Laos which bound it on the North side. It hath the Indian Sea to the west, and the Chinese to the east, so that it would seem to make only a Peninsula. The provinces that lie up in the country towards the north are but little known, and our geographical maps mark not their situation and limits well. We have found already by two observations of an eclipse of the moon, that the longitude thereof is very ill determined. The King of Siam intimated to our Fathers that he wished he had an exact map of his own dominions and the Kingdoms about, having bid the Lord Constance tell us, that he would give us letters of recommendation to the Princes his neighbours, to the end we might have the liberty to travel over their countries, and make an exact description of them. I do not think that since my departure our Fathers have had time to obey the orders of the King of Siam, because they were in haste to be gone for China, waiting only for the opportunity of a passage. That will be the first work we shall undertake so soon as we have learnt the language.

A description of the Kingdom of Siam

This Kingdom is divided by many rivers, and watered with frequent rains, which for six months of the year and more, overflow all the country, that abounds in rice, fruits and cattle. The houses are commonly of wood, and raised upon pillars because of the inundations, without anything of the grandeur or regularity that is to be found in the houses of Europe. The Chinese and Moors have built several pretty neat stone-houses in Siam. The wealth of the country appears in the temples, by the many works of gold, and most lovely gilding, which are the ornaments of them, these pagodas being, besides, of a singular structure, and in very great number. They are in no want of timber, and they have some excellently good for building of ships.

The capital city is called Siam; and that is the name the Portuguese have given it. The Siamese call it *Crung si ayu tha ya*, and not Juthia or Odia. Crung si, signifies excellent town. Their histories call it also Crung theppa

Plate 27. A Siamese pagoda

ppra ma bà nà kom.[39] The meaning of that is, Angelical, admirable and extraordinary town; and they call it Angelical, because they think it impregnable to men. Seeing all nations are well received at Siam, and that people are suffered to live there in the free exercise of their religion, there are some of almost all nations in that country. The Chinese are the greatest traders there, and besides the commodities of China deal also in those of Japan. The King of Siam sends ships to trade at Surrat, Bengal, Moca and other places. But the Siamese being no better at navigation than the other people of the East, Europeans have the sailing of their vessels. He hath also several Junks[40] which are Chinese vessels, and are manned by Chinese. But tho that Nation brag that they have had the use of the compass for above these two thousand years; yet they come very far short of the Europeans in the art of navigation. They have no other instruments for sailing but the lead or sound. They keep reckoning as we do, and run some time upon such a point of wind, the currents, mountains which they discover on land, the colour, fineness and mixture of the sand, with other experiences are the rules they go by.

The habits of the Siamese The Siamese are not magnificent in their apparel. The inferior sort of people men and women are clothed much alike. They have a l onguis which is a piece of very simple stuff about two ells and a half long, and three quarters of an ell broad. They put this longuis about their body, so that it makes as it were, a kind of coat reaching from the girdle below the knee, but the women's come down as low as the ankle. The women have besides that a piece of white betille, almost three ells long which they put about them in manner of a scarf to cover the rest of their body, for that purpose the men have another longuis, which they never use but when it is cold, rains or when the sun shines too clear. The habits of the mandarins when they are in their home dress, differ only from those of the common people by the fineness of the stuff. But when they go abroad they have a longuis of silk or painted cloth six or seven ells long, which they have the knack of adjusting so well about their body, that it reaches no lower than their knee. The considerable Mandarins have

Mandarin qui parle a vn de ses gens

Plate 28. A mandarin speaks with one of his people

under this Longuis a narrow pair of drawers; the extremities whereof are embroidered with gold and silver. They have also vests with bodies and sleeves pretty wide. They have shoes shaped like the shoes of the Indians. On the days of ceremony when they are to appear before the King, they have a cap of betille starched, which tapers into a point like a sugar-loaf, and is tied with a string under the chin. The King gives to some Mandarins according to their quality, crowns of gold or silver, made much after the shape of the coronets of our Dukes and Marquesses, to be put about their cap, which is a mark of great distinction.

A Character of the Siamese and their manners

The Siamese are very good natured and civil, they live in good intelligence one with another, and they are not wanting in compleasance to strangers. The good conduct of the French, and especially the wisdom and virtuous examples of the Chevalier de Chaumont, gave them so high a notion of France, that Mandarins of the best quality earnestly sued for the honour of going thither in quality of the Ambassadors of the King their master, or in the retinue of those whom he sent. So to speak generally, there is a great union in families amongst them, and out of principle of tenderness for their parents and relations, they accuse us of somewhat of hard heartedness, because we leave ours, and go live far from them in remote countries, telling us that they may stand in need of us. Justice has no less sway among them than friendship and peace. When any ship is cast away upon their coast, there is a law that obliges those who have taken up anything of the wreck to bring it to the chief town, to be afterwards given to those to whom the effects belonged; which is also observed in relation to strangers.

The property of Betel and Areca

The persuasion they are in, that it is indecent for a man to have his teeth white like beasts, makes them take a great deal of pains to blacken them. For that end they make use of a varnish made for the purpose, which they renew from time to time when it begins to wear off. That they may give the colour time to stick on, they eat nothing for some days, and even dispense with betel and areca. The betel we have often spoken of is the leaf of a tree of the same name, and shape of our acorns. They cut that fruit into four parts, and having mingled it with lime of shells, they wrap it up in the betel leaf. This mixture is so very savoury to them, either because they are accustomed to it, or because of the great effects they feel from it, that all eat of it of what quality, or in what place soever they be. They pretend that it is a specific remedy to fortify the gums, help digestion, and above all to make the breath sweet.

The property of tea

It is a civility amongst them to present betel and tea to all that visit them. Their own country supplies them with betel and areca, but they have their tea from China and Japan. All the Orientals have a particular esteem for it, because of the great virtues they find to be in it. Their physicians say that it is a sovereign medicine, against the stone and pains of the head; that it allays vapours; that it cheers the mind, and strengthens the stomach. In all kinds of fevers they take it stronger than commonly when they begin to feel the heat of the fit, and then the patient covers himself up to sweat, and it hath been very often found that this sweat wholly drives away the fever.

The manner of preparing tea

In the East they prepare the tea in this manner, when the water is well boiled, they pour it upon the tea which they have put into an earthen pot, proportionally to what they intend to take (the ordinary proportion is as much as one can take up with the finger and thumb, for a pint of water) then they cover the pot until the leaves are sunk to the bottom of it, and afterward give it about in China dishes to be drank as hot as can be without sugar, or else with a little sugar candy in the mouth; and upon that tea more boiling water may be poured and so it may be made to serve twice. These people drink of it several times a day, but do not think it wholesome to take it fasting.

What ginseng is and its virtues

Of all the plants of the East the ginseng is most esteemed. There are several kinds of it; but the best is that which grows in China in the province of Laocung. It is of a yellow colour, the flesh or pulp of it smooth, having little threads like hair. They find of these roots some that are shaped like a man, and it is from thence they have their name, for Gin in the Chinese language, signifies a man, and seng sometimes to kill, according as it is differently pronounced; because that root being taken seasonably or out of season, produces quite contrary effects. There is ginseng also in the Kingdom of Korea,[41] nay and in Siam too, as some say; but it is not so good as that which grows in the shade in low valleys, and that it must be gathered at the end of autumn, because that which is gathered in the spring has ten times less virtue.

The way of preparing ginseng

The Chinese physicians who make most use of it, affirm that it is a sovereign remedy for cleansing the blood, and recruiting the strength that has been weakened by long sickness, that he who has that root in his mouth, will hold out at labour as long again as he that hath it not; that corpulent people who have a white skin may take more of it than dry persons who have swarthy complexion, and whose countenance speaks heat; that it is never to be taken in distempers caused by an internal heat, nor when one hath a cough or spitteth blood. For preparing of it, they put water into a cup, and having made it boil well, they throw into it ginseng cut into small bits; they cover the cup very close, that the ginseng may be infused, and when the water becomes lukewarm, they drink it alone in the morning fasting. They keep that ginseng and prepare it the same way in the evening as they did in the morning, saving that they put but half the quantity of water, and drink it when it is already a little cold. Then they dry the ginseng that hath already served, in the sun, and if one please, he may again infuse it in wine and use it. The quantity of the ginseng is proportioned according to the age of the person who is to take it. From ten to twenty years of age they take a little more than half the weight of a groat

Plate 29. A depiction of some of the flora of Siam

of it; from twenty to thirty, about the weight of six pence; from thirty to threescore and ten and upwards, they take of it to the weight of about a shilling, and never more .

Some particulars concerning certain birds Nest

We saw at Siam certain birds nests which these people find to be rarely good for ragouts, and excellent for the health, when ginseng is mingled therewith. These nests are only found in Cochin-China upon vast steep rocks. Thus they make use of them. They take a pullet, (such as have the flesh and bones black are the best,) they gut it well. And then taking the birds nests, which have been steeped in water till they are soft, they tear them into small shreds, and having mingled them with ginseng cut into little bits, they put all together into the body of the pullet, which they boil in a pot closely shut until it be enough boiled. This pot or pipkin is left upon the coals all night, and in the morning they eat the pullet, the birds nests and the ginseng without any other seasoning. After they have taken this remedy sometimes they sweat, and if they can they'll sleep upon it.

Various customs of the Siamese

Nobility is not hereditary amongst the Siamese, the places given by the Prince make the nobles, and the distinction of quality with that people. Though their religion allow them polygamy, yet few of them have above one or two wives. As for the ladies, they think the greatest respect that can be shown to them, is for a man to turn his back and not to look upon them as they pass.

The multitude and magnificence of their pagodas, and their liberalities to the *talapoins*, are arguments of their piety. They say that in the Kingdom there are above fourteen thousand pagodas and fifty thousand *talapoins*. What ever is within those temples is looked upon as sacred, and to steal anything from thence is death; about five years ago five robbers were surprised in a pagoda, and they were roasted alive by a gentle fire. They fastened every one of them to a great pole, and then having kindled a fire, all round them, they were turned there till they expired. In their morning prayers which they never miss, they call to mind three things. God and the law which he hath left them to observe; their parents and the benefits which they have received from them; their priests and the reverence they owe them; when a missionary would speak to them of our religion, for a present he may have free access to them, and that also will dispose them to hear him.

The curiosity of the Siamese to know things future

Seeing they live upon a small matter, and that their country supplies them with all that is necessary for life without much labour and husbandry, they spend their time in idleness. They improve not their minds by any science and are curious about nothing but future contingencies. To know such they not only consult astrologers, but make use also of other means full of superstitions. The Lord Constance told me that there is a cave where the Siamese go and offer sacrifices to the spirit that presides in it, when they have a mind to know anything that they are in pain about. After they have said their prayers there they come out and take the first word they hear spoken for the response of the oracle which they have consulted. It sometimes happens that to punish their criminal curiosity God permits that the event confirms what they have learnt by this way. Thus some of the wives of the first ambassadors that were sent to France on board the Sun of the East, being anxious to know the destiny of their husbands, whom they feared they should never see again, made their sacrifices in the cave I mentioned; and being afterwards come back again to the town, in the evening they heard a woman saying to her slaves, "Shut the door, they'll return no more." They took these words as a presage of the misfortune that happened in the sequel, and from that time bewailed the loss of their husbands.

The reverence the Siamese have for their King

The respect they have for the King goes as far as adoration. The posture wherein they are to be in his presence is a visible mark of it. Nay even in the council which sometimes lasts four hours, the ministers lie all the while prostrate before the King; and if any of them chance to faint, he dares not rise upon his knees, nor sit up upon the ground, though the Prince command him so to do till a curtain he drawn before his throne. When the King goes abroad, all must withdraw, and nobody dares to be in his way but they who have express orders for it, unless it be when he had a mind to show himself to his people on certain days of ceremony. Strangers also have notice given them to keep within doors when the King is to go abroad. No man is suffered to come near the Palace whilst he is there.

One day as I was returning from a pagoda with a Mandarin who had carried me thither in his *balon*, our water-men going along with the stream, came a little too near the walls of the Palace. But they soon stood off again when they felt a shower of pease flying about their ears, which the soldiers upon the guard shot at them with trunks, to make them withdraw.

The King holds council several times a day

The King holds several councils daily, and that's his greatest exercise. None of his counsellors dares be absent, and if any of them chanced to have extraordinary business, or to fall sick, he ought before the hour of council ask leave of the King to be absent. Without that leave no hurry of business nor sickness will excuse him from incurring grievous punishments, if he be able to go; for the King never fails to send to know the reasons of his absence, and the officer whom the King sends has orders to speak to the person himself.

The King's daughter hath her court and council

The Princess the King's only daughter, hath her court and council consisting of the wives of the chief Mandarins. She is witty and active, and in the government of the provinces which the King hath given her, shows a great deal of wisdom and moderation; she is only served by women, and no man ever saw her neither publicly nor privately. When she goes abroad upon an elephant, she is shut up in a kind of chair that hinders her from being seen.

The Kingdom of Siam descends not from father to son

In the Kingdom of Siam the King's brothers are preferred before his children in the succession to the crown, but it returns to these after the death of their uncles. The present King has two brothers who live with him in the Palace, he hath also, according to the custom of the Orientals, an adoptive son who accompanies him in all places, and who has peculiar honours rendered unto him.

The religion of the Siamese is very odd, and cannot be perfectly understood but by the books that are written in the Pali[42] language, which is the learned language, and hardly understood by any, except some of their doctors. Nor do these books neither always agree amongst themselves. This following account of their religion is the most exact that possibly I could attain to.

What the Siamese believe of their God

The Siamese believe a God, but they have not the same notion of him that we have. By that word they understand a being perfect after their manner, consisting of spirit and body, whose property it is to assist men. That assistance consists in giving them a law, prescribing them the ways of living well, teaching them the true religion, and the sciences that are necessary unto them. The perfections which they attribute unto him are all the moral virtues, possessed by him in an eminent degree acquired by many acts, and confirmed by a continual exercise in all the bodies he hath passed through.

He is free from passions, and feels no motion that can alter his tranquillity; but they affirm that before he arrived at that state, he made so prodigious a change in his body by struggling to overcome his passions, that his blood is become white. He hath the power to appear when he pleases, and also to render himself invisible to the eyes of men; and he hath such wonderful agility, that in a moment he can be in any place of the world he pleases.

The knowledge of the God of the Siamese

He knoweth all without having ever learnt anything from men, whose doctor and master he himself is, and that universal knowledge is inherent in his state, having possessed it from the instant that he was born God; it consists not as ours does, in a train of consequences, but in a clear, simple and intuitive vision, which all at once represents to him the precepts of the law, vices, virtues, and the most hidden secrets of nature, things past, present and [to] come, Heaven, Earth, Paradise, Hell, this universe which we see, and even what is done in the other worlds which we know not. He distinctly remembers all that hath ever befallen him from the first transmigration of his soul, even to the last.

His body is infinitely more radiant then the sun, it lights that which is most hidden, and by the help of the light that it diffuses, a man here below upon earth, might, that I may make use of their expression, see a grain of mustard seed placed in the highest Heavens.

Wherein consists his happiness

The happiness of that God is not complete, but when he dies never to be born again: for then he appears no more upon the earth, nor is he any more subject to misery. They compare that death to a torch extinct, or to a sleep that renders us insensible of the evils of life, with this difference that when God dies, he is exempted from them for ever, whereas a man asleep is but free from them for a certain time.

The reign of every deity lasts not eternally, it is confined to a certain number of years, that's to say, until the number of the elect who are to be sanctified by his merits be accomplished; after which he appears no more in the world but slides into on eternal repose, which was thought to have been a real annihilation, because they were not rightly understood. Then another God succeeds to him, and governs the universe in his place, which is nothing else but to teach men the true religion.

Men may become Gods

Men may become Gods, but not till after a very considerable time; for they must needs have required a consummate virtue. Nor is it enough to have done a great many good works in their bodies where their souls have lodged, they must also at every good action they do, have an intention of meriting divinity, they must have intimated that intention, by invoking and taking to witness the Angels who preside in the four parts of the world, at the beginning of their good work; and they must have poured out water, imploring the succours of the She-tutelary Angel of the Earth, called Naang pprathorani; for they believe, as we shall show hereafter, that there is a diversity of sex amongst Angels as well as amongst men. They who desire to be Gods carefully observe that practice.

The Siamese acknowledge a permanent state of sanctity

Besides that state of divinity to which the most perfect aspire, there is another not so high, which they call the state of sanctity. It is enough for being a saint, that having passed through several bodies, one has acquired many virtues, and that in the acts which men do they have proposed the acquisition of sanctity. The properties of sanctity are the same with those of divinity. The saints possess them, as well as God does, but in a far more imperfect degree, besides that, God has them of himself, without receiving them from another, whereas the saints derive them from him by the instructions he gives them. It is he who teaches them all those secrets whereof he hath a perfect knowledge. And therefore it is that if they be not born whilst he is in the world, since they cannot receive his documents, they are not sanctified. So that it is their custom in doing good works, to desire the grace to be born again at the same time their God is. What we have said of the deity, that it is not consummated till God dying upon Earth, ascends up into Heaven, that he may no more appear here below, ought in like manner to be understood of sanctity; for it is not perfect till the saints die, not to be born again, and till their souls be carried into paradise, there to enjoy eternal felicity.

The Siamese believe a Heaven and a Hell

These and the like are the sentiments of these people touching the deity. And seeing they have sense enough to know that vice is to be punished, and virtue rewarded, they believe a paradise, where the just enjoy the pleasure which their good works have merited, and a Hell, where the wicked receive the chastisement due unto their crimes. They place paradise in the highest Heaven, and Hell in the centre of the Earth. The pleasures of paradise and the pains of Hell are not eternal; they shall be there but for a certain time, which is longer or shorter according as they have done more or less good works, or committed more or fewer sins.

What the Siamese believe of Hell

They say, that in Hell there are Angels who administer Justice, and take care to mark exactly all the bad actions of men, examine them after their death, and with extreme severity punish them for the same. They have a ridiculous imagination as to the judgement that then passes; they are persuaded that the first of these judges, whom they call Prayomppaban, hath a book, wherein the life of every particular man is registered, that he continually reads it over, and that when he comes to the page which contains the history of that man, he never fails to sneeze. Therefore it is, say they, that we sneeze upon Earth, and thence proceeds the custom they have of wishing a happy and long life to all that sneeze.

Hell is divided into eight habitations, which are, as it were, eight degrees of pain; nay, they believe also that there is a fire which burns the damned.

What they believe of Heaven

They fancy to themselves also in Heaven eight degrees of beatitude. They'll have the same things to happen there as upon Earth; and affirm that there are Kings, Princes and people there; that there they wage war, fight battles, and obtain victories; that marriage itself is not banished from thence; that in the first, second and third habitations, the saints may have children; that in the fourth in fine, there is no more concupiscence nor marriage; and so purity daily increases till one come to the last Heaven, which is properly paradise, called in their language Niruppan, where the souls of the saints and Gods live in perfect purity and sovereign felicity.

They maintain, that all the good or evil that happens to men, is the effect of their good or bad works, and that one is never unfortunate and innocent at the same time. Thus wealth, honours, sanctity and divinity are the rewards of a virtuous life; and on the contrary, infamy, poverty, diseases, death and Hell, are the punishments of sins which men have committed. And whether one be born again under human shape, or under the figure of any animal, they attribute the advantages where with one comes into the world, as goodness, gracefulness, wit, or nobility, to the merit of good works and natural defects; as ugliness, mutilation of members, and the like to the debauches of this or the other lives which went before it. All these things, say they, so many certain marks which discover to us what lives men have led before they were born in this state, and this is the source of that prodigious diversity which appears in their conditions, their lives and their death. Being prepossessed with these errors, they slight what you tell them of original sin and the effects thereof, and they call the disobedience and punishment of our first Father a mere fiction.

Upon a religious account the Siamese respect those who are any ways eminent by the advantages of body, mind or fortune

The souls of men that are born again in the world, come from three different places, from Heaven, from Hell, or out of the bodies of animals. They whose souls come from Heaven, are distinguished by some advantageous signs; they have for their share, virtue, beauty, health, wealth, and they are born great men and handsome Princes. Upon this principle these people show great respect for men of dignity, or of an illustrious extraction, because they look upon them as those who are shortly to be deified or sanctified, seeing they have done good works enough to merit that high rank of honour to which they are raised.

They whose souls come out of the bodies of other animals, are less perfect than the former, but far more however, than those that come from Hell. They look upon these last as rogues, whose crimes make them deserve all kinds of disasters. And thence proceeds the horror which the Siamese have for the cross of Christ. For, in short, do they answer when one speaks to them about that, if he had been a just man, his Justice and good works would have saved him from the shameful punishment he suffered, and protected him from the fury of his enemies.

They know the punishment and guilt of sin

They distinguish two things in sin, the guilt and the punishment reserved in Hell for the sinner. The punishment may very well be remitted or lessened in this life by good works and good resolutions, but the guilt is never blotted out till one be first punished by death or other miseries. In the punishing of sins, the law of like for like is exactly observed; for if you have killed a man, you shall die a violent death in this life or in another. If you have killed a serpent, a serpent shall sting you to death; if you have robbed any birds nest, and carried away her young, you shall one day be, after one or more transmigrations, snatched out of the arms of your parents in your tenderest infancy, and forsaken of those that could any way assist you. Nay their God hath not the power to exempt himself from that rigorous law; for at the age of fourscore and two years he was put to death by a monster called Man, whom heretofore he had killed at the like age under the shape of a pig.

If the fault a man hath committed in his lifetime be but slight, he may by the good he does, or by the good will he has to do so, merit that the punishment which he ought to suffer in Hell, be remitted either wholly, or in part at least. But if the sin be grievous, no good works can expiate it; he must blot out by suffering in Hell all the pains that it deserves. And this hath given ground to a tradition received amongst them, that God neither could, nor as yet can deliver his brother from the pains of Hell, to which he is condemned.

So, there is not any good action but what is rewarded in Heaven, nor any crime but what is punished in Hell. Hence they conclude, that when a man dies upon Earth, he acquires a new life in Heaven, that here he may enjoy the happiness that is due to his good works; and that the time of his reward being finished, he dies in Heaven that he may be born again in Hell; if he lie under any considerable sin; that if it be only a slight fault he is guilty of, he enters again into the world under the shape of some animal, and having in that state satisfied justice, becomes man again as before. In this manner they explain the metempsychosis, which is one of the fundamental points of their religion so that the life of man is spent in continual transmigrations, until he be sanctified, or hath deserved to be a God. They allow of spirits; but these spirits are nothing else but souls which still inform somebody until they attain to sanctity or divinity.

They believe Angels to be corporal

Angels are corporal, and as there are different sexes amongst them, so they may beget sons and daughters. These Angels are never sanctified nor deified. It is their part only to take continual care of the preservation of men, and of the Government of the Universe. They distribute them into seven orders or hierarchies; whereof some are more perfect and noble than others, and they place them in so many different Heavens. Each part of the world hath one of these intelligences, that presides over all that is done there. They assign them also to stars, the Earth, towns, mountains, forests, nay even to the wind and rain. And because they are persuaded that these Angels are constantly busied in examining the conduct of men, and that they are witnesses of all their actions, to reward such as are laudable, by virtue of the merits of their God it is to these intelligences, and not to their God, that they are wont to apply themselves in their necessities and miseries; and they thank them for the favours which they think they have received from them.

They acknowledge no other devils but damned souls

They acknowledge no other devils but the souls of the wicked, which coming out of Hell where they were detained, for a certain time roam about the world, and do men all the mischief they can. Among those wretched spirits, they also reckon children stillborn, women that die in childbed, those that are killed in duels, or who are guilty of some other crimes of that nature.

They tell strange stories of certain anchorites

They relate strange things of some anchorites, whom they call Pra Rasi, who retreating into dismal solitudes and thick woods, lead a most holy and most austere life. These solitaries, according to their books, have almost perfect knowledge of the most hidden secrets of nature. They can make gold, silver and the most precious metals. The most astonishing miracle is not above their power. They take all the shapes they please, fly in the air, and in an instant are where they have a mind to be. But though these extraordinary men might render themselves immortal, because they know the means of prolonging life, yet every thousand years they sacrifice it to God, by consuming themselves upon a funeral pyre, all but one, who remains to raise the rest by virtue of his charms. It is no less dangerous than difficult, to meet with these miraculous men; for nothing less than life is risked by the encounter. Nevertheless one may learn in the books of the *talapoins*, the way that is to be taken, and the means which are to be made use of for attaining to the places where they are.

Their belief touching the eternity of the world

They reckon the Heaven and Earth to be uncreated and eternal, and cannot conceive how the world could ever have a beginning, or that it should have an end. They believe every star and planet to be the habitation of a particular Angel. They reckon only seven planets, and the names they give them serve also for the seven days of the week, as in the Latin tongue. After all, the stars are fastened to no body, they hang in the air, and have their particular motions.

The Earth in the opinion of the Siamese is flat and square

The Earth, in their philosophy, is not round, it is only a flat surface; they divide it into four square parts, which they call Thavip. The waters, by which those four parts are separated, not being navigable, because of their extreme subtlety, hinder the commerce that they might have one with another. The whole Earth is encompassed with an extremely strong and very high wall. On this wall all the secrets of nature are engraven in great characters, and there it is that these wonderful hermits whom I mentioned, learn all the admirable things they know; for they easily convey themselves thither with that surprising agility they are endowed with. As to the men of the other three parts of the world, they have a countenance much different from ours: for the inhabitants of the first have a square face, of the second a round, and of the third a triangular.

Whatsoever diversity of faces there may be amongst the inhabitants of those three several parts of the world, yet in every particular part they look so like one another, that it would be hard to tell who is who, if men hath not another way to distinguish those with whom they live. The different inclinations that people have for different persons, is the standard of discrimination. Thus a Father distinguishes his son from his wife and friend, because he finds the love he has for his son to be quite different from that which he has for his wife or his friend. There is this difference besides betwixt the three other parts and ours, that all good things abound in those without any mixture of evil; and that what things they eat takes what relish one pleases by virtue of a certain tree which they invoke when at any time they are in need. Hence it is that no charity nor virtue can be practised there. And because there is no occasion of meriting there, men cannot acquire sanctity, nor receive any punishment, which makes them earnestly desire to be born again in the part which we inhabit, where many occasions of well doing are to be found. They obtain that favour when they beg it by the merits of God, who hath run over all those places, though they be inaccessible to us.

The system of the Siamese In the middle of the four parts of the world there is an exceeding high mountain, called in Siamese Ppukhan Pprasamen. It rests upon three precious stones, very little ones, its true, but strong and solid enough to support it. Round this mountain the sun and moon continually turn, and by the daily revolution of those two luminaries, day and night are made. This great mountain is environed by three rows of lesser hills, of which, there is one all of gold. The great mountain is inaccessible, because the water that surrounds it is not navigable. As for the Mountain of Gold, a fearful gulf renders the approach to it most difficult. It is true, a rich man heretofore got to it, but it was with extreme danger of being lost in that abyss, whither all the waters come and muster, and from whence afterward they gush out to make the sea and rivers.

The whole mass of Earth hath underneath it a vast extent of waters, which support it as the sea bears up a ship. These inferior waters have a communication with those that are upon the Earth, by means of the gulf I have been speaking of. An impetuous wind holds the waters under the Earth suspended, and this wind, which exists of itself, and has no cause, blowing from all eternity with incredible violence, drives them continually back, and hinders them falling. When the time is come that the God of the Siamese hath foretold, that he shall cease to reign, then the fire of Heaven falling upon the Earth, shall reduce into ashes everything that comes in its way, and the Earth being so purified, shall be restored again to its former state. But you must know what is to go before this universal renovation.

Prodigies which the Siamese expect before the birth of a new God

They say, that heretofore when God was still living upon Earth, men had the stature of giants, enjoyed perfect health during several ages, were ignorant of nothing, and above all, being instructed in the oblig-ations of the law, led a pure and innocent life, and were religious observers of their promises. In process of time they lost all these advantages, and at long run they will become so weak and little, that hardly will they be a foot high. In that state their life will be very short, and nevertheless they'll grow up in wickedness, until at length, in the last times they'll give themselves over to the most ignominious crimes. Then they shall have no more law nor scriptures; but being buried in most profound ignorance, shall forget the very name of virtue. And that makes them say that the end of the world draws nigh, because there is nothing now but corruption in it, and so little sincerity and faithfulness amongst men, that they seem to be arrived at the highest pitch of wickedness. Moreover these great changes shall be observed in beasts as well as men, and they shall degenerate by little and little. Nay, they have already lost the use of speech, which, whilst God lived upon the Earth, was granted them through his merits. They gave liberty to beasts, thinking them capable of good and evil, and worthy of punishment and reward. In the three last ages six new suns shall successively appear, and every one of them shall enlighten the world for the space of sixty years. These six new luminaries shall by degrees, dry up the sea, kill the trees and animals, and even consume mankind. After all these prodigies, a fire, which they call *Phai Balaran*, descending from Heaven, shall burn the Earth; the heights thereof shall be made plain by it, and no more inequalities will remain therein.

Then the Earth covered over with dust and ashes, shall be purified by the blast of a boisterous wind, which shall carry off these remains of the worlds conflagration; and after that, it shall breath out so sweet a smell as shall draw a female Angel down from Heaven, that will eat of this purified Earth. She is to pay dear for that pleasure; for to expiate it, she shall be obliged to live here below, and never be able to ascend to Heaven again. This intelligence shall by the piece she hath eaten, conceive twelve sons and as many daughters, who will re-people the world. The men that spring from them shall be ignorant, blockish, not knowing one another at first; and after they shall come to know one another, they shall be ignorant of the law, and not come to the knowledge of it till after a long space of time, which they call *Cap*. To explain the duration of that time, they suppose a deep well twenty fathom square; if there be a grain of mustard seed yearly thrown into this well, the time that is required to fill it up, is that which they call *Cap*.

This space of time being expired, a God shall be born again, who shall scatter the darkness of the ignorance wherein they were, by teaching them the true religion, discovering to them the virtues that are to be practised, and the vices to be shunned, and instructing them in all sciences. He will give them scriptures that shall explain these things, and the holy law that for a long time hath been blotted out of the minds of men, shall be of new again graven in them by the cares and merits of that deity. This is the only employment which they think suitable to the dignity of God, whilst he is upon Earth; for they reckon it below him to mind the Government of the World, to take care of men and beasts, and to produce all that the Universe brings forth: and in this manner it is that the world shall be from time to time renewed to all eternity.

Sommonokhodom is the last God of the Siamese

I thought it fit to premise all these things before I came to speak of Sommonokhodom (so the Siamese call the God whom at present they adore) because they are necessary to the understanding of his history. That history, after all, is a monstrous mixture of Christianity and the most ridiculous fables. It is at first supposed that Sommonokhodom was born God by his own virtue; and that immediately after his birth, without the help of any master, to instruct him, he acquired by a mere glance of his mind, a perfect knowledge of all things relating to Heaven, the Earth, Paradise, Hell, and the most impenetrable secrets of nature; that at the same time he remembered all that ever he had done in the different lives he had led; and that after he had taught the people those great matters, he left them written in books, that posterity might be the better for them.

Fables which the talapoins *relate of their God*

In these books he reports of himself, that being become God, one day he desired to manifest his divinity to men by some extraordinary prodigy, he then sat under a tree called *Ton Ppo* which for that reason the Siamese reverence as some sacred thing, and look upon it as a happy presage for the places where it grows, being persuaded that it would be a great sin to do the least hurt to that tree. He adds, that presently he found himself carried up into the air in a throne all shining with gold and precious stones, which came out of the Earth in the place where he was; and that at the same instant Angels coming down from Heaven, rendered him the honours and adoration that were due unto him.

Thevathat Sommonokhodom's younger brother makes war against him

His brother Thevathat and his followers could not without extreme jealousy behold the glory and majesty that environed him.

They conspired his ruin, and having stirred up the beasts against him, engaged with him in a war. Though he was all alone, he was not terrified by that multitude of enemies, he resisted all their attempts without being shaken, and by virtue of his good works which defended him, the shafts they darted at him, were changed into so many flowers, which far from hurting him, served only to increase his honour. In the mean time he confesses that in the brunt of the battle, when he was most in danger, it was but in vain that he had his recourse to the good works he had done in keeping the nine first commandments of the law, which he found were not sufficient to defend him in this pressing necessity. But being armed with the tenth command, which he had inviolably observed, and which enjoins the practice of charity towards men and beasts, he easily triumphed over his enemies; and in this manner he obtained that victory.

Sommonokhodom assisted by the female tutelary Angel of the Earth triumphs over his enemies

The female guardian-Angel of the Earth (for we have already distinguished two sexes amongst the Angels) coming to him, at first adored him, then turning towards Thevathat and his adherents, she made known to them that Sommonokhodom was really become God. She told them, that she had been a witness of his good works; and to convince them of that showed them her own hand still dropping with the waters that he poured out in the beginning of his good actions. Hence come the superstitious custom of the Siamese of shedding water in the beginning of their good works, whereof we have spoken several times already, and which the Siamese religiously observe since that time. In fine, she exhorted them to render him the adoration that he deserved; but finding them to be hardened and obstinately resolved not to hearken to her remonstrances, she squeezed her wet hair and pressed out of them an ocean of water wherein they were all drowned.

The Foppery which the talapoins *tell of Sommonokhodom*

It is also found written in the books of Sommonokhodom, that from the time he aspired to be God, he had returned into the world five hundred and fifty times under various shapes; that in every regeneration, he had been always the chief, and, as it were, Prince of the animals under whose shape he was born; that many times he had given his life for his subjects, and that being a monkey, he had delivered a town from a horrible monster that wasted it; that he had been a most potent King, and that seven days before he obtained the sovereign dominion of the Universe, he had retired in imitation of some anchorites, with his wife and two children into remote solitude; that there he was dead to the world and his passions in such a degree that without being moved he suffered a Brahmin who had a mind to try his patience and carry away his son and daughter, and torment them before his face. Nay his mortification went a great deal farther, for he even gave his wife to a poor man that begged an alms, and having put out his own eyes he sacrificed himself by distributing his flesh amongst the beasts, to stay the hunger that pressed them. From thence they take occasion again to find fault with the Christian religion, which enjoins not men to comfort and assist beasts in their necessities. These are the rare actions which the *talapoins* in their sermons propose to the people for imitation, and the examples they make use of to incline them to virtue.

Thevathat killed his brother Sommonokhodom when they were apes

What is recorded of Thevathat in the same books is no less extraordinary nor fabulous. There we learn that he was always born again with his brother Sommonokhodom, in the same kind as he was: but still inferior in dignity, because Sommonokhodom was the Prince of the animals whose shape he took. But Thevathat aspiring also to divinity, and not endeavouring anything above himself, would never submit to his brother. On the contrary, he endeavoured by continual revolts to disturb his reign, and omitted nothing that he might deprive him of the Empire, wherein, at length he succeeded in some manner; for he killed him when both of them were apes. What we saw during our abode in Siam, did but too much convince us, how far the people are infatuated with such fables. A young churchman maintaining a position of civility in presence of my Lord Ambassador, some *talapoins* came thither out of curiosity, and amongst others the superior of one of their most famous monasteries. This man asked what they were disputing about with so much heat, and being answered that they were speaking of God, and of matters concerning that first being. Likely enough, replied the *talapoin*, the stress of the disputation rests upon the great labours and the death his enemies made him suffer, whilst he was a monkey. Let us now return to the fabulous story of Thevathat.

Thevathat makes a schism and declares himself against his brother

Being a person of much wit and address, he found the way to make a new sect, wherein he engaged several Kings and much people, who embraced his doctrine and imitated his examples. That was the original of a schism which divided the world into two parts, and gave a beginning to two religions, whereas before that all mankind had but one. Some, of whom they reckon us for the reasons we shall presently allege, became the disciples of Thevathat, and the rest of Sommonokhodom. Thevathat tho he was but the younger, finding himself supported by so many Princes, who espoused his quarrel, employed open force and treason to ruin his elder brother. He invented the most heinous calumnies to blacken his reputation; but these designs succeeded not. Nay he was oftener than once overcome, when to confirm his followers in the faith which he had taught them, he had the boldness to contend with his brother who should work the greatest Miracles.

Thevathat conspiring to be God, is with his followers deprived of many knowledges

Ambition made his desire to be God, but not being really so, he was ignorant of a great many things, which his brother perfectly knew, and because his haughtiness would not suffer him to listen to Sommonokhodom, he did not learn of him what was done in Hell and Paradise, nor the doctrine of the transmigration of souls, nor yet the changes that had been and were to be in all ages, from whence they conclude that it is not to be wondered at, if we who are his disciples find nothing of all those things in the books he hath left us; if our scriptures be full of obscurities and doubts, and that if being wholly ignorant of divinity, we have so great a mind to reason and dispute with them. For since Thevathat our master knew nothing of that himself, he could not instruct us therein.

Hence is it also that we are ignorant of the secret of curing men, of preserving them from all evils, of making gold and silver, and of discovering those precious metals in the places where they are hid. For they believe that there are vast treasures in certain unknown places, but that I know not what supernatural virtue hinders us from perceiving them; or if we do see them, it makes them appear to us under a shape and figure which imposes upon our sight. They also object to us that we cannot work many prodigies, which they pretend they can do, and are the effect of magic, because Thevathat having as little skill that way as in all the rest, he could not teach us.

But tho' Thevathat was not God, and that by consequence he had neither the agility nor subtlety of body, nor the other perfections of divinity, yet he excelled in several sciences especially in the mathematics and geometry. Now as it is of him, if we'll take their word for it, that we have received these knowledges, it is no wonder if we be good geometricians, and be perfectly well skilled in other arts.

The talapoins *persuade the Siamese that the Christian religion is taken out of the law which Sommonokhodom taught them.*

In the new doctrine which he published he foisted in a great many things, which he had taken out of his brothers religion: and that had rendered both laws so like one another in several points. They differ however, in that Thevathat law is far less severe than that of Sommonokhodom; for it allows men a great liberty of killing and eating animals, tho' the use of them be unlawful and criminal. From the doctrine of Thevathat, as out of a force of schism, seven other sects are sprung which have a great deal of affinity one with another, and that tradition they apply to the heresies of the Dutch, English, and other people separated from the Church of Rome; for they look upon them as so many shoots sprung from our religion, and that confirms them the more in their opinions.

Thevathat is punished in Hell for having persecuted his brother

After all the outrages that Thevathat had done to his brother without any respect to nature or even to divinity. It was but just he should be punished. And so the Siamese scriptures make mention of his punishment, and Sommonokhodom himself relates that after he became God, he saw that wicked brother of his in the deepest place of Hell. He was in the eighth Habitation, that is to say, in the place where the greatest offenders are tormented, and there by a terrible punishment, he expiated, all the sins that he had committed, and especially the injuries he had done to me. Explaining afterwards the pains which Thevathat was made to suffer, he says that he was fastened to a cross with great nails, which piercing his hands and feet, put him to extreme pain, that on his head he had a crown of thorns, that his body was full of wounds, and to complete his misery, the infernal place burnt him without consuming of him. So sad a spectacle moved him to compassion; he forgot all the wrongs his brother had dome him, and could not see him in that condition without taking a resolution to help him. He proposed to him then these three words to be adored, *Pputhang, Thamang, Samgkhang*; sacred and mysterious words for which the Siamese have a profound veneration, and whereof the first signifies God, the second the word of God, and the third the imitator of God; promising him, that if he would accept so easy and reasonable a condition, to deliver him from all the pains to which he was condemned. Thevathat consented to adore the first two words, but he never would adore the third, because it signified priest or imitator of God, protesting that priests were sinful men that deserved no respect. To punish him for that pride, he still suffers and will suffer for a great many years to come.

The talapoins take the Siamese off from turning Christians, by persuading them that Jesus Christ is Thevathat the brother of their God.

Tho' there be many things that keep the Siamese at a distance from the Christian law, yet one may say, nothing makes them more averse from it than this thought. The similitude that is to be found in some points betwixt their religion and ours, making them believe that Jesus Christ, is the very same with that Thevathat mentioned in their scriptures, they are persuaded that seeing we are the disciples of the one, we are also the followers of the other, and the fear they have of falling into Hell with Thevathat, if they follow his doctrine, suffers them not to hearken to the propositions that are made to them of embracing Christianity. That which most confirms them in their prejudice, is that we adore the image of our crucified saviour, which plainly represents the punishment of Thevathat. So when we would explain to them the articles of our faith; they take us always up short, saying that they do not need our instructions, and that they know already better than we do, what we have a mind to tell them.

But it is time to return to Sommonokhodom whose story we have interrupted; he had run over the world, declaring to mankind good and evil, and teaching them the true religion, which he himself wrought that he might leave it to posterity. He had even gained several disciples, who in the condition of priests were to make a particular profession of imitating him, in wearing a habit like to his, and in observing the rules that he gave them, when, at length, he attained to the fourscore and second year of his age, which was also the age of that monster, which heretofore he killed as we have already said. One day as he sat in the middle of his disciples teaching them, he saw the same monster in shape of a pig, running with incredible fury, and he made no doubt but that it had a design to be revenged. Knowing then that the time of his departure out of the world drew nigh, he foretold it to his disciples, and shortly after having eaten a piece of the pig which he had seen, he was taken with a violent colic which killed him.

Wherein consists the annihilation of the Siamese God

His soul ascended to the eighth Heaven, which is properly paradise called Niruppan,[43] it is no more subject to miseries and pain, but there enjoys perfect bliss. For that reason it will never be born again, and that is the thing they call being annihilated. For by that term they understand not the total destruction of a thing reduced to nothing; but their meaning is, that one appears no more upon Earth, tho' he live in Heaven. His body was burnt; and his bones, as they say, have been preserved to this present. One part of them are in the Kingdom of Pegu, and the other in Siam. They attribute a wonderful virtue to these bones, and they affirm that they shine with a divine splendour. Before he died, he ordered his picture to be drawn after his death, for fear men might by little and little suffer his person to wear out of their remembrance, and at long run forget him for good and all. He left also the print of one of his feet in three different places, in the Kingdom of Siam, the Kingdom of Pegu and the Isle of Ceylon. People go thither in pilgrimage from all parts, and yearly honour these prints with singular devotion.

The Siamese with great reverence preserve the hair

The Siamese pretend also that they have part of Sommonokhodom's hair, which he had cut off after he became God: The other part was by Angels carried up into Heaven. It is their custom to upbraid us that we have not respect enough for holy images, for sacred books, and for the priests. The truth is, no people can have greater veneration for those things than they have. By a precept of their law they are commanded to honour them: but it is not enough for them to respect the priests and the divine scriptures; the vestments of the one, and the characters of the other wherein their law is written, is to them also an object of religious worship. Nay they think it a most laudable action, and excellent virtue to do good to the *talapoins*, and that their clothes and the beads which they receive from them have the power to cure diseases. They imagine also that in their books there is a divine virtue, and that if one understood it and knew how to use the words of them, he might work great wonders. And therefore of the three ways of working miracles; the first is to understand aright how to make use of the word of God; the second, to be instructed in the doctrine of the anchorites; and the third is the assistance of devils. This last, however, they condemn, but they mightily approve of the two former, boasting that they alone know these admirable secrets.

False oracles whereby the Siamese authorise their religion

For the proof of their religion they reckon up several fables, which pass amongst them for so many authentic miracles. And these are some of the chief of them.

1. In the Kingdom of Pegu, where the relics of Sommonokhodom are kept, his bones partly changed into several metals, and partly in their natural state shine with an extraordinary brightness.
2. In the same Kingdom there is a little isle in the middle of a river, wherein there is a temple of their God, this little isle, let the waters be never so high, even when the highest places are overflowed, remains dry. They add, that the presents which are offered to God by casting them into the river, according to the custom of that country, run along with the stream, until arriving at the isle, they stop there, and will go no farther.
3. In storms at sea, when seamen are in danger of being cast away, they throw a ring into the sea with an intention to offer it to the temple of the isle, and all of a sudden the seas become calm, and the ship is out of danger.
4. Upon the borders of the Kingdom of Pegu, there is a little hill, where they have a tradition that God went often. A vast multitude of people go thither yearly in pilgrimage, and tho' the top of it be very narrow, yet it holds all that come upon it, and is never full of pilgrims.
5. They also say that on the top of that little hill, there is a great treasure of gold, silver, and other precious things, which there pilgrims offer to God, when they come there. They tell how an army of Chinese having one day carried away that treasure, was next day wholly destroyed, and the riches carried back by Angels to the place where it was before.

6. Tho the top of the little hill be altogether exposed to the weather, and heat of the sun, yet there is always a shade upon it; that even at noon, guards the people; from the excessive heats which they would suffer there without that.
7. In the town of Sokhotai there is an idol all of gold: they pretend that is a miraculous statue, and that if when rain is wanting, it be carried into the fields, as usually it is, immediately rain falls in great abundance.
8. In another town which is called Campeng, there is, as they say, a lake, wherein to this day there is to be seen a living fish, which hath but the half of its body, and the manner how that prodigy was wrought is remarkable. Heretofore a holy man lived in that town; who having a broiled fish presented before him, he ate but one half of it, and threw the other into the lake desiring that it might live. His wish was granted him, in consideration of his great merits; for at this very present the same half fish is still alive in the lake.

It would be too tedious here to relate all their other reveries, we shall only take notice that building upon an infinite number of prodigies of this nature, in disputing with us, they challenge us to show some miracles in confirmation of the doctrine we preach. They brag to us of certain brass and stone-statues, which they believe were heretofore men, and by a divine virtue rendered inanimate. They have also, as they say, many ancient works, made by the hand of Angels. In conclusion all the effects which we attribute to magic, they take to be so many amazing wonders, and they are proud that they alone have the art to do them.

There are certain *talapoins* amongst them who have embraced a state of life called *Vipisana*. Nothing can be more austere, they observe perpetual silence, always applied to the contemplation of divine things, and they have the reputation of being great saints. The Siamese believe that they continually converse with Angels, that what is most admirable in nature, is always present to their mind, and that their eyes pierce even into the most hidden mines, where they clearly see, gold, silver, all metals and all sorts of precious stones.

As to manners and the way of living, a Christian cannot enjoin anything more perfect than what their religion prescribes to them. It commands them to do good, and not only prohibits them bad actions but also every sinful desire, thought and intention. And that makes them say that their law is impracticable, or at least, very hard to be kept as it ought to be, and, indeed they think that they shall all go to Hell.

The law of the Siamese contains ten very severe precepts

Their whole law is comprehended in ten commandments as ours is; but it is much severer, for besides that with them neither necessity nor any other circumstance excuses a man that sins, many things which among Christians are only of perfection and council, pass with them for indispensable precepts.

The use of all intoxicating liquors are forbidden to them. They are not so much as permitted to taste wine whatsoever need they may be in, or whatsoever occasion may press them, and they are extremely scandalized when they see Christian priests drink of it. They cannot without a sin kill any living creature, and it is a crime to go a hunting, to strike a beast, and to do it hurt any manner of way. The reason they give for that is that beasts having life as well as we, are sensible of pain as well as we, and since we are not willing that any body should hurt us, it is not reasonable that we should hurt them. Nay they accuse us of ingratitude, because we put to death innocent creatures who have rendered us so many services. For that reason they are obliged to practise charity not only towards men, but towards beasts also, and to assist them in their necessities. They have so great a respect to their scriptures, that they dare not trust them in our hands, no nor explain their law to us, lest that exposing it to our derision, we might be guilty of some irreverence, and the sin of that be imputed to them. They often upbraid us with the way we carry holy images, and read the holy scriptures, as being not respectful enough. After all, the *talapoins* who are their priests, monks and doctors are looked upon as the true

Plate 30. A *talapoin* on a city street

followers of God. They have little commerce with the world, never salute a layman no not the King. And that's the reason why it offends the Siamese to see the European priests use familiarity with seculars.

The *talapoins* go every morning a begging and the opinion people have of their virtue makes every one give them somewhat. And indeed the most essential part of morality which they preach, is that to be saved, men must erect or repair Pagodas, and above all things assist the *talapoins*.

The laymen have eight principal commandments which consist, 1. In adoring God, his word, and those who imitate his virtues. 2. Not to steal. 3. Not to drink wine, nor any liquor that intoxicates. 4. Not to lie nor to deceive any body. 5. Not to kill men nor beasts. 6. Not to commit adultery. 7. To fast on holy-days. 8. Not to labour on those days. These are the duties which the priests explain to the people, and instruct them in, in their sermons.

The monasteries of the *talapoins* are so many seminaries where youth are bred. Thither are all children of quality sent, as soon as they are capable of instruction, and whilst they continue there, they are made to lead a very austere life. They are called *nin*; and have their particular rules and precepts, which consists in wearing a yellow garment, and having their head and eyebrows shaved twice a month, the fourteenth and twenty ninth of the moon, to fast those two days, and also three other holy days, which happen the fifteenth, twenty third, and last day of the moon, to eat only twice a day, in the morning and at noon, without permission to take a bit of food more till next day, to have no commerce with any woman, never to sing a song, nor to hear those that do sing, not to play upon any instruments, to avoid public shows and rejoicing, not to use perfumes, not to love money, which they are not so much as to touch, far less to hoard it up, not to take pleasure in the taste of what they eat, and to divert their thought from that; which is the reason that several of them mingle somewhat with what is given them, to render it less agreeable; in fine to honour their priests, to give them the hand, and to sit always below them.

The *talapoins* lead a more austere life; for besides that they have all the obligations of laymen and of the youth whom they breed, they have over and above more than sixscore rules proper to their station, whereof these are the chief. To go twice every day to the temple morning and evening to say their prayers, to be wholly covered, never to touch women, not to speak to them hand to hand, nay and not to look upon them when they meet them in the streets, to walk with great modesty, looking downwards and not turning the head, to carry always a fan and to cover their face with it, to hinder their eyes from wandering, never to consent to any ill thought, not to dress their own victuals, but to take such food as is given them, to live on alms which they beg about the town, but not to enter into houses, neither to wait at doors longer than an ox is a drinking, to teach the law to their disciples and to the people, to mortify themselves and do penance a whole year, part whereof consists in staying abroad fifteen days in the month of February, exposed to the dew of Heaven in the middle of the open fields; to confess their sins one to another, to fast three months in the year, July, August, and September, to eat but once a day all that time, which they call their great fast, and nevertheless to preach every day, to say over a kind of chaplet made up of an hundred and fourscore beads, and divided by tens, not to salute any layman, to be merciful and mild towards all people, not to be angry, and never to strike anybody, never to have the head covered especially in the temples, not to sit but upon a certain leathery seat which they carry about with them, particularly in places where women sit, never to lie abroad out of the monastery, and not to be seen out of it alone: To have but one habit, not to play at any game, not to receive the money that is given them, but by the hand of him that serves them for a steward, and to employ it in good works, as paying the poor's debts, and redeeming slaves, to lodge pilgrims, and to do them all the good they can to be sincere and true, and when they must affirm or deny anything, to say only it is so or it is not so. In fine never to suffer in their mind the least doubt about their religion.

The Talapoins make frequent discourses to the people to exhort them to the practice of virtue, and particularly of charity towards men and beasts.

He that preaches, sits, after the manner of the country, upon a little theatre or stage, covered with carpet, and very high above the auditory. When the people are gathered together, he begins and reads a sentence of Sommonokhodom with a modest and grave countenance; looking always down with his eyes, and using no gestures, then he unfolds the fabulous mysteries of that book, and draws from thence some moral doctrine for the instruction of his auditory, making use of metaphors, parables, and above all of comparisons taken from natural things, as it is the custom of the Orientals. The people sit huddling and listen with much reverence and attention, and men being on the one side, and the women on the other. The rest of the *talapoins* are at the preachers side, but separated from the people, and sitting on a half pace. All the hearers have their hands joined, and as soon as the preacher hath spoken the text, they cry all together with hands lifted up to Heaven, and bowing down the head, the word of God, most pure truth. They have like us a kind of Sunday every seventh day, which they spend in fasting and prayer, besides some other more solemn holy-days, which last three days, and which are celebrated sometimes in one pagoda, and sometimes in another, with an extraordinary concourse of people. The women are the most solicitous to go to those meetings of piety. During that time they preach from six of the clock in the morning to six o'clock at night, fresh preachers succeeding one another, and preaching six whole hours by turns. These long discourses are not tedious to the auditory, who always hearken with reverence without coughing or turning the head.

And thus you have what I could learn of the Siamese religion, which till now hath been so unknown in Europe. But if one do but in the least examine what we have said of it; he'll find so many things that have some resemblance with the Christian doctrine, that it may be easily judged the Gospel hath been heretofore preached to that nation, which in progress of time hath been altered and corrupted by the ignorance of their priests.

[44]I can say nothing in particular as to the present state of Christianity in Siam. It is strange that the Gospel should make so small progress amongst

people, who are zealously and carefully cultivated, who daily see the majesty of our ceremonies, so proper for giving an idea of our mysteries, who besides have no vice that may make them dislike our maxims, and who have so great an esteem for the *talapoins*, because they make profession of an austere life. This might make men think that they had something of blockishness and rusticity, if the gentle carriage and pleasant repartees of the Ambassadors that were in France, made it not apparent that they are witty and polite. But it belongs not to us to pry into the secret judgements of God. Let us only make fervent prayers to that Father of mercies, that he would illuminate them.

Notes

[1] Mohammed (and derivatives) originally spelt Mahomet.
[2] Originally written as "for most part".
[3] Surgeons, doctors. Archaic.
[4] Batavia, Java.
[5] Original states "at two several times…."
[6] Written "limon" in original.
[7] Written "emersion" in the original.
[8] Written "satelles" in the original.
[9] *Oxford English Dictionary*: Also kaffir, one of a South African race of Blacks belonging to the Bantu family.
[10] Spelt, variously betle and betel, in the original.
[11] Illustration.
[12] Spelt variously "flagellet" and "flagelet" in the original.
[13] Written "Maurice" in the original.
[14] Written as "Javaners" in the original.
[15] Sometimes spelt "praux" in the original.
[16] Written as "Neuter" in the original.
[17] Written "His Excellence" in the original.
[18] Written "Tunquin" in the original.
[19] Written "Cochinchine" in the original.
[20] *Oxford English Dictionary*: to appreciate, to be sensible of, feel grateful for.
[21] *Oxford English Dictionary*: Champaign etc., a stretch of flat and level country.
[22] *Oxford English Dictionary*: A small roll of aromatic paste for burning as a perfume, now esp. as a fumigator, deodorizer or disinfectant.

[23] *Oxford English Dictionary*: (Obs.) load, freight.
[24] Spelt "livers" in the original.
[25] Written "Ceilan" in the original.
[26] In the original the obsolete "Bolt-sprit" used.
[27] Spelt "Bancok" in the original.
[28] Spelt "musquitoes" in the original.
[29] *Oxford English Dictionary*: A Buddhist monk or priest, properly of Pegu, extended by Europeans to those of Siam.
[30] In the original written as "pilotis".
[31] *Oxford English Dictionary*: A rowing boat, now only poetically and vaguely.
[32] Written "Camboye" in the original.
[33] Written in original as "Pekin".
[34] Spelt "cimeter" in the original.
[35] Written "lanthorns" in the original.
[36] Written "porcullises" in the original.
[37] Written "Alcoran" in the original.
[38] Spelt "bason" [tray] in the original.
[39] The author possibly confused the historical record with Bangkok, called (in part) Krung Thep, or the City of Angels.
[40] Written as "Jonkos" in the original.
[41] Written "Goree" in the original.
[42] Written "Balis" in the original.
[43] Sometimes written "Nyruppaam" in the original.
[44] A marginal note in seventeenth century hand script, written with a quill pen, has been made here, possibly by the owner of a first edition: "*What a most extraordinary observation is this for a Jesuit to make? Alas what is human nature?*"